Dorthy

SHAUN ALLAN

Dorthy by Shaun Allan

First Printing: 2019

ISBN: 978-1-910484-27-2

Singularity Books
www.shaunallan.co.uk

DEDICATION

To everyone who has shown me this Cowardly Lion's Yellow Brick Road leads to lots of laughter, smiles and love.

ACKNOWLEDGEMENTS

The yellow brick road is long and windy and scary, and you don't always have a lion or a tiger or a bear by your side, oh my. So, following Dorothy into an Oz with much darker creatures than flying monkeys is a daunting task.

I couldn't have done so without all of you, my Sinners.

I need to thank Mel Hall for both the original front cover and title. The book was originally going to called Dorothy, except for a mistake by Mel when she automatically put Dorthy, the name of her grandmother. The name fits and it, in fact, quite important, as you'll see.

In this book, you'll see new twists on old characters, and sympathise with ones you would think you never could.

There's no place like home, so, welcome home to Dorthy.

Contents

1

When your parents die, even if you hated them, there's an echo inside of you. A pit which, like an empty stomach, aches to be filled. But it never can be. The meal which you might eat to placate its grumblings loses a sliver of taste. It will never be just like she used to make, never just to her special recipe. The hug of a friend or loved one will never have the same protective blanket his did. No matter who they are or what they say or how they act, there will always be an aftertaste that you don't even notice unless you think about it. Then it's bitter. You swallow. Wash your mouth out with water, but the sour flavour never leaves you.

Dorothy tried *not* to think about it. Most days, she succeeded. She didn't dream about the accident as much. She no longer, most nights at least, woke from a nightmare where she felt she was drowning. She'd stopped seeing them, her parents, everywhere. It was only somewhere, now. Just the occasional glimpse of them in places they could never be.

Her friends rallied around, as friends do. When she needed space, she had it. When she needed to cry, they offered their shoulders. When she had to get out and forget everything, they supplied the venue, the laughter and the alcohol. And the kebab.

Dorothy's aunt and uncle felt helpless. They had taken her in. She had a room, decorated just how she wanted it, and was well fed and looked after. She had all the love they could give, which was a copious amount. They had never had children of their own and had always been close to both Dorothy and her parents, her mother and aunt being sisters. They gave her everything they could to help bury the pain she'd felt. A shovel in the shape of a hug. A JCB digger in the form of a smile and support. It wasn't that she clung to it, like a treasured teddy she couldn't quite relinquish, it was more the memory held on to her as if her parents refused to let their little girl go even though they were no longer alive.

Dorothy loved her surrogate mother and father. She really did. She told them as often as she felt able to. And, though they were not her real parents, they gave her all they had. But the sorrow, loss and pit of darkness which so often threatened to engulf her was something she could not give up. It linked her to their lingering spirit. It connected her to their memory, and she felt, if she let it go, she would suddenly lose them completely. Their memory would fade. Whilst she still cried or her mood swung down like the Reaper's scythe to tear through her smiles, it was almost like holding her mother's hand.

"Don't be out too late," her aunt Susan said.

Dorothy wouldn't be. She never was. Hanging around parks or shopping malls was something she'd never seen the attraction of. If she was shopping, it was for a reason. To buy things. Not to loiter or intimidate or sit smoking and blocking the way to other shoppers while listening to music that practically sat up and offered you a razor blade to caress your wrists with. She needed a new pair of jeans. The ones she wore most often, the most comfortable item of clothing she owned, were becoming tired. The knees were starting to tear like a yawn in the material. Dorothy knew this was fashionable. It was unusual to see someone wearing jeans without slashes at the knees. But hers were not by design. Hers were from the fatigue of a material worn out from being worn, washed and reworn so many times. She'd had them since... before and though they were never a reminder of past times, she was reluctant to part with them. Buying new ones meant she could keep them for those times when memories swept through her, like her aunt during the big Spring Clean (or a Monday afternoon, as it was also called) and she needed something to take her back for a moment. Or an hour. Or more.

The temperature was dropping rapidly when she left the house. It had been warm throughout the day and she'd dressed for earlier rather than the cooler later. She contemplated going back inside to change from the jeans, light t-shirt and shoes into a sweater and boots. But no, she wouldn't be long. Besides, she'd be inside for most of the time, once there. She'd just grab a jacket and be on her way. The sooner she was there the faster she'd be back, something her Uncle James would often tell her when he felt she was dawdling or procrastinating.

"You should put something else on," Aunt Susan told her when she returned inside. "The weather's looking like it's after changing. You don't want to get caught in the rain or catch a chill, do you?"

"I'll be fine," Dorothy said. "I'm going to take a coat and I'll be either on the bus or at the shopping centre."

"Still," Susan said. "Don't you think you should put something warmer on? It's not summer now."

It wasn't summer. She was right. In fact, summer hadn't been summer. The heat wave promised by the weather men on the television had either forgotten it was meant to be dropping by or it had already happened and she'd blinked and missed it. Perhaps it had been like a team building paintballing game, peppering the landscape with pellets of brief sunshine. Odd days, like this one, did their best to suck some heat from the distant sun, but even they gave up before evening came and admitted defeat.

"Aunt Susan," she said, hugging the precious woman and taking a deep inhalation - she loved the smell of her aunt's long red hair, all cherry or coconut, depending on what shampoo was on sale that week. "I'm a big girl and I'm not going to be long. Trust me."

"Well, if you're sure."

"I am, honest."

Susan kissed Dorothy on the cheek and wondered, not for the first time, where this grown up girl came from. She still felt her niece should still be running around with felt tip covering her hands, crying out for a chocolate biscuit and a sugary drink. Those days were long gone and Susan had to admit she missed them. She'd only been the visiting older sister of Sophia, Dorothy's mother, so didn't have such an active part of the girl's formative years. She had, though, been there as much as she could so had a strong bond, almost in readiness for when, well, when things changed.

"See you soon," Susan said.

"Love you," called Dorothy as she ran from the hallway.

2

The bus to town was about to leave as Dorothy arrived at the bus stop. She hurried to the just closing doors and breathed a sigh of relief when the driver stopped and reopened them. She bought her ticket and walked along the aisle, avoiding eye contact with most of the other passengers apart from a brief smile of recognition for a neighbour. She took a vacant seat at the back and settled in for the ride. Dorothy took out her headphones and put them on. The other end of the wire wasn't plugged into her phone so there was no music playing, but she found it a suitable deterrent for anyone who might feel like starting up a conversation. She wasn't particularly anti-social, she was just in a quiet mood and wanted to do what she had to do and get home. She always seemed to do better on a test after a good night's sleep and tomorrow's maths exam would need the full eight hours with extra bonus time.

Rain started to tap on the window next to her, as if it were asking to be let in out of the cold. She folded her arms, hugging herself to encourage some body heat to spread, even though the temperature hadn't changed. The bus stopped occasionally to allow people to board or alight, but Dorothy didn't notice any of them. She stared out of the window at the gathering darkness and watched the streaks of rain as they ran down the glass, merging with other drops which either gave them more momentum or stopped them dead, out of the race for good.

"Hey Dottie."

Dorothy hated the abbreviation of her name. If her parents had wanted it to be shortened, they'd have forgone the extra letters and christened her that way. Everyone who knew her knew she would rarely answer to anything other than her full first name. She ignored the person speaking to her. She knew the voice anyway and could see him in the reflection from the window. Julian Hornsby. Class joker and a boy too intelligent for the little work he put in to his studies. Dorothy had to show effort and diligence to achieve the grades she had. Granted, she was doing well at school, but it didn't come easy. She often thought that she was wading through treacle in her attempts to understand the topics she was being taught. Julian skated through his lessons on a rink of laughter, wit and cheekiness. His ready charm was lost on her however. They were friends of a sort, but she could happily punch him sometimes. The fact she disliked the name 'Dottie' only made him use it all the more.

He dropped into the seat next to her with enough force to make her bounce in her own.

"You got the kangaroo chair, then?" he said, his voice bright. An elbow jabbed in her arm to emphasise the 'hilarious' joke he'd made only served to annoy her.

"Julie," she said in a flat voice. If he could lose a few letters of her name, she would happily mislay some of his.

His face dropped and he turned away from her. She was happy with that. Even though he was in close proximity, he was quiet. That was all she needed. The rain held her attention. Julian held her dismissal. After a moment, he turned back to her.

"I'm only messing, you know?"

"I know," said Dorothy. "But if you can't take, don't give."

"What's made you so grumpy?"

"People who deliberately do things to people when they know they don't like them."

"Who would do...?" Julian paused. "Oh yeah." He hung his head, staring at his shoes. "Soz."

Dorothy relaxed. Julian couldn't help being an idiot. He was a clever boy, but didn't really know what to do with his intelligence and so wrapped it up in nonsense, hoping some meaning would walk into his life, take his hand and lead him on the correct path. Until that happened, he'd make do with fun, frolics and frowns from those he made the target of his jibes.

"Don't worry about it," she told him. "I just need to get to town and get home before this rain really kicks in."

"What you getting?"

"I need some new jeans. These have had it."

"I don't know," said Julian, shaking his head. "They look as if they've definitely still 'got it' on you."

Typical. Give the boy a chance and he had to resort to being a sexist pig like the rest of his gang at school. Why couldn't he just say 'Oh, cool.' or something and leave it at that? Why did he have to let his mind swim about in the gutter? He probably thought he was paying a compliment.

Well, thanks.

Really.

She sighed and turned back to the water streaming down the window. It looked as if she was already too late. The rain had kicked in and was not going to relent in its onslaught of the bus and its passengers. She realised the top she was wearing should have been the coat her aunt had suggested. She'd get wet. She'd get cold. She turned to Julian, hoping he could redeem himself by being gallant.

"Lend me your coat, please?"

Julian looked past her at the weather. He pursed his lips, either because he was thinking about her request or for a kiss which was never going to come. Not from his present company, at least. His carefree attitude did work on some girls, Dorothy knew. Occasionally, she'd even catch herself falling under his spell. It was only ever a momentary lapse and she mentally slapped herself each time, in lieu of slapping him.

He looked back at her.

"Nah," he said. "I would but... nah."

He stood, realising the frosty reception he was receiving was not likely to thaw quickly. His winning ways did, on occasion, lose. You couldn't win 'em all. He'd sit elsewhere rather than constantly running against the brick wall of her stuck up...

The bus lurched, throwing Julian onto Dorothy's lap. Her head whipped sideways, slamming into the glass. Through the bright spots bursting in her eyes and the explosive stab of pain in her temple, she managed to push him off, cursing. He stumbled to his feet, mumbling apologies, trying to steady himself so he could make sure she was ok. The blood oozing from her head worried him. He wasn't used to being worried. Perhaps it was purely a touch of guilt for refusing her the loan of his coat. He was as unfamiliar with guilt as he was with concern. Such things were water from his duck's back. Or rain off the bus window.

The bus had skidded to a halt. The few other passengers aboard were similarly shaken, though it appeared Dorothy was the only one hurt.

"Is everyone all right?" shouted the driver. His head poked from behind his small cubicle where his chair, the wheel and his hidden-because-it-wasn't-allowed phone shared space. "A tree was just blown in front of the bus! The wind has picked up from nowhere!"

There were mutters and groans in reply. One man, larger than his clothes but not as big as his ego advanced on the driver, fist and teeth clenched.

"What the hell was that?" he bellowed. "Did you get your license from the back of a cereal pack? Cut out three tokens and send 'em off with a fiver? You coulda killed us!"

He reached the driver and raised his hand to grab the man who was scrambling to close the security door which prevented exactly the sort of attack that was imminent. As his shirt was taken in the passenger's grip, the bus was thrown to the side again, a car crashing into it head on.

The windscreen shattered, sending a spider's web of cracks across its surface. The impact separated the driver and his attacker, hurling them both backwards along with the others. The driver fell over his chair, the glass missing him completely. The other man's face hit the metal framework that was used to hold folded pushchairs. Blood sprayed from his broken nose, then spewed from the gashes as a thick branch smashing through the windscreen found a target. His back. His legs. His neck.

He slumped forwards. Two of his fellow passengers were screaming already. As he came to rest against the feet of a woman, just managing to hold her fear in check, her resolve snapped as easily as the bone in his nose. She vomited across his body and began to scream too.

Julian climbed next to Dorothy and took her in his arms. She didn't try to resist and pulled him closer. They huddled there, at the back, staring at the carnage before them. The dead man. The screaming couple. The now crying woman. The unconscious teenager and his frantic girlfriend, desperately trying to shake him awake.

Julian heard a sob and turned to Dorothy. She was still looking straight ahead, shock paralysing her. He realised the sound had come from himself.

3

The bus rocked. It seemed to shiver in great tremors as if a huge hand were shaking it, trying to force the occupants out. There were no thick fingers, however. There was only the unseen wind, buffeting the vehicle with the ferocity of a bull throwing a red caped matador into the air.

Julian gulped down his fright, a solid lump in his throat, and tried to rouse Dorothy from her trance. He took her chin and turned her face to his.

"Dorothy?"

She looked at him, oblivious to his identity and, possibly, his presence.

"Dorothy? Come on, focus. We need to get off this bus."

He was trying to keep his voice calm but, with every shudder of the bus, a similar tremble rippled through him. Dorothy continued to stare. People continued to scream and cry. Outside, he heard windows smash as objects being blown through the air hit them. The storm had increased suddenly and they needed to take shelter. They were close to the mall. They'd be safe in there. He'd make up for his lewd comment. He'd pay recompense for being a constant fool. He could do this.

"Dottie!" he shouted, emotion gravelling his voice to give it the edge of feet crunching across a pebbled driveway.

Dorothy blinked and looked up into his eyes, recognition lifting their veil. She raised her hand to slap him and he grabbed it before it could make contact.

"We need to move," he said as calmly as his nerves would allow. "Now."

Dorothy looked around the bus and gasped.

"What happened?"

"I don't know. We swerved to miss a tree, then that guy threatened the driver. Next thing a car hit us and... I don't know. The storm came out of nowhere. We need to take shelter."

When Julian indicated the dead body in the aisle, Dorothy looked and turned away. The corpse could have been a rug or a log. Or perhaps one of the pushchairs rolled from the metal storage area. There was no trace of shock or disgust.

"We can't leave," she said.

She seemed calm, in contrast to the raging violence outside the bus and the madness inside. She had been snapped out of her reverie and was back to being her sometimes too-sensible self. Outside, the wind was strong enough to lift them and toss them where it wished, ragdolls onto the floor of a child's bedroom. And the rain was heavy enough to drench them in a heartbeat. They should stay. Dry and contained and safe. Wait until the emergency services came or the storm abated.

"Listen to everyone," insisted Julian. "They're panicking. One guy is already dead. The mall's not far. I can see the lights from here. We'll be much better off there."

To Dorothy, it sounded as if the other passengers were not the only ones panicking. Julian himself was clearly badly shaken. He was also delirious. They would never make it to the mall. The winds were too strong and the rain too heavy. They needed to stay.

"We can't," she said quietly. "It's too dangerous out there. We'll never make it."

"Suit yourself," said Julian. His moment of chivalry had passed, blown away by the high winds of self-preservation. He moved to the doors and forced them open. They were stiff, the emergency locking mechanism broken and unyielding. "Give me a hand!"

Dorothy shook her head. If he couldn't leave, he couldn't be hurt. By remaining in her seat, she was saving him - though he didn't see it. The storm seemed alive, tearing at the world with invisible, but tangibly savage, claws. She could shut out the others. Make them white noise. But she knew Julian. She didn't care about *them*. She didn't particularly care about him, either, but her lack of concern was... less.

"I'm not staying. You can, but I'm not. I'm getting off this bus one way or another. Help me or I'll kick the doors down."

Dorothy had a fleeting image of him being the Big Bad Wolf, huffing and puffing away but, in her head, something bigger huffed and puffed. Julian was the house blown down. She sighed. Fine. She'd help him. It was his life. It could be his death. Not that she'd wish him dead. He *might* make it. She could hope.

She stood and began to pull the doors open with him. Using their feet to push against the inner surfaces of the bus, the doors slowly began to move.

Then Dorothy happened to look up. And she gasped. And let go of the doors.

Released, they suddenly slammed shut, the hydraulics hissing in relief. Julian cried out as they shut on his fingers. He wrenched his hands back and held his hands up. There was no damage, the rubber coating which ran up the edges of the door frames protecting him, but he inspected them anyway. He turned to the girl who, under other circumstances, he'd barely talk to apart from making - to him - good natured jibes.

"What the..."

Then he saw the look on her face. The wide eyes. The open mouth. He followed her gaze and promptly forgot his fingers. Together, they backed away from the doors. They didn't notice the bus had gone silent. The screaming had stopped. The crying too. As the tornado, a tall funnel of chaos, approached, devouring all in its path, the screaming began again. This time, the voices were joined by two others as both Dorothy and Julian fell back against the seat they'd occupied when their only concerns were a pair of jeans and a bit of a laugh.

The bus was lifted effortlessly. A leaf on a breeze. A feather detached from the wing. At first, it simply raised up, straight and level. The entire company of passengers held their collective breath, a breath that was expelled suddenly as the tornado's current ripped at the vehicle, throwing it around and around. Julian vomited, feeling as if he were caught up in the spout of an eternally emptying bath.

Dorothy buried her head in her hands, bending forward and bracing herself against the seat, wishing she had done as she had promised her Aunt Susan and brought a coat.

4

Hope is a fragile thing. You hope to succeed, only to have your success shredded by a casual word. You hope to find love and find, instead, betrayal wrapped in a smile and tied with a promise. You hope for health while disease devours your organs in a silent feast.

You hope for hope when your eyes are blinded by despair.

Dorothy and hope were best friends. They were life-long companions who walked hand in hand through the slings and arrows of outrageous life. She hoped her parents would return, though she knew they could not. She hoped Susan and James would live forever so she wouldn't have to face the grief her own parents' deaths had visited upon her again. She hoped she would be able to achieve the grades she needed for the career she thought she wanted but didn't know if she really craved. It would come. Inspiration, one day, would hit and she would discover her calling. She hoped the day would be soon.

She hoped the crying would stop. The pain would ease. Her breath would be less ragged. The weight on her legs would lift. The drip that was falling on her face would cease.

Family, on the other hand, are attached by an invisible cord that binds them together regardless of how hate might push them apart. A brother is a brother. A mother, a mother. Friends can be chosen and discarded, to be cast adrift if your own life takes you on another journey or if they forget the meaning of the word 'friend'. Family is a lofty title for something - or someone - stitched to you by the thread of birth. And, often, you can feel the needle's prick throughout your life.

The sibling of Hope is Hopelessness. Dorothy was drowning in this part of the Emotion dynasty. Her eyes were closed, too heavy to open, the fear of what they might see preventing them from even taking a peek. She wished for her bed. Her home. Her aunt's arms. Her mother's embrace.

Instead, she had noise and pain and breathlessness, all wrapped up in a shroud of anxiety.

A cough and moan close by startled her. She recognised the sound. Julian. She forced her eyes to open and looked around.

The bus was on its side. The exit doors were open above her, with one hanging limply and the other missing completely. The other passengers were... crumpled. It was the only thing she could think to call them. They were lying strewn across the length of the bus, looking like the ragdolls thrown by that impatient, tantrumming child whose bottom lip was stuck so far out they ran the risk of tripping over it.

A young girl had fallen across the back of a seat. Backwards. She was bent all wrong. The human spine was not meant to go that way. That far. Her eyes were closed and blood trickled from her nose, a feeble attempt to escape the broken body before life faded.

The driver was face down against the entrance. The door to his cubicle was open and his hand was still holding onto the handle, as if he'd tried to open it whilst they were in flight. It gripped the handle but was attached to nothing else. The stump dangled down, almost beseechingly, reaching out towards the rest of him. Dorothy couldn't see his unfinished arm. She was thankful.

A head a short distance from her turned and a boy looked at her. He was roughly her age. Handsome. Well... he would have been. One eye was bloodshot. The other was swollen shut, a crack in the nectarine of its socket. She smiled at him. It was empty of spirit, but all she had. He smiled back, his as devoid of meaning as hers. They were too stunned for anything to mean anything.

The moan again. She looked up and saw Julian. He was trapped above her, his legs caught between the seat opposite where they'd been - and Dorothy somehow still was - and the one in front. The back of the latter was pushed back and twisted, holding Julian's legs as firmly as the driver's hand clutched its handle. Luckily, the remainder of his torso had not become separated. He groaned and moved slowly, but at least he was alive.

Dorothy realised she needed to check herself for injury. She ached, but didn't think she was really hurt. Thankfully the bus had landed on the side she was already on. The seat had cushioned the fall and, miraculously, the window next to her was intact. Her head throbbed. Her ribs felt as if she'd been punched hard in the chest, but none seemed to be broken. Finally, she looked at her legs. The weight on them had made them numb and her brief, awkward movements told the blood it could begin to flow once more, taking with it a thousand tiny pins to prick her extremities.

The weight was a little boy. Small. Well dressed. Short blonde hair. Leg twisted. Face, thankfully, hidden. Dorothy watched his back, laying her hand in the centre to feel for either breath or beat. After too long, she felt both. Barely, but there. Carefully, she lifted him up so she could slide out from beneath him. She eased his body down onto the side of the bus - her floor, now - doing her best not to stand on the glass of the window. His head rested slightly to the side. Dorothy recognised him. He lived further along her street. Too far to be a neighbour, but close enough to warrant a nodded 'hello' if they happened to pass each other in the street. Tom? Tim? Something like that.

She reached up to Julian, taking his hand in hers. His eyes opened slowly. He looked from her to the seat holding him in place.

"Wha...?"

"I don't know," she said. "Some kind of freak storm. A tornado or something. It grabbed us and now it's let us go."

"Is everyone dead?"

"No." Dorothy shook her head. "That lad over there is alive. Someone was crying a minute ago, but they've stopped now. That little boy is still breathing. And there's us."

"Can you help me down, please?"

"I'll try."

Dorothy reached up and took Julian's shoulders, supporting as much of his weight as she could. Luckily, he was a skinny runt. Built for speed rather than stamina. He wore it well however, and that, coupled with his ever present charm, was an endearing combination. If he'd have been any bulkier, he would probably have found his legs partially missing rather than just trapped. He tried to pull the back of the seat away to give him some room to move, but couldn't. It wouldn't shift more than a few millimetres.

"I can't get out!" he said, his voice a fearful octave above its usual tone.

"Calm down," Dorothy told him. "Let me help."

She let go of his shoulders and jumped. On the first attempt, she missed her target, but succeeded on the second, grabbing hold of the metal bar running across the chair's upper back. She pulled herself up and turned on her side, planting her feet firmly either side of Julian. His eyes remained firmly fixed on hers and she was silently grateful for his timely courtesy. He could easily have taken the opportunity to look elsewhere on her anatomy. She'd have retaliated, of course, but his predicament was clearly more important to him than his libido.

"When I say 'go,' we pull together," she said. "But hurry, I can't keep this position for long."

He bit his tongue, avoiding the leading comment which prompted an automatically lewd response. Instead, he nodded. Dorothy took a deep breath and counted down.

"Three, two, one... *GO!*"

Simultaneously, the pair pulled. Dorothy knew neither she nor he were particularly strong individuals, but perhaps, working together...? The chair moved slightly. A minor triumph, but one which spurred them on to find an extra burst of vigour. They pulled harder. The chair moved further. Julian pushed against the floor and, suddenly, was free. With nothing to hold him in place, he fell, taking Dorothy with him, landing on the boy.

Ignoring the sharp pain in her arm and the yelp from Julian, Dorothy scrambled up. She was intertwined with him and felt as if she were untying herself. Her haste made the job more difficult but she was sure she'd heard the crack of something breaking.

A bone.

She knew it wasn't hers and really wanted it to be the arm, leg or rib of the older boy, leaving the younger one to not have anything else to suffer from. She forced Julian away, his scream indicating the crack had, actually, been a part of his body. Gently, she moved Tim. Yes, it was Tim, she was certain. She whispered his name. She felt his neck. She touched his back.

Nothing.

She tried to shake him. To rouse him. To get some sort of reaction.

Nothing.

"*Tim!*"

Dorothy slumped, defeated. She was no doctor. Her first aid ability extended to little more than asking her aunt to put some salve on to ease a graze or her uncle to apply a plaster. When she hurt herself, she often reverted to being a little girl, one who needed her surrogate mother to look after her. But, she recognised death. It had been her companion since the accident that had taken her parents. Even though it had taken a step back and remained in shadow, it had been ever present.

Now, Death had moved forward once more. It had reached down and taken the poor boy away. And their fall must have been the straw which severed the boy's back. She turned him over, wanting to look into the dead eyes of the child she had killed. When she saw his crushed face and neck, she clasped her hand to her mouth, wanting the shriek to be swallowed along with her guilt.

"That wasn't us," said Julian quietly, his hand on her shoulder. "We couldn't have done that. He would already have been gone."

"No!" cried Dorothy, yanking herself away. "He was breathing! His heart was beating!"

"Then he must have died just after you touched him! He couldn't have survived that. No way."

"He..."

Julian was right. Of course he was. She'd not actually looked at anything more than the side of his face, just enough to recognise him. She hadn't seen the damage already done. She had just wanted to ease his pain.

"I just wanted to help him," she said.

"You did. His last moments would have been of someone caring."

Dorothy didn't say anything. She didn't need to. The tears running down her cheeks spoke volumes.

A scream. A scuffle. A shout choked violently off.

The pair looked up sharply. Someone was dropping into the bus through the entrance at the front. Someone else already had. One of the surviving passengers, who Dorothy hadn't noticed previously, jumped on the first newcomer who was bent over the driver, only to have the second land on them, knocking them over. Dorothy and Julian couldn't see, at first, what was happening.

Then the passenger was thrown back, flying through the air as if they were a bus caught in a tornado. He landed on the window, next to Tim's body, smashing the glass. His neck was ripped out. His eyes were rolled up in their sockets. His body was trembling as if a multitude of small electric shocks were passing through it.

Julian dropped to a crouch, holding in the vomit threatening to fill the void where the man's gullet should have been. He stopped, suddenly, as the interlopers growled. The one in front leaped onto the boy who had smiled at Dorothy, bending his head down. There was a shake and the head came back up. In the mouth was the other's throat. Blood flooded the chin, painting it like a child's self-portrait. The contents of Julian's stomach could not be held back at that point and they spewed forth, splattering across the man and the boy.

The attacker roared, his head going back and his arms held high, fists clenched. It was a jubilant yell that was echoed by his companion. A cry that froze the hearts of Dorothy and Julian but spurred them into action. They needed no words to tell each other they had to escape. Words would have used breath more valuable as energy. They would have alerted the two... whatever they were. Otherwise occupied with feasting on the other passengers, they appeared ignorant of the friends' - because even enemies can become friends in times of despair - movements.

Dorothy gestured upwards towards the exit. The single, still in place door was like an outstretched hand, offering assistance and the hope she so desperately coveted. It was an offer she gladly accepted. Julian nodded and clasped his hands together for the boost she would need. Not daring to look at the horrors further down the bus lest they feel the attention on them, she quickly, and as quietly as she could, lifted her leg. With a grunt, she jumped, grabbing for the door, climbing quickly.

Julian followed, using the end of the side-on seat for the hike he needed. Dorothy took his arm to help him up and out.

His foot slipped, kicking the door.

The silence was broken by the thud and the creak and the gasp.

Hands grabbed his foot. His leg. Pulling, savagely. Her grip lost, Dorothy stumbled, her own foot twisting beneath her. She fell hard, sliding against the side of the bus. She tried to stop herself but there was nothing to take hold of. She landed on the ground, a thick layer of grass cushioning her but forcing the air from her lungs.

She couldn't move as she heard Julian call her name. Her limbs felt too heavy as she heard the animalistic roar, the sound weighing them down with fear. She tried to shout to him, but could only manage a hoarse rasp.

His scream began.

And abruptly ended.

5

As soon as Dorothy's breath was near-normal, she rolled over and crawled against the bus. She could hear movement inside but Julian was quiet. What should she do? Run? Climb up to see if she could help? Run was the obvious, sensible choice and she was, most of the time, very sensible. But she couldn't just leave her friend.

She looked around for some sort of weapon. The best she could see was a stone that would have been as effective as a fly to be swatted away. Just climb up, she told herself. Have a look. A peek.

She was at the bottom of the bus, the axles and exhaust system creating an easily mounted climbing frame. She took hold, set her foot in place and was about to start up when she realised. She didn't have to climb up. The bus was on its side. She just had to creep around to the back, close to where they'd been sitting, to see.

That's all she had to do.

That's all.

Not much, was it?

Right... Go. Except...

Except, she couldn't move. She felt fixed to the floor, as if the grass had reached up and bound her with Gulliver's ropes. Her pulse's rapidity was a time bomb's ticking, increasing in speed until it was ready to explode.

She was Dorothy. Just a girl. Too normal. Too sensible. Too ready to do the right thing and too unprepared to face whatever was happening. Only a short time ago, she had kissed her aunt goodbye and forgotten her coat. Such simple things felt a world away. A lifetime ago. Perhaps she was actually unconscious. She'd hit her head. This was a dream or a nightmare induced by the crash. She would wake up in hospital or her bed at home. Let it ride out.

But did sleeping people know they were dreaming? Was this the lucid dreaming she'd heard about? Maybe all this was just the playtime of her mind occupying itself until she woke up. She could go along with it. It wasn't real and she wouldn't really get hurt.

Except, her ankle *did* hurt from her landing. Her head *was* pounding from the impact with the window. She *was* afraid and no amount of telling herself it was in her imagination would calm her nerves.

There were no sounds from within the bus. The silence beckoned to Dorothy, enticing her to stand and investigate. *Come on*, it told her. *It's fine. You're fine. Take a look!* She was tempted, for a moment. The feeling passed quickly. Whatever had attacked her friend and the others was still in there. Julian was too, and he was beyond her help.

No, tears! Stay away!

She would not cry. She must not. It would alert the *things* inside. It would crumble what little resolve she was clinging onto and scatter it as dust on the wind. It would ensure she'd suffer the same fate as Julian.

Poor Julian.

She caught the sob in the back of her throat just before it had the chance to escape, swallowing it back down and standing defiant against its mutiny. There was only one thing she could do. Only one course of action.

Go.

Closing her eyes, Dorothy took a deep breath. The air felt different. It was cleaner. Fresher. The storm had washed it clean and was sharpening it as it entered her lungs. She held onto it before letting it out slowly through her nose. She felt cleansed, the aches in her body lessened as if the act of breathing deeply had anaesthetised her injuries. She looked around, seeing her surroundings for the first time.

The road, houses and street lights had gone. There was no large shopping mall nearby, proclaiming that the sales were now on and she could save up to fifty percent in the very shop she had intended to visit. There was a swathe of the greenest grass she had ever seen, with no hint of dog fouling or litter dropping to spoil its emerald flawlessness. This merged with tall, proud trees that looked down upon the shattered vehicle and occupants with disdain. It was dark among the thick trunks, as if the light was unsure of venturing under the canopy of leaves and only tentatively reached in to afford minimal illumination.

Dorothy had to move. She was telling herself to get away from the bus, to take cover in the trees. Perhaps, there, she would be safe. She'd have the chance to either recover or wake up, depending on whether this was reality or not. Her body was refusing to cooperate, however. Her brain had forgotten how to command her limbs and she was thankful that the act of breathing was autonomic, otherwise she would suffocate where she sat.

All she wanted was a pair of jeans.

She heard scratching. She looked around to see where the noise was coming from but, at first, could see nothing. The sound came again. It was close to her. Next to her. She looked down.

Two things. Both horrific.

Dorothy, luckily, couldn't see the upper torso of the woman who had been crushed by the bus. She had seen enough of Death's visage in the boy who had died from her touch and was happy not to see such a thing again. Of course, the right arm and leg that still protruded made her gag and fight the urge to throw up. The fact that they were unscathed only lent to the abhorrence at their appearance. The perfectly manicured nails, tipping the fingers of the hand that lay relaxed against the grass, shouldn't have belonged to someone who'd had around 12 tonnes of metal dropped on them. It should have been that of a woman chilling by a pool after a morning being pampered on her day off from work. She should have been having some 'me' time after spending so much time dedicated to everyone around her. She would have spent the morning laughing with her hairdresser, drinking latte and remembering what peace was like.

Her leg, encased in a shimmering, silken material that Dorothy wished could hang in her own wardrobe, ended in a sparkling red shoe that seemed to reflect the entire world around them. Dorothy couldn't help but reach out to it. Before her hand made contact, the scratching came again.

That was number two. The dog. Or the snout of the dog. It was a mass of thick brown fur with a white streak sneaking through. One of the fangs was missing. A short distance from the snout towards Dorothy, was the paw and lower leg. The front right, mirroring the animal's master. It jittered, slightly. A twitch as if Life wasn't quite willing to hand over the baton to its darker counterpart. As it shook, its dewclaw touched metal.

It was the prompt she needed. Dorothy ignored the pain in her ankle, minor compared to that of others, and pushed herself up. The trees had changed their attitude. They were no longer condescending. They were inviting. Offering refuge. She limped into their embrace.

She collapsed against one of the trunks. Her ankle had swelled and it was struggling to carry her weight, even though she'd only travelled a short distance. The tree was wide enough to shield her from the view of anything that might exit the bus and she welcomed its protection. The tears pricked at her eyes, announcing their intent, but she pushed them back again. She knew, if suppressed, they had a habit of multiplying to the point they would overflow her defences and wash her resolve away.

A howl splintered her thoughts.

She squatted down, holding her breath. The howl was answered by a second, both coming from the direction she'd come. Slowly, she dared to peek around the tree. The two attackers were standing on top of the bus. Their arms were in the air and one of the pair held aloft a severed arm. He shook it, the hand flapping and looking as if it were waving to Dorothy. Or beckoning. They howled again, then leapt to the ground on the far side. She could hear them baying at each other as they ran off.

She waited. They might come back. They might be hiding, fooling her into thinking they were gone when, in fact, they were watching for her return so they could pounce and finish their work.

The pull was too strong, however. Julian was still inside, though he was certainly dead. The others, too. She needed to see if anyone had survived.

She had no idea where they were. Dorothy knew her surrounding area well enough. She'd tried jogging but, when that became more of a chore than a recreation, she reverted to going for long walks. She *would* plug her headphones in on those occasions, and would lose herself in her varied playlists while the step count accumulated. As such, she had explored most of the areas around her home. There was a large park not far from where she lived, but the grass was kept buzz-cut short and there were only odd trees here and there to break the monotony of paths that led in circles but didn't get anywhere. Her aunt and uncle, as she was growing up, would take her out for picnics and to play soccer. She knew the few open spaces. This place was unknown to her. The storm must have transported them a fair distance, but nowhere had she heard of people being attacked and…*eaten*! She wished they had been animals. Bears or lions or wolves that had been equally carried away from either their natural habitats or nearby zoos. They weren't. They were very much human. Male. Rabid and vicious, but people, nonetheless.

She walked back, slowly. Her footsteps were light and tentative, but they were prepared to change if necessary, carrying Dorothy away if the men reappeared. Her ankle protested at each step, but she gritted her teeth through the pain. If she needed to run, that's what she would do.

She stopped by the two victims of the vehicle's fall. The dog's leg had stilled and a cold chill settled on Dorothy as she stared at them. She noticed a ring on the woman's finger and she stooped to look closer. It was narrow silver band with veins of deep red running around its circumference. Dorothy touched the metal, careful not to come into contact with the dead flesh.

"D… D…"

She spun around, scooting away as a figure loomed over her. She contained the cry that was desperate to be released, but a quiet squeak managed to leak out, a mouse before a ferocious feline.

"D… D…"

Julian!

Dorothy couldn't hold herself back as the feeling of relief unlocked the damn and let her tears flow. He was alive! She couldn't imagine how, but she didn't care. Not too long ago but a lifetime away, she would have very much preferred him to sit elsewhere and leave her alone rather than try his personal version of charm on her. Now, she couldn't think of anyone she would want to see more. Through blurry eyes, she looked at him. He was injured, his steps shuffling rather than sure. She wiped her eyes and steadied herself. He needed her. She must help him.

"Julian, are you…?"

She didn't need to finish the sentence. She could see the answer. He wasn't all right. He was missing the majority of his neck, muscles and tendons and… spine?... being visible in the void where flesh should have been, causing his head to loll to one side. His face was covered in dried blood and muck. His eyes stared forward, dull as if the light behind them had been somehow switched off.

"Julian?"

"D…"

"Dorothy," she said quietly, her voice breaking. "I'm Dorothy."

Julian took a faltering step forward. Though his eyes were lifeless, his expression was imploring. Fumbling, he moved his hand up his neck, the fingers becoming momentarily lost in the exposed inner workings of his body. He managed to reach up to his cheek and pushed his head upright. He released his hold and his head fell again. He staggered and Dorothy thought he might fall. He didn't. Instead, he hobbled towards her again.

"D…"

"Dorothy!"

"D… Dor…

"Dorthy!"

6

Love. A many splintered thing.

The love Dorothy had for her parents had been broken in the accident that killed them. The love the mother and father had for their child was smashed by the oncoming car that had forced them off the road and into the lake. That of an aunt and uncle was well meaning and genuine, but was a pale shadow of what a girl might need to help her walk through life on the right side of self-esteem and confidence.

Love was a whisper of a song on the wind. It could fill you with meaning and light your soul with its flame, yet be snatched away by an errant breeze that extinguished its warmth in a heartbeat.

The axe was keen. Its edge was finer than a human hair and could, indeed, slice one in two, twice over. It had been sharpened and polished and sharpened again, the blade being given the attention a loved one might afford. It was caressed late at night. Greeted with a smile in the early morning light as dawn's sun reflected brightly off its surface.

And it could, with a single swipe, take a life.

It would not need much effort in bringing the blade down down, as if the axe itself was helping the swing, eager to touch the intended target. A lover's kiss, deep and passionate and leaving the other breathless.

In this case, however, the lack of breath was due to the equal lack of life.

Love. Something Edward Simmons could never truly know. To feel the emotion – to feel anything – you needed a heart. Edward was lacking that particular organ. In truth, Edward was lacking many organs, but he was doing his utmost to remedy that situation.

The man was called Stephen Decker. A wife and two children told him they loved him on a daily basis. It wasn't a reflex response to a member of the same family. It wasn't something you just said because it was expected, though you meant it, though it was sort of automatic. No. They told him they loved him, a comment he readily reciprocated, because they did. Because they liked to say the words and to hear them. Stephen Decker said the so-called 'three little words' because they rolled off his tongue and, in the process, filled each of them with a feeling that would energise them for the whole day.

He was returning home. He had worked for long hours in the fields surrounding his farm house and was ready for his dinner and his bath. Stephen had never wanted to be a farmer. He wanted to explore and to learn and to be a man of substance. His father dying younger than he should have and ore and debt than he needed to be had forced Stephen to take over the family farm to pay off the moneys owed that fell to him as the firstborn. Onlyborn, in fact.

His dreams died with his father. The day after the funeral, his mother walked out of the front door and was never seen again. She had yet to shed a single tear for the loss of her husband, though she loved him dearly and was a devoted wife. Regardless of the grown son she was turning her back on, Edina Decker felt she had lost everything and her life was over.

So she stepped over the threshold of her home, and let her feet lead her to a brand new life.

They did, indeed, though she walked for four weeks to find it. She was weak and starving and dehydrated when she was found hiding in a coal house from the rain. The woman, a widow herself, took Edina in. She could see a kindred spirit that was a shade darker than it should have been. A strong friendship developed between the ladies. When questioned about her past, Edina never mentioned her son. She remained oblivious of the grandchildren that would have blessed her life. She, in a way, forgot she'd even had a previous family. The woman, Katherine, became her family. A sister in all but blood.

Life was good. Life was new.

For Stephen, her lost son, life was also over. No longer would he seek out new lands. No more could he gain an understanding of things outside his experience. His father's farm became his prison. He worked it as hard as he could, and dedicated his time to its maintenance as the dutiful offspring he was. He married his wife and had a son of his own, followed soon by a daughter. Within the walls of his house, Stephen was happy. Blissfully so. Beyond, he felt as if he were stepping into a pit. One that was determined to drag him down and swallow him whole.

When he stepped over his threshold, he might easily have been walking in the cold footsteps of his mother. They were fading and led the abandoned man, who often felt he was still a boy, nowhere.

The trees in the copse that he'd cut down disappeared as a consequence of his frustrations. He took his axe to them with a fervour that had decimated the long-standing wooded acreage, and it had taken a time short enough to be insulting to their longevity.

The animals that had lived within its space were further victims of Stephen's anger. He had enjoyed their squeals of fright and slowly diminishing whimpers more than he would have expected. Killing them was something he was hesitant of at first but grew to enjoy and even hunger for. He did, in the end, learn. He discovered that a sliver of spite ran through him. He found that slipping a knife across the throat of a deer or between the ribs of a rabbit gave him a chill that vibrated through him as if he had been touched by lightning.

He loved his family, and they loved him. Totally.

He wouldn't extend his newfound passion to them.

He just *wouldn't.*

Edward Simmons could imagine the feelings warring with the confines of Stephen's body. He pictured the internal carnage that was ensuing as the temptations grew to be more than a single man could contain. He couldn't feel it, for he was yet to have that ability, but Edward knew he was still a work in progress. He was a canvas that was yet, in part, in need of the brushstrokes that would render him complete.

Edward was his own artist. He had to be. The one who had started his landscape had long since cast him aside. Edward had to finish the work started. He would probably have enjoyed it, if he was able.

He crouched in the field. He had been in that position for four days, waiting until the time was right, unmoving apart from the occasional need to lubricate his joints lest they set him in place. He spent his time thinking about his forthcoming actions, as he did each time. He wondered what remorse would be like. Would it eat away inside of him, devouring his heart until he inflicted upon himself that which he did to others? Or would he celebrate those who fell before him in the knowledge they were fulfilling a destiny they didn't know they had?

Edward thought about feelings most of the time. He wished he could enjoy the sensations they would give him. Perhaps, before his canvas was filled, he might find a way to paint some onto himself.

His thoughts whirred and spun in his head, cogs turning and belts running silently on spindles as fine as a spider's web. When he was finished, he was sure that he'd be a masterpiece, and those who had helped him become complete would be honoured in doing so.

The tingling started in his fingertips and ran up his arm to where it joined his shoulder. It stopped there, of course. Where the flesh met the metal was a cold, impassable wall that pins and needles could never prick. He flexed his fingers to relieve the bristling of the nerves and watched his fingers with a wonder that had yet to diminish. Bremen, the original owner of the arm, had been a vile man who crept into the houses of single women and stole from them. It was not for monetary gain, as he never sold anything he took. There was no specific reason he took any single thing – it didn't need to be valuable or unusual. He took what he liked, purely because he wanted to.

He would stand over the slumbering forms for hours, watching them until the sun began to stretch its fingers into the early morning sky. Then he would leave.

If they awoke early, or were disturbed, he would still leave, but there would be a flush to his cheeks after a strangled cry and a broken neck.

Edward thought Bremen should be proud of the new use his arm was being put to. After he had been killed the limb was transferred, replacing Edward's own metal appendage. Taking the lives of those not deserving of drawing breath was a fitting compensation for the man's victims.

Stephen Decker strode with a smile on his face. He was going home. He would be embracing his family. He would tell his children bedtime stories and would retire to his own bed with his wife, where they would enjoy each other before falling asleep in each other's arms.

He would just need to stop by the stream first to wipe the blood from his hands and face. He would need to rinse his shirt. He tried to avoid splatters normally, but he was starting to me more aggressive – no, enthusiastic – in his work. The wild boar had proved to be a formidable quarry, but it had fallen, as it must. This marked the first time he had tasted one of his kills. Previously, he left the carcasses for other animals to feast upon but, when one of the sprays of blood hit his mouth and, instead of recoiling or wiping it away, he had licked his lips, he could not help his urge.

Still warm, the animal had proved delicious. A large part of the taste had to be the spice of the adrenaline coursing through him, but even without that, Stephen found the beast filled with flavour.

He would still eat the meal his wife set in front of him when at sat at the table. He would still enjoy it and compliment her cooking, but it would be lacking a certain something. The added ingredients of his own hands and blade.

As he walked, he saw those hands push that blade into his wife through her stomach, pulling it up between her ample chest to the neck he loved to gently kiss. He stopped and breathed deeply, banishing the image. She was his beloved. He would never.

Never.

Edward stepped up behind Stephen. His metal legs moved easily from the position he had remained in for so long and Bremen's hand wrapped around the axe's handle as if they were old friends.

Stephen let out his last breath explosively, his life leaving with the same exhalation. His broken skull split like the trunk of one of the trees he had so vigorously felled.

Edward looked the dead man's body over, even though his choice had already been made. It didn't hurt to be sure. As ever, he agreed with his first decision. The left leg. Stephen's body was well muscled and in the condition one would expect from many days of hard labour and evenings of soft comfort. It was both looked after and enjoyed.

Edward would like to experience that same enjoyment at some point. Perhaps he even could.

The axe came down a second time and the man made of metal, machinery and science, set about replacing his leg with that of the man made of flesh, feelings and increasingly sickening appetites.

7

Fight is one of the first impulses of a threatened animal. Depending on the creature, the response to being cornered can be instantaneous and instinctive. And deadly.

Alternatively, the urge to flee can be the primary response to potential injury or death.

When the half eaten figure of her friend stood over her, attempting to say her name, Dorothy chose the latter. She didn't take the time to correct him or ask if he needed assistance.

She ran.

She forced herself to disregard the look of longing on Julian's face. It didn't matter what he wanted. It couldn't. She could see his *muscles*! She could see the ligaments doing their best to stay connected when they had been almost chewed through. Bone. Dorothy could see *bone*!

She was back in the cover of the trees before she had taken a breath. She was far enough from the bus to not be able to see it before she had taken a second. The cannibals, if that's what they were, had vanished in the opposite direction, and she had to put distance between them. Julian should not have been standing, let along speaking, and Dorothy wanted to leave him far behind too.

When she had taken and expelled her third breath, the pain in her ankle became too much for her to ignore and she had to stop. She sank to the ground, taking shelter in a ditch that was nowhere near deep enough to effectively hide her. She broke some branches off a bush and held them around her for camouflage.

Then, as silently as she could, Dorothy sobbed.

She was adept at crying with barely making a sound and with tears that were more a red rimmed eye than a soaked cheek. She had the chance to perfect her skills multiple times with her aunt and uncle when the emotions suppressed from the loss of her parents bubbled to the surface.

The episode lasted only briefly. She was also proficient at controlling her errant emotions.

When she was able to see once more without sentiment clouding her sight, Dorothy peered through the branches, listening intently for sounds of movement. There were none. Slowly, she lowered them, keeping herself flat against the bottom if the dip.

She needed to take stock of her situation. Be practical. Be sensible – she usually did that so well. She had to find out where she was and what had happened. And she needed to stay alive.

She woke suddenly. Darkness had fallen, creeping up on her while the sleep she hadn't needed had taken her anyway. The forest obscured the sky in the main, but she could still see it was a cloudless night. The lack of any street lighting enabled the stars to be much more visible than she was used to but she couldn't see a moon. She stretched out, groaning softly.

"Dorthy!"

Dorothy froze, grogginess dulling her body's natural responses. She could neither fight nor flee. She could only stare.

"Dorthy!"

Julian was standing at the lip of the ditch, looking down. His head was practically resting on his shoulder, the tendons on the opposite side dangling where they snapped. He looked to be trying to push it up every so often, but he couldn't grip properly, so his hand slipped over his face. His other hand reached out to her.

"Stay away!" she snapped, backing up along the gully.

"Dorthy!" he followed her movement, his feet shuffling. At any moment, he was likely to fall in, on top of her.

"Go away! Leave me alone!"

"Dorthy!"

"Dorothy! I'm *Dorothy!* Why can't you ever get my name right?"

"Dorthy."

Dorothy stopped moving. Julian wasn't attacking her. Although he was in worse shape than the road kill she occasionally passed when she was driving along the motorways, he could still have hurt her. Yet, he wasn't trying to.

Dorothy loved to watch horror films and would laugh at her friend, Sara, who would keep a cushion or pillow handy for when she was too afraid to watch the screen. She knew what happened if you were bitten by a zombie or vampire or other supernatural creature. Not that she thought there was anything supernatural going on. The bus had been caught up in the storm and had been dropped somewhere she didn't recognise. It had sent those men crazy and they'd attacked the passengers. Still, she was not one to believe in any of the bizarre things that occurred in her favourite movie genre.

But...

If you were bitten by a zombie, you became one. It was the same for vampires and werewolves.

And Julian had clearly been bitten. He hardly had any neck left, yet he was walking and, almost, talking. Did that mean...? Could he be...?

"Are you ok?" she asked him. Maybe he could still hold a conversation. He would be traumatised by the attack and needed her help. PTSD, that was it. He was shell-shocked.

And, to think, she had run from him and been afraid.

"Dorthy," he said, sadness apparent in his tone.

"Julian," she said, climbing out of the ditch.

She didn't bother to correct his mistaken pronunciation of her name. She could see his throat move as he spoke. She wanted to minimise the image. She took his hand and squeezed it.

"Let's see if we can get you some help, shall we?"

"Dorthy," he answered.

Dorothy sighed. She preferred 'Dottie' to' Dorthy', but it was too late to tell Julian that. She doubted he would be able to process the information.

8

His eyes opened. His head throbbed. His joints, particularly his back, ached at every involuntary twitch of his body. He moaned and the sound was hollow in his ears. Oddly, he felt his voice should have been fuller. Had more substance to it. He sounded, to himself, as if his voice was missing a part of itself. There was a hollowness that his was confusing his ears. He began to cough, the jerking causing the headache he hadn't really noticed over his other pains to explode and make him press his temples to the point they could almost cave in.

The coughing subsided. He lay there, trying to bring his breathing under control and subdue any further fits. Steadily, he started to feel more normal. The headache eased quickly and, apart from his back, the soreness in the rest of his body reduced to more manageable levels. He had always felt an ache that was permanently settled under the surface of his skin, as if, at any moment, it would reveal itself and reduce him to a quivering ball of agony. It was a thunder on the edge of his sensations, and it was ever present.

But this was different. This wasn't *that.* This was... he couldn't quite describe it. His mind was thick with forgetfulness and it was causing his thoughts to push against a current he was struggling to fight. He didn't know where he was. He couldn't remember how he came to be there. He needed to concentrate to remember his own name. Even when he had, he wasn't sure he was correct.

He lifted his hand to rub his eyes.

The palm of his hand was covered in scratches. He looked at his other and found the same criss-cross of red, sore lines etching his skin. The pattern continued up his forearms to where the biceps tunnelled into the sleeves of his shirt. He touched one of the slashes on his wrist and winced. Where had they come from? What had he done? Had he been attacked?

He pushed himself up and stood. The world started to spin around him and he crouched down to try and let it whirl its way still once more. His back cracked loudly as he bent down and he could feel the joints freeing up, as if they'd been fused together and he was breaking their bonds. He looked at his clothing and the tears in the cloth.

What?

He stood again, ignoring the much fainter wave of nausea that washed over him.

"Come on… Adam. Get it together."

Saying the words – his name – out loud seemed to cement his identity in his mind. He felt a little surer about himself, though he still couldn't recall what had happened. Adam. His name was Adam. He was… a… baker? The smell of bread, fresh from the oven and perfectly risen, filled his nostrils. Yes, he was! Suddenly, his memories returned, slamming into his mind with enough force to take his breath away. He lived alone, but was courting Melody whose father sold his sheep every Thursday morning in the market square. She was lovely, rather than beautiful, and her smile bound him as if with a spell.

He'd seen Melody earlier that day. They had shared an evening meal, in fact. When they parted company, their kiss was filled with the promise of boundaries and barriers crumbling. He'd intended to go home, but had decided to walk along the river that ran through town. The cygnets had recently hatched, as they did each year, and he enjoyed watching them grow and become swans themselves. Melody told him that, one day, he would grow into a swan. He would be strong and proud and beautiful. He was, of course, those things already, to her, but she hoped he wouldn't fly away and leave her.

"Why would I want to grow up at all?" he asked and she smiled that smile.

He tickled her sides and they laughed until the tears came and the passion ignited. But, they had promised each other they would wait, so they shared that kiss.

He had stood by the water's edge and watched the young birds as the sun set and the moon and her sisters, the stars, flooded the heavens. The cob, the cygnets' father, hissed at him in warning. He intended them no harm. Adam thought nature was beautiful. If he had a choice, he could spend all day appreciating its wonder. But, at the implied behest of the swan, he backed away and continued his walk. The sky was clear and the moon was full.

There was nothing else. Nothing except…

Hunger.

9

The more Edward walked, the easier it became to do so. Stephen's leg was slightly shorter than his own, metal, appendage and he had to walk with a permanent limp or risk falling over. He had overestimated the man's height, something he didn't usually do. He needed to be more careful. More accurate. Otherwise, his attempts to rebuild himself would fail and he would be what his creator always said he was.

Useless.

The Tinkerer was a tall man. Woefully thin, as if the meat had been sucked from his bones while the skin still clung to them, he towered above everyone who came into stood in his presence. He always wore black, and had a battered top that took his height a good foot further towards the ceiling. It gave him the appearance of a ghost of sorts that was only emphasised by the deep, inset eyes that were permanently in shadow. He was an unnerving man that could shake the core of the most defiant visitor.

He enjoyed the effect he had on others. He welcomed and nurtured the look to ensure those he met were perpetually uncomfortable around him. He, when younger, spoke with a voice that was pitched higher than those of his friends, so he determined to bring it down an octave or three. He wanted to speak from his boots, the journey from sole to mouth being long enough for him to lose the pitch and gain the power.

The Tinkerer, his name being cast aside long before in remembrance of the day he had been cast out by his parents, enjoyed the taste of fear that accompanied those he met. He liked to dine on it and would spend his meetings licking his lips, honestly believing he could taste their dread.

The stream of visitors had reduced to a trickle in recent years as his reputation for animosity grew and his status as an inventor diminished. He had once been the friend to royalty and those of great eminence. The Tinkerer had created such fine devices for them that he had, before the darkness descended on the world, almost been seen as gentry himself.

From mechanical pets to contrivances that could dress you where you stood, the Tinkerer was a master of his craft. He could look at a problem or a request and the solution would start to grown in his mind like a flower blossoming, ready to be picked once in full bloom and handed to the requestor. He would closet himself away in his workshop, not eating and with only minimal drinking, until the planted seed was ready for plucking.

It was the only time there was any light in his life. It was the only place he felt he belonged – with his contraptions. They were his real friends after, when he was young, he had built the tiny spiders that had injected those his father had insisted were his friends. But they weren't. His father was wrong.

Real friends didn't push you or pull your hair or call you names or hurt you. So, the Tinkerer made his own, and they did his bidding and slipped their tiny needles into the sleeping necks.

The Tinkerer wasn't used to poisons. He was more at home with parts than potions. He meant to make them sleep for a couple of days. Awaken with a throbbing head. When they didn't wake at all, his father sent him away. Enough food for lunch and a small dinner and a spare set of clothes was hastily thrust into a bag and the door was opened.

Not a single word was said. His mother remained seated in the lounge, staring at her hands wringing in her lap. The Tinkerer understood. He left and he didn't return. He didn't understand tears so shed none. His mother did, but she did so away from her husband.

When he arrived in the capital city and opened his shop and captivated the population, he rebuilt his spiders. Just in case. He also, *just in case*, studied poisons.

He thought himself to be a decent man. He *wanted* to be a decent man. He simply had devilish tastes. He didn't, at first, wish to be feared. He longed to be liked rather than be the brunt of people's jibes. Unfortunately, his upbringing and the treatment from his peers had warped his sense of what 'liked' really was. Thus, he began to relish his darker side.

It was, he felt, a spiral staircase he could not help but descend, so he should accept the situation. A part of him flickered in the recesses of his shadowed spirit. This part was Possibility. Possibly, he could redeem himself. Possibly, he could step out of the night and make it all right. Possibly, he could be who he had wanted to be.

But, while he waited for that to happen, he would revel in his reputation.

The Tinkerer was lonely. He had his spiders, and they were attentive to his needs and his moods. They carried the weight of his temper. They listened to both his rants and his meandering, wistful wonderings. There was not, even remote, understanding of his words, however. And he knew this.

His face was unused to a smile. When one did chance by and settle on his lips, it looked shocked, as if it didn't belong and had ended up there by mistake. It had taken a wrong turn on the way to someone whose life was filled with happiness but didn't realise until it was too late. It had to stay. It had to do its best to look sincere. It, in the main, failed. When he was faced with the problem of a lack of companionship, the smile was unlike any he had worn previously in his life. It was *real*. It was warm. It would not be seen by anyone else, but that didn't matter. For a time, the Tinkerer felt something called, he believed, happiness.

For more days than he could count, he worked on his creation. His already slender form grew skinny. Boney. His eyes sank deeper into their sockets. He was a whirlwind of creativity, spinning up a mass of intricate gadgets that fitted together to build…

Edward took his first steps only one month after the Tinkerer had started making him. Of those steps, only the first three were unsteady. After that, he was sure footed, his balance perfectly measured and his coordination better than that of his creator.

Edward spoke within an hour. He held a full conversation within two. He made a joke by the time the third hour had passed. When he smiled, one and a half minutes after that, the Tinkerer did as any normal father would do in such circumstances. He followed his own parents' example. He sent his newborn, mechanical son out into the world, branding him a failure.

Edward had smiled. The Tinkerer had seen that smile and, rather than be proud of the life he had created, he could feel only jealousy. His metal monster was more human than he.

Edward knew that he was not like his father. Mortal. Frail. Prone to emotional piques. He was pure. Superior. *Forever.* Yet, he wasn't complete. Blood didn't pulse through his veins. He had no veins. He couldn't breathe. He had no lungs. He also had no heart, yet he felt it break.

The more Edward walked, the easier it was to do so. The more he lived, the harder it became. His decision was made within his sixth hour of opening his eyes for the first time. He would rebuild himself. He would be what his father really needed. He only needed the body parts. He discovered, in the feast of knowledge he'd been given as part of his birth, that there were those who should not have been allowed to have their own.

Edward would find them. He'd seek out those who soiled the gift of life they had been given by tainting that of others. He would, systematically, replace the various parts of his own physique.

Then he would find his father.

And he would kill him.

10

"Dor..."

"Stop!"

Dorothy held up her hand and hung her head. Her eyes were closed and her breath was shallow through gritted teeth. She'd had enough.

"Yes. I'm Dorthy. I give in. Please, just stop repeating it over and over!"

Julian looked at her. She could see nothing in his expression that implied he might have any idea what she was saying but, at least, he didn't speak. He was acting like a lost puppy in the way he was following her and she was torn between trying to escape him and wanting to help him. Not as torn as his neck, of course, and it was that which gave her pause.

She should be mourning him. She should be trying to find her way home, alone, crying over his ravaged body back at the bus. Instead, he was shuffling along with her, occasionally tripping over the most obvious obstacles – roots and bushes and so on – without trying to step over or around them. His eyes were on her at all times. She couldn't help but feel sorry for her friend. She'd admitted to herself that he *was* a friend, even though he taunted her and wound her up. They were in this mess together and, as he could clearly not help himself, she felt obliged to look after him. Somehow.

But...

He should be dead.

No one could have survived the attack that he'd suffered. No one could still be moving and breathing and speaking with so much damage to their body. Yet he was. The legacy of Hollywood was making her uneasy, however abjectly ridiculous it was to contemplate the fact he might be some sort of zombie.

Zombies ate brains. Hers, she thought was a decent example of that food. She did fairly well at school. She thought things through. She didn't abuse it with drugs or too much alcohol. It would be in fine shape. Full, no doubt, of flavour.

So what if Julian was only following her because he could sense a tasty snack?

But, she couldn't leave him behind. She'd tried. She had run away from him, but the pain in her ankle meant she could only keep the burst of speed up for a limited time before she had to stop and rest. Before she could move on again, Julian was by her side, saying that abortive attempt at her name. She had zigzagged. She had looped back on herself. She had hidden. It mattered not. He found her.

Perhaps her brain smelled, as well as tasted, good. Maybe it was the fresh baked bread of the zombie world. Just being in the vicinity of the aroma could make your stomach grumble and your mouth salivate.

Dorthy... no *Dorothy...* needed to stop such thoughts. She was becoming frantic. She was lost. She was hurt. It was building up over her and she was ready to drop. It reminded her of the time she had gone skiing with her school. She had injured her ankle then, too. She was standing outside the cabin, drinking in the fresh, crisp air and the stunning landscape, when a well placed snowball from one of her friends hit the large clump of snow precariously balanced on the edge of the roof.

They laughed when it landed on her. She didn't.

She wasn't laughing now. She was afraid and she was angry at herself for *being* afraid. She was sensible. She didn't get scared, not really, and she needed to get her brain into gear and figure this out.

If Julian didn't get there first.

STOP!

"D..."

"No," she said. "Don't."

He didn't. Instead, he stood and looked at her. Her, not her head, as if picturing the contents of her skull in the same way Wile E. Coyote imagined the Roadrunner. Lunch. He was waiting. At first, she didn't know for what, but then it dawned on her. He was waiting for her to move. To do something. Then, she guessed, he'd follow.

Fair enough. The blood wasn't gushing out of his open wounds. His head seemed fine resting on his shoulder. She was getting used to the glimpses of spine that seemed to be exposing itself to her like a park pervert.

Dorothy looked around. Rather than simply running away from something, she needed to be moving towards it. There had been no sign of the things that had attacked them on the bus, and nothing else seemed to be moving amongst the trees. She realised she'd been foolish in her rush through the forest. Having no idea if there was anything else here that could hurt her, she should have been more careful. More *sensible.* It was her middle name, her uncle had told her.

Fine. Think. Use the brain Julian wasn't drooling over.

She was hungry. She needed something to drink. She should find shelter. She had no idea where those things might be, or if they actually existed, but it gave her a sense of purpose. She closed her eyes to try and think, slowing her breathing down to calm herself. Panic wasn't going to help.

"Dorthy."

Dorothy ignored him. She had to focus. To figure a way out. She had no idea how she could explain what had happened to Julian when they made it back home. She was fairly certain the doctors at the hospital had yet to come across injuries like his, particularly where the victim was still walking around. Before that, though, she had to *get* home. It was a difficult task when you had no idea where you where in the first place.

"Dorthy."

"Shush!"

She was trying to think. He needed to stay quiet. Maybe she could block him out as if he were one of the soap operas her aunt would watch every single night of the week. It got to the point where Dorothy could be in the same room, reading a book or doing her homework, and not hear a word of what was said on screen. Julian was one of the actors. He was a niggle in her ear that she would happily forget about, at least until she had a plan.

"Dorthy!"

"*What?*" she snapped, turning to him.

Julian was still standing where he had been when she closed her eyes. His head was still balanced precariously. His arms hung limply by his side. He looked pitiful. She sighed.

"What?" she asked, the edge gone from her voice. She didn't expect an answer, as he had yet to say anything else, but she could hope.

"Dorthy," he said.

"Yes, I know."

He turned to look behind her. Dorothy turned to follow his gaze, realising he was, actually, trying to tell her something.

Oh...

The dog was sitting calmly, its tail wagging and its tongue hanging out. It was watching her. She, at first, couldn't do anything else but watch it back. The animal was so ordinary. So normal. So completely out of place.

"Hey there, boy," she said, crouching.

She held out her hand, palm upwards, inviting it forward. It didn't move. Its eyes didn't blink or divert their attention from Dorothy's own eyes. It ignored her hand. Its tail continued to happily wag and it remained sitting in place.

"Are you lost? Do you have an owner?"

She looked for a collar around the dog's neck but couldn't see one. It appeared healthy, so she assumed there would be a home for it somewhere close by. She'd always been taught to be wary of dogs she didn't know. One could never tell if they were friendly or not, and the most passive pet could bite without warning. Still, this one seemed friendly. It didn't feel threatening. Besides, it was only small. A ball of fluff with legs and ears. And a tongue.

Slowly, Dorothy moved forwards, closer to the animal. She kept her arm out, avoiding any sudden movements. It didn't seem to mind her approach, indicated by its tail flapping faster from side to side. Dorothy smiled. She liked dogs. She moved her hand down to stroke the head it dipped slightly to allow her access.

Her hand didn't stop when it came into contact with the dog's head. Her hand *didn't* come into contact with it! Her hand carried on moving down, moving through the animal's head and body until it was touching the ground.

She stared. The dog lifted its leg and brought it down on the back of her hand. It slid through, as disappearing into the flesh. She felt a slight chill in her skin as it passed through.

Dorothy watched the paw when it was pulled back. She saw the shape and the colour. She knew them. She knew the dewclaw. It had been twitching. She had seen it scratching the surface of the bus.

11

"Dorthy," said Julian.

"Yes," answered Dorothy. "It's a ghost."

A ghost. She laughed to herself. *At* herself. A ghost. What was she thinking? She had banged her head. She was still in the bus, unconscious, just as she had thought before. Or, like Julian, she was dead and this was the hereafter. Had she been bad whilst alive? If this was Hell, she wanted a recount. Or a refund.

Convinced she was imagining the dog, she stood and walked past it, deliberately sweeping her foot so it passed through its body. Julian followed, as she expected. She didn't look back had decided it didn't matter which direction she went in. She didn't know where she was and there was no way of knowing if she was heading towards danger. She was keeping the bus and its assailants behind her and that was all she could do. Maybe she'd find a house. A phone. A police officer. Someone normal?

One way was as good as another.

"Come on Julian," she said, setting off with a stride that belied her uncertainty.

"Dorthy," he said, following.

"Indeed," she said.

The dog that wasn't there watched them go and then scampered after them.

The sun was rising. The stars were fading as the sky brightened, disappearing into the dawn like the dream Dorothy wished she was having. She carried on walking, not looking back to see if Julian was still with her. She could hear him. His footfalls were heavy and he wheezed as he breathed, although that could have been the air weeping from a hole in his trachea.

After a while, she stopped. There'd been a sound she had been able to hear but, with the noise from Julian, she wasn't quite sure what it was. Finally, she could tell. Running water. There was a river nearby.

"We're near water," she said to Julian, the dialogue starting before it could remember that he couldn't reciprocate. "Excellent! I'm thirsty!" she answered to herself.

She turned to him, happy to have his ravaged company. It took her mind off her predicament. She refused to look down at the dog that was sitting by her leg. It wasn't there. It couldn't be. Again, almost out of spite, she let her foot enter and exit its body. It didn't move or react. It just wagged its tail and waited.

"Do you see the dog?" she asked Julian, not expecting an answer.

"Dorthy," he said. He tilted his head slightly and regarded it. "*Dorthy.*"

"Of course," she said.

So, if he could see it, either he was a part of her dream, or a party to her delusion. She didn't suppose it mattered which was the case. She bent down to scratch between the dog's ears. Its tail thumped against the ground and Dorothy was sure she couldn't actually hear its beat. She couldn't feel the fur but held her hand there as if she could. The dog responded and licked her hand, its tongue looking as if it were cutting through her fingers but leaving no wound. Her grin was natural and genuine.

Being finally accepted by her, the dog jumped up and pranced around their feet. Dorothy laughed, stepping around it, not able to get around the feeling that she'd trip over it.

"I'll call him Frank," she said. "I always wanted a dog called Frank."

"Dorthy," said Julian.

"You're right," she told him. "He is adorable, even for a ghost."

It wasn't lost on Dorothy that she was interpreting what Julian was saying as if they were having a real conversation and the spirit of a dog she'd seen crushed was playing with her and she was happy about it. The world had gone mad, or she had. Go with the flow and she'd end up washed on the beach of salvation. Or wake up.

"Come on," she said, responsibility settling back on her shoulders. "We should go."

The trio set off again through the forest. Dorothy was feeling refreshed and energised. She was smiling. Stranded, in pain, lost and afraid, but smiling. The river was calling to them and she wanted to answer its call.

The sound of rapidly flowing water grew as they neared, following the noise like dogs to the crinkle of an opening packet of anything. When they broke the line of trees, expecting to see a wide expanse splitting the land and a far bank that was unreachable because of currents and distance, Dorothy was surprised to encounter quite the opposite. The river was narrow, being only a little wider than she could jump with a good run up. The banks dropped sharply to its depths – and it did look deep – but the flow was almost lazy compared to the implication from the din it was making.

She stood on the edge, looking down, wondering why it was so loud. She could see, close to the middle, a mass of sharp rocks thrusting up from the riverbed. They were causing the water above and around them to bubble and froth, as if dancing on the points of the stony blades.

"We should be careful," she said quietly. "I wouldn't want to swim in there."

"Dorthy."

"I agree."

Dorothy had no real idea what Julian had said, but her agreement seemed to fit. Was she actually starting to understand him? That was ludicrous. He said the same word in the same tone, more or less, each time. She sighed. The feeling of being alone was threatening to overwhelm her. She shook her head. Flow. Go with it. Whatever is going to happen *will* do. Her mood won't change that, so there was no point in being in one.

"Come on."

She decided to follow the river's flow, rather than go against it. It gave her the impression that she *wasn't* fighting against a tide of circumstance that was about to sweep her over into an abyss. Because she *wasn't*. She was handling this. Quite well, she thought.

Frank, their new companion ran a few feet in front of her and stopped. He raised himself up onto his hind legs and barked. It was silent, but Dorothy's mind filled in the silence. She could imagine what he sounded like and wished she could actually hear it.

"Good dog," she said. "We're coming."

She slapped her neck as she felt something bite her and felt a small splinter jab her hand. She pulled the hand away and looked at it. Had whatever that had bitten...?

She saw the small dart protruding from her palm, transferred from her neck by the impact of her hand on it. Her vision blurred. Her head filled with fog. Her mouth became dry. The strength drained from her legs into the river to be sucked under and torn into pieces by the sharp rocks.

She collapsed.

"Dorthy," said Julian.

Frank, the dog, jumped on Dorothy's chest. He stood on the surface, rather than sinking through, and licked her cheek. When she didn't respond, he looked up at Julian and barked.

"Dorthy!" Julian said, a sigh evident in his tone.

As the bushes that filled the gaps between the trees along the bank parted and small figures stepped out, Frank vanished.

12

They had hidden in the cellars when the creatures came.

There had been shouts. Tears. Hastened goodbyes. Then the screams had come. Screams and yells and manic laughter. They didn't move. They daren't. Some of them cried, but others offered hugs and hands over mouths and fingers on lips.

Days begin and days end. Often, the two opposite ends of the hours offer similar experiences. Tiredness. Yawns. Looking forward to the day that follows and the one that has passed. Often, also, they can be as different as the light from the darkness. The one can be full of well rested vigour with the other being laden with the arguments or the accidents that were scattered by Fate's hand upon your life. A day may be filled with laughter or flooded with sorrow.

In the main, days follow each other in a relay of mundanity. They race to the finale faster than anyone can dream of equalling. We are slaves to their competition and are lost in the moments that are cast aside in their wake.

A day has an expectation. It has a plan. It has a supposed agenda.

When a Tinkerer lets loose with an invention, and that invention goes awry, a day breaks upon the world like the tears of a parentless child.

When they awoke, Frederick Watkins and his wife Emelda kissed, just as they always did. Penelope and Peter, their children, ran into their room and jumped on the bed. The two youngsters had an unerring ability to know when their parents were no longer asleep. They were in the room and on the bed within seconds of the good morning kiss.

The family were happy. Even though the world had soured recently, they took the positives from their life and used them to sweeten their world. It was easy to ignore things when they had each other. They wouldn't out after dark. They wouldn't go outside the town limits. They wouldn't drink the water from the river, instead queuing for hours to use the well at the back of the Hodgen's house. It was ancient and deeper than anyone knew and the water tasted stale, but it was safe. It didn't kill you and… It didn't turn you.

Penelope and Peter were ushered out of the bedroom to get dressed. They would have to leave for school soon. Life still went on, despite the terrors that stalked the hills only a few miles away.

"Come on, gang," shouted Frederick.

He was standing at the front door, always the first ready and the one to be prompting the others to hurry or they'd be late. They never were, but Frederick would leave nothing to chance. Routine kept his children alive and his wife kissing him each morning.

They left within moments of the time they needed to, but Frederick was still uneasy. Moments were precious. They should be spent wisely. Emelda squeezed his hand, feeling his frustration and sharing his nerves. There was no reason to worry, of course. Nothing had happened for months. When the creatures had been driven from the town and the funerals had been held for the Carrons' and the Pierson's, the defences were improved. The walls were raised. Lights were installed. Sirens would activate and the gates, massive sheets of razor wire topped metal, could be closed within seconds. The guards were doubled and patrolled endlessly.

Peter and Penelope ran ahead, racing each other to the next tree or street corner, giggling as they went.

The laughter stopped abruptly when the siren wailed its warning. The children stared at their parents, not sure, exactly, what the sound was, though they could guess what it implied. Frederick and Emelda looked first at each other, shock immobilising them, then they ran, gathering up their son and daughter.

The streets filled rapidly, panic blistering on the normally smooth surface of the townsfolk. They knew what the sirens meant. They had to act, and quickly. The adults were agitated but managed to contain their urge to stampede, trampling each other in the process.

That happened before. The last time. They could not let that happen again. The children couldn't see their parents afraid. They couldn't witness the injuries caused by a mass of people fuelled by the knowledge that Death was descending upon them. They shepherded the children along, as fast as they could, their minds filled with the choice made months before but only now being carried out.

The cellar of the school was a series of interlinked rooms that had been extended along with the town defences. Storerooms were filled with all manner of foods and drinks to sustain everyone in the village for weeks, if necessary. The plan wasn't to hide everybody down there, though. That would be preferred, but would be foolhardy.

The Terrors, those manic creatures changed by the Tinkerer's meddling into something savage and cannibalistic, would not stop if they found no victims. The town would be ravaged. The houses ransacked and wrecked. Eventually, they would be discovered, and then everyone would die.

This way…

The roar was heard above the sirens, almost an aural battle for supremacy. The preparations were complete. The adults were back in their homes. Some held weapons, knowing they would be ineffective but hoping they would, at least, inflict some measure of damage. Some sat in a final, loving embrace, ready to meet the end together.

Some lay together, hands held, dead eyes staring at the ceiling, self-slit throats bleeding out.

The Terrors. Still, mostly, human, but with an unnatural and all-consuming hunger. They feasted on anything that lived, desiring only to still a beating heart and savour its flavour. They besieged the streets, tearing the town apart.

Those that had taken their own lives were shredded in anger.

Those that raised a weapon when the door or window was smashed open managed to prolong the end for a few seconds. Scant moments to try and drive back the demons that infested their homes.

Those that had chosen to hold each other and find strength in a shared resignation, gave themselves to the demons. Fighting would be a wasted effort. Only one husband, Shapiro Bryant, dared to defend his wife. He threw himself forward into the mob, screaming at them. His limbs were torn from his body. His screams intensified, being cut off as his throat was ripped out. Jubilant, the beasts clawed at him until his organs were uncovered and devoured themselves.

Rolanda, his wife of forty years, mostly good but tainted by a too strong hand when arguments raised their ugly heads, sat on the couch. Her hands were clasped tightly together. Her eyes were closed. She rocked forward and backward. She was crying softly. Her husband's sacrifice had not saved her. She was still taken. Still eaten. Still alive and aware far into the assault. Shapiro had only extended her pain.

The children were quiet. If any tears were shed, they were silent ones. Even the youngest understood what to make any sound would mean. Secreted in below the school, they didn't see the light of day for two weeks. Two children died in that fortnight. Understanding that they would never see their parents again – or would only find the ruined remains – they couldn't bring themselves to eat or drink. Their friends tried to encourage them or, when they grew weaker, force them, but they had lost hope. They both died in their sleep, a painless death in an otherwise pain-filled life.

When they crept out of the school, they were changed. The sun had set on their spirit. They could only, now, walk with darkness in their souls.

And they would do what needed to be done to survive.

13

"Dorthy," said Julian.

The children, seven of them, circled him, nail filled clubs and javelins held in readiness. He didn't move or show he had seen them. His gaze was fixed on the girl crumpled at his feet. When the children realised he was no threat and saw he had no neck for their dart to find a target, they turned their attention to Dorothy.

The tallest of them, James Bryant, son of a foolhardy and arrogant man, stepped forward. He held the point of his homemade but no less effective spear close to her throat and nodded to the child opposite. His sister shook her head, too afraid to move closer to the stranger. James gestured again, angry at being disobeyed. The girl next to his sister pushed her forward, a sly smile dancing across her lips. She liked James, even more so since he had taken leadership of their group. His sister stood in the way, not allowing anyone to get too close to her brother. She needed his love for herself, lacking that of their dead parents. Eva, the girl, gave Brie, the sibling, a shove to show James she could be decisive too. If the stranger tried anything, then Brie could also be removed as an obstruction to her intentions.

The unconscious girl, close enough to being an adult's age to warrant taking, didn't move when Brie fell against her. Eva's smile morphed into a quickly masked scowl. There would be other chances.

Brie knew of Eva's infatuation and could guess the real reasons behind the hand on her back. She spun and leapt on the other girl, forcing them both to the ground in a wild mass of shouts and punches.

James signalled to the others in the search party. Bring the girl, forget the other two. He would let them fight. They'd stop eventually and realise they were alone. They'd then decide they needed each other and hastily return to the safety of the town.

The four others took a limb each and lifted Dorothy, following the boy who would be a man.

"Dorthy," said Julian quietly. He lumbered after the children. After Dorothy.

14

Adam, lost in the forest, was afraid.

The sun was rising rapidly, but it was struggling to push its rays through the thick canopy and reach for the flora below. Adam longed for its touch. Recently, the night had been a beast that stalked him at the end of each day. It was one that relentlessly galloped after him and one he was powerless to outrun.

He tried to fight the growing feelings of dread that would creep through him when twilight drew in, bringing nightfall with it. He failed each time.

He was never one to know fear, normally. He'd been an arrogant child, unmindful of the effect his harsh words and actions had on those around him. He took what he wanted, physically and emotionally, and made those who gave him it suffer if they showed reticence.

His father's death changed him. The man was strong willed but decent. He had nothing but kind words for those around him and would have been appalled if he knew the sort of boy his son was. Adam Sr. lived by a precise set of rules that he had tried to instil in his offspring. They dictated how he treated others and how he expected to be treat. How to react in certain circumstances. How to be with his family and his peers. It was regimented, but he was a man proud of his life and his ways. And, obliviously, of his son.

Adam had rebelled. He didn't want to be forced into a mould of his father's making. Though it was the template to a life of respect, it wasn't one that the boy, himself, had created. He would build himself in his own image. And he did. It did not earn him respect. He was friendless, where his father had many. He was avoided, while his father would be surrounded by people eager to see him and ask how he was.

When Adam Sr. died, his funeral was attended by so many people, they spilled over into the street. The wake was a celebration of a life rather than the mourning of a loss. Adam realised that, if anything happened to him, his would be a lonely affair with an audience there to ensure he had, indeed, died. The next day, he visited those he felt he had wronged. He apologised. He took the beatings. He accepted the doors slammed in his face.

His father did, finally, offer a guiding hand to his son's future. Adam started to be liked. It was a slow process indeed, but he had turned the tide of his life and the turnout for his death. His arrogance stepped over into the land of confidence.

Except, in the previous months, he could feel thoughts nibble on his nerves. There was nothing coherent he could take a bite out of, but there were whispers in the back of his mind. He tried to shut them out and to silence them with bravado, but they were insistent. And nocturnal.

From dawn until dusk, he was Adam, son of Adam in ways he would not have thought possible. When the sun had set, he was just Adam. Agitated. Stressed. Scared.

When he was with Melody, the murmurs were quiet. He rarely heard them, his mind concentrating on love and libido. Until that night. Until the hissing of the swans joined the susurration in his head, to the point he had his hands pressed to his ears.

As he made his aimless way through the trees, his memories were returning. He could remember who he was and who he had been. He could remember his father's handshake. His mother's smile. Melody's touch. He still could not recall the final moments before he awoke in the forest, but he was sure that would come.

His body had its own memory. It retained the dread and presented it to the man like a trophy at an awards ceremony, almost proud of the fact that it could recall such a thing and bring it to the fore without hesitation.

His heart was beating fast in his chest. It thudded as if it, too, felt his fear and wanted to be free of his torso's confines. The sun was doing its best to ease his panic but, until he was able to walk freely beneath its smile, he would continue to tremble. The trees towered above him, bars of a prison he could not escape from. The cuts on his hands and arms stung like hundreds of violent nips at his skin.

His chest itched and he scratched it as he stumbled along. The irritation grew to the point he had to open his shirt to see the cause. He was shocked to see an angry rash covered his entire upper body, bloody from where his nails had raked at it through the material.

He could hear water. A river. It was nearby and he increased his speed, eager to be clear of the overbearing trunks and the suffocating expanse of leaves. He stopped suddenly when he heard a voice.

"Dorthy!"

Movement!

He ducked, hiding behind one of the very trees he felt so imprisoned him. He could tell whoever was approaching was trying to be quiet, but they were failing. Their voices, subdued but loud enough to be heard, carried through the forest as if the trees were passing the words along themselves. Adam was shocked to see a group of children pass him by, followed by an older boy with a head that was barely attached to his body. Four of the children were carrying a girl. One was leading. He was about to step out from his cover when two other children, girls, ran past. They were pushing each other, arguing, but staying together.

They were going back into the forest. He desperately wanted to be out in the daylight. He needed to be away from the trees. But… They were *children!* He had to follow. Making much less noise than they had, he did so.

15

"Do you think he's dangerous?" Brie asked quietly.

She had her knives. They rested flat against her forearms, ready to spin out in well-practised flicks of the wrists. She watched Julian carefully, sure that he was biding his time until the chance came to eat them all. He had been a victim of the Terrors, that much was obvious. The damage to his throat should have killed him, but they liked to occasionally only part devour a victim. It was how they filled their ranks. How they turned people.

A bite, savage and deep enough to almost kill the prey but just short of fatal. It gave and took a small part of either side. Life. Savagery. Longevity, Bloodthirst.

The bitten became the biter, the attacked the attacker. Usually, the transformation was instant. Between one heartbeat and what would have been the next if the heart had not stopped beating, A new Terror was born. They had yet to encounter one in whom the change was delayed or stalled. It didn't mean it wasn't going to happen. It just meant it hadn't yet.

"Yes," answered Eva.

Eva and Brie were once best friends but, when Eva's brother matured – something that the destruction of their village and murder of their parents had accelerated – Brie's interest had changed from a common dislike to a one-sided desire. When it came to the Terrors, however, they were once again united.

"I think he's going to kill us all," Eva said.

"He can try," laughed Brie, bringing one of the blades up to the exposed side of Julian's neck. "He won't succeed."

"Don't kill him all yourself," snarled Eva. "I want some, too."

"Nobody is killing anyone!"

The girls stiffened at the sound of James' voice. He was only slightly older than his sister but he had a paternal hand pushing him forward. He was an easy choice for a leader. Having the mayor as a father gave him an inherited authority that was emphasised by his manner. He was automatically deferred to and tried to be the leader he hoped he would have become when he succeeded office as planned. Those aspirations were dust now, but he could still make demands and have them carried out. He was mayor in all but ceremony and title.

Brie and Eva stared at each other. Their brief alliance had dissolved in the boy's words. They were, once more, sister and devotee.

"Why not?" asked Brie.

She was the only one who dared stand up to her brother. She was wise enough to exercise this ability only when alone, but Eva didn't count. Eva didn't matter. Eva needed to see that Brie, by blood, had a measure of authority herself.

"Because, we only kill Terrors and their like."

"Look at him!" said Eva, daring to step on the coat tails of Brie's licence. "He *is* one of them!"

"I don't agree," said James.

He stepped forward to stand in front of Julian, close enough for the latter to bite a chunk out of his face if he so desired. Julian looked to the floor, not making eye contact with his captor.

"Dorthy," he said.

"Of course he is," Brie insisted. "He's bitten. He's turning!"

"He's not." James turned to them, his back to the creature. "If he was, he would have by now. It can go slower, but it's never taken this long."

He gestured towards Julian. He was feeling calm in the presence of the oddity. Elated, even. With it and the girl, they had something to bargain with.

"Look at his clothes," he said. "He's not from around here. Maybe the virus hasn't reached that far yet. Maybe it means there's somewhere we can go to be safe."

"I say kill him," said Eva.

The killing of her parents had changed her from a fairly timid, pleasant girl into an angry, antagonistic young woman. She would prefer to strike first and not bother to ask any questions. It was a rash attitude that had, more than once, put the group of survivors in danger, but she wanted revenge for what had happened and didn't care how she exacted it.

"No," James said. "He's valuable."

"Why do we need him, when we have the girl?" Brie didn't like siding with Eva, but James was being foolish. The Terror-in-waiting was a risk and it was one they couldn't tolerate.

"Look at him," James said. He was walking around the creature, looking at it with contempt. "He's pathetic. We don't need to be afraid of him. We can study him. Find out what makes the Terrors what they are."

"Why do we need to know that? Just kill them all!" Brie said, moving to stand beside Eva.

The pair, for their diminutive stature and age, looked a formidable force. They stood defiant in the face of James' idiocy and thought they could stare him down from his lofty tower. He seemed oblivious to them, though. He wasn't, in fact, but he wasn't about to show them he was concerned by their actions. His sister was an excellent second in command and Eva, though she seemed to be showing him more attention than he'd like, had a newborn streak of spite that would prove useful in the future. He knew he was right about this and so would ignore their objections. He was in charge. That was that.

"Two reasons," he said. "Firstly, we know nothing about why the Terrors are like they are. Secondly, he and the girl were together. He's leverage."

Both of the girls had to admit (to themselves) that they were impressed. They hadn't thought of that.

"If he tries anything…" started Brie.

"You can kill him," said her brother. "You can kill them both."

The creature, part Terror and part person or all of neither, stared at the floor. He seemed to have no idea of where he was. He simply stood there, occasionally uttering that same word: 'Dorthy.' James could see no threat in him. If nothing else, any sudden movement would probably result in his head becoming detached from his neck. He didn't share the girls' opinion. He wouldn't allow them to voice their dissent among the others. Anything resembling even a slight disagreement with their leader would undermine his position and, perhaps, the new foundations they were trying to build a community upon.

He turned to leave.

"Come on Brie, we have a prisoner to attend to."

Brie hurried after her brother. As they left the room, she stuck her tongue out at Eva. Eva scowled. She'd have her revenge. When she realised she was alone with the thing, she was suddenly not so brave and hastened after the others.

Julian didn't watch them go. He was staring at the floor. There was a smudge. It was doing nothing out of the ordinary except marking the floor, as smudges do. Julian kept looking at it, however. In the absence of Dor*o*thy, it was all he had.

16

"Dorothy."

"Dorothy!"

"Dorothy!"

Dorothy opened her eyes and immediately wished she hadn't. The sun streamed in through a high window, drilling into her brain as if it had been waiting for her to wake up and had stored the energy it was building up until just the right moment for it to impale itself in her retinas.

She had been dreaming. She was home, asleep in bed. The aroma of fresh baked bread, her aunt's speciality, filled the room and the call from downstairs roused her to a grumbling stomach, hungry for a slice.

But she wasn't in bed, she was in a wooden chair, her hands tied. The only smell was a dank, sweaty odour that felt like a greasy smear in her nostrils. There was no sign of her aunt and there was no-one to call her. The room she was in was empty.

She looked around, flexing her wrists to try and free them. The ropes which bound her were tight and unyielding. Her ankles were similarly restrained.

"Hello!" she called.

The room ignored her. It was large and mostly empty, apart from half a dozen small wooden chairs, similar to the one she was tied to, stacked against the far wall. Dorothy could see some short white sticks sitting in dust on the windowsill. They looked like chalk.

In fact, the whole room had a schoolish feel to it. Was this a classroom?

"Hello!"

She strained to hear any sounds outside the soft, cold echo of her own movements. There were none. Still...

"HELLO!"

There was no response. She struggled again against the ropes and, again, failed to budge them. She wanted her aunt, a need fuelled by the dream she'd had. She wanted the mall. Her friends. *Home.*

"HELLOOOOOO!"

Resigned, she stretched up to try and see out of the window. Unable to, she shuffled on the chair, performing a series of mini-hops to scrape across the floor. She didn't care about the noise she was making. If nobody was going to come to her calls, she doubted they'd hear her now. Once at the window, she peered out. The sun was bright and she had to squint to see anything with no hands to shield her eyes.

She could see a town. It appeared to be partially destroyed, perhaps by the tornado that had so casually tossed her bus about. The houses were missing roofs. Windows were smashed. Walls were collapsing. She couldn't see any cars or people walking about. Maybe they'd left before the storm. Well, someone was still there, or she would still be back at the forest with...

"Julian?"

"JULIAN!"

"Who's Julian?"

Dorothy spun, or tried to. The voice was from behind her and she couldn't see who was there. They sounded young. Perhaps they could get help! She twisted around, trying to repeat the movements that had helped her reach the window. She tried a little too hard and cried out as the chair tipped over and she fell on her side. She couldn't move.

Feet appeared in front of her face. The shoes were shiny, as if recently polished, but small. A child. She knew she wasn't far out of childhood herself, so was hoping she could convince whoever this was to assist her. She followed the legs up to see it was a boy. He was about thirteen or fourteen. Maybe not even as old as that. His stance and the mess of hair on his head made deciphering his age difficult.

"Can you help me up? Is your mum or dad around?"

"Who's Julian?" James asked again. "Is he that *thing* that was with you?"

"Thing? Who are you? Where am I?"

"Yes. The thing. The Terror that's not turned properly yet."

"I don't understand. Where am I?"

"You're here," said James.

"Where's that? Get me up!"

"No," said James. "You can stay there. It's safer that way."

"Safer for who?" Dorothy was starting to lose her temper. Her usually even, sensible mood was fraying at the edges and was in danger of becoming sharper than she'd like in such a situation. She needed to keep her head and find answers rather than start ranting and fighting when she was trussed up like her aunt's Sunday roast.

"Us, of course," James said. "If you're down there, you can't escape."

"I won't escape. I don't even know where I am or who you are. I just want to get home."

"You are home. Our home. And we're not going to let it be destroyed. Not again."

"What do you mean? Just let me go!"

Dorothy closed her eyes to try and contain her growing frustration. This child needed to listen to her!

"Can't you just get an adult? Please? We can sort all this out."

"Sorry," said James, his voice levelled into an emotionless monotone. "I can't do that."

"Why not?"

"Because they're all dead."

Dorothy's eyes snapped open and she stared at the boy. This nightmare was getting more and more bizarre. She needed to wake up!

"*What?* Look, just get me an adult. Let me out of here with my friend."

James crouched down next to her, moving a strand of hair away from her face in a surprisingly tender gesture. He smiled, though the curve of his mouth failed to reach any other part of his face.

"I said, I can't. There aren't any. They're all dead. Or turned, which is the same thing."

"I don't understand!" Dorothy was giving in to her temper. She wasn't in the mood for stupid games from a child. It wasn't funny. The ropes were starting to cut into her wrists. She was hungry and she needed to urinate.

"It's easy," James said. He was still stroking her face and the contact was making Dorothy want to squirm and pull away, but she had nowhere to go. "The adults, our parents are dead. We survived and we'll continue to survive."

He chuckled, a sound of genuine mirth.

"You're going to help with that."

"Yes!" Dorothy exclaimed. "I'll help! Of course I will!"

James stood. He looked down at her, his face briefly conflicted. Then he shrugged.

"Yes, you will."

"Tell me how," Dorothy said. "I'll do anything you need."

"You're going to be an offering," he said.

"An offering? What do you mean? What sort of offering? Who to?"

James turned and started walking to the door. He opened it and stopped before stepping out.

"We're going to feed you to them."

"*What?* Feed me to who?"

"The Terrors."

The door swung slowly shut as he left. The click of the latch seemed to seal the door and her fate. The ensuing silence was filled with a hushed promise.

"Come back!" she yelled. "Come back! Please!"

Eva moved from her hiding place behind a second door into the room. She watched the girl writhing on the floor and listened to her shouts. She saw the tears fall to the floor. She was unmoved by the girl's plight. She felt only hatred towards her. This stranger. This intruder.

She'd seen James stroke her face. She'd seen the look on his face as he was talking to her. He never looked her at that way. She didn't like it.

17

Adam moved quickly through the town, careful not to be seen. He could see that something terrible had happened and he was uneasy.

The houses were spread evenly along streets lined with colourful, blossoming trees that were beginning to coat the ground at their feet with a layer of golden leaves. At one time, the buildings would have been a delightful line of cream and wood structures, calming on the eye and reflecting the peaceful nature of the residents. Adam could imagine what had happened.

The Tinkerer.

He had heard of, though never experienced, the results of the strange man's experiments. He had a fierce reputation for innovation, enriching the lives of those rich enough to pay his prices, but there were stories of darker trials, with more sinister outcomes. The tales were unproven, as far as Adam knew, but the rumours had too much meat on them not to have the substantial flavour of truth.

The land had a growing shadow spreading over it and there could only be one person responsible for its expansion.

Adam couldn't help that, however. He was just a man in a country of bigger, braver men. He had simple needs. His Melody was one of them. Thinking of her, he almost turned back. He still didn't know how he had woken up in the forest. He should be working on that and finding out where he was. He should be getting back to his love.

Instead, he was creeping through a town he didn't know. One that had been the victim of a brutal attack. The houses bore the scars of the battle. Their previous dignity was broken and lay shattered, the fallen walls and smashed windows being open wounds that let the inner furnishing fall out like entrails from an eviscerated corpse.

In the forest, he'd lost track of the children before it ended and the town began. There was a wide gap between the two, strewn with low cut tree stumps. The area had been cleared of all foliage. Adam had seen this before. Where a town had stretched its boundaries and was encroaching too close to a forest, the edge of trees would be removed. No more houses would be built, and so causing deforestation, and the stumps that were left prevented this anyway. It was done to create a sort of barrier that marked the change of territory and also gave the illusion of space.

More than that, particularly recently, it meant that anything prowling with savage intent could not appear unannounced.

A wall had been built just beyond the stumps. It was far too high to climb and the only option was to choose a direction and walk.

Adam had to stop himself from running out from the canopy of thick branches and into the sun. He longed to feel its warmth on his skin. The subdued light from within the forest's folds clung to him. He could feel its cloying touch dripping from his body and was eager to wash it away by being clear of its grip. He'd waited, however. The children and their prisoner were gone. He couldn't see any adults and he could tell from the buildings that something horrifying had occurred.

He had taken a deep breath to steel himself so he could walk out. Then he took another and after that, a third. Adam, son of Adam seemed to be waiting out there in the open space. *Just* Adam had to build himself up to stepping across the threshold. It wasn't until he looked back around him, startled at the movement of some leaves – a breeze or small animal – that he ran forward and transformed into his father's son. He turned to the right. No choice was still a choice, and a lack of knowledge of the extent of the wall meant his direction mattered little.

The gates, when he reached them, were wide open. One had only a single, massive hinge holding it in place. Rammed into the other were numerous wooden stakes.

Atop each stake was a decapitated human head.

Adam looked at each in turn. The eyes of all were open, staring forward. In returning their gaze, he felt he was apologising for their sudden demise. He knew he wasn't at fault, but they needed someone to care. Someone to acknowledge their passing and the method of their death.

As he moved to walk through the gates, the head closest to him moved. It was a simple matter of gravity, of course. The weight of the skull and its contents impaled by the wooden shaft was causing it to slip down. His stomach lurched at the thought yet he couldn't help but look up at it. It was a man, about his age. The eyes, as with the others, were looking forward.

Until he stepped in front of it. Until it looked back at him.

Adam gasped, his hands reaching up without him realising. He was about to lift the head down, or set its position, or something.

The mouth opened wide. It was missing teeth and those that remained had been filed to points. It began to snap at him, snarling and growling. Adam stumbled backwards, landing heavily against the other gate. He groaned in pain and, for a moment, couldn't move. The head was rocking on the stake, moving, sliding, dropping.

It fell to the ground and rolled to his feet. The snapping had stopped but the eyes were fixed on his. The man, what was left of him, began to laugh.

Adam ran.

There should have been adults. Whether they were rebuilding their town or in hiding with their offspring, he couldn't know, but he had to find out. The macabre trophies at the gate had shaken him and Melody was calling him. He couldn't turn back, though. Adam Sr. would never have done so. Adam Sr. would have taken the children home with him. He would have fed them. He'd give them a bed each and ensured they had a home. Adam, the son, could not, perhaps, do that but he would offer aid.

He kept to the ruined houses. He felt guilty as he climbed through the wreckage, dashing from one building to the next once he'd confirmed nobody was watching. He felt he was violating the graves of the dead. The headstones were shredded sofas. The limp, decaying flowers were upturned drawers or discarded clothes. It was easy to feel that there had, actually, been no real people living there and the houses and belongings had been dropped as if by a giant hand. Only once did Adam see anything that had been a part of an actual person. It was a hand. Slender with painted nails.

It was severed at the wrist.

He turned his back to it and continued his exploration.

Before long, he saw a fat, sprawling building. It was low, a single story, and was in need of repair but not from attack. Largely intact, Adam could see that most of the windows were in one piece and, apart from one wall being cut in half as if a giant scythe had cut through it, swung carelessly by the spirit of Death that had taken the lives of those at the gate, the structure seemed to have escaped the wrath of whatever had attacked the rest of the town.

A large sign lay on the floor at the entrance to the building. It proclaimed that the school was an outstanding seat of learning for children and the adults they would become.

Adam stayed where he was, a short distance from the school and waited. He was hidden in the trashed summer house of the closest house and it afforded enough shelter for him to see without being seen. He still hadn't seen anyone, alive or dead, in the town. Perhaps the school was some sort of haven from the attackers. Perhaps it could be one for him, at least until he could make sense of what was happening.

The heads, the *head*, his strange displacement and lack of total recall.

When he was sure he would not be discovered, he ran across to the school. With it being a single floor, he had myriad windows to smash and gain entry. He didn't need to, though. When he tried the front door, it swung open easily. Unlocked.

He pulled it and slipped inside, ensuring it closed behind him. Ahead of him was a long corridor lined by classrooms. The first was an office. It was empty. Swiftly, he made his way along the hallway, trying each door as he came to it. All were locked. All except one. Adam paused, breathed, and pulled. It opened easily.

He'd barely stepped inside when he heard the cries from deeper into the school.

The girl! It had to be!

His caution was forgotten and he ran on. His footsteps echoed in the silent dust that had fallen across the floor. Anyone nearby couldn't fail to hear his passing, but Adam didn't care. He needed to save her. The gates had shown him how easily life could be taken away.

If he could save one, he might prove them wrong.

In her room, Dorothy heard the heavy footfalls of someone coming towards her. In the previous stillness, filled only with her shouts, they carried an ominous, threatening weight. She squirmed against her bindings, pushing against the floor to move the chair she was tied to back against the wall. She wanted to face whoever was coming for her. It certainly wasn't the child who had been with there before. She stopped yelling and held her breath.

She felt the ropes around her wrists move slightly and increased her pulling at them. Finally, she had loosened them enough to twist her hands free. The footsteps stopped outside the door. Dorothy kept her hands behind her, fists clenched, prepared for whatever might come in.

Adam stood, panting. The cries had ceased and he was unsure which room they had come from. Had the girl been struggling with one of the beasts that had caused the town's ruin? Was she now dead? If so, he would avenge her. Melody would want him to, rather than return to her. The girl's blood would be on his hands if he didn't try.

He heard the scrape of something moving in the room he was standing outside of. He thought about opening the door carefully and entering slowly. There was no point. Whoever was inside would have heard his approach. He cursed himself for not being more discreet. The time for caution had gone, so he had only one course of action. He barged through the door, shouting angrily. As he entered, he ducked and rolled, landing in a crouch, ready for a fight.

When Adam saw the girl alone and tied to the chair, with the rest of the room empty, he hurried to her.

When Dorothy saw the man burst in, she gulped back her fright. If he was there to hurt her, she would return the favour. When he moved to her, she brought her hands out, hitting the side of his head as hard as she could.

Adam fell back and swore. He pushed himself up and grabbed hold of the girl's arms. She was frantically trying to hit him again and shaking her upper body to loosen his grip.

"Get off me!" she screamed, leaning her head forward to bite at him.

"I'm trying to help you!" he shouted.

"Get off!"

"Stop it!"

Suddenly, Adam slumped forward, the crack to the back of his head knocking him unconscious. He fell onto Dorothy, the wind leaving her forcibly. She looked up as his limp body was pulled from her. A girl, younger than the boy who had visited her earlier, looked back at her. The contempt in her face was unmistakeable. Dorothy opened her mouth to speak, but didn't get the chance to say anything. The staff that had been used on Adam came down hard on the side of her head.

18

"Who is he?" Brie asked.

She was angry and agitated, pacing. Her knives hung down from her belt and her hands rested on their hilts as if willing something to happen so she could pull them forth and strike. She was a caged animal, its claws sharpened, desiring a target.

"We'll find out when he wakes up," James answered.

James was keeping his emotions tightly under control. He wasn't willing to vent his fury at his sister in front of the rest of their group, but he was finding it difficult not to. She insisted on trying his patience. If she didn't stop being so rash, she would put them all in danger.

"Did you have to hit him so hard?" Eva asked. She was unconcerned either way, but could see James' ire at Brie and wanted to play on it.

"Shut up," Brie snapped.

Before Eva could respond, James stepped between them. He glared at his sister and she closed her mouth. She could push him, she knew, but she also knew that look when her big brother gave it.

They were in the large sports field behind the school. Even with the wall around the town, the area felt exposed and James wanted to be done with this and back inside as quickly as possible. His authority was being put into question by those closest to him. He needed to bring them all into line. His plan should ensure that and keep the Terrors at bay.

Brie scowled at Eva's smug expression. She'd enjoy wiping it off the other's face as soon as she had the chance.

James moved to stand behind the two stakes that had been erected. The man and girl were tied upright to them, a task that had shown teamwork within his camp still existed. He had hope that the frayed edges could be trimmed and normality, parentless and fraught with danger as it was, could return. He stepped through the gap between the prisoners, imagining doing so gave him an entrance that would impress those he led.

The survivors of the Terrors' attack had once looked as lost as they had felt. When they resurfaced from their hiding place in the school cellars, they were hardened, but they were still children. Some of them were far too young to face the horrors of what had befallen them, but their time below ground had aged them emotionally. They knew, before seeing it, what they would encounter. Disposing of the bodies in a massive bonfire had been difficult, but they had persevered. Killing those who had turned had honed their, or given them, combat skills. It had stripped away their innocence and left behind a carcass of grim determination.

James was proud of them. He was proud of his sister. They'd overcome their trials and had become much stronger because of it, but the tests were not, and now would never be, over.

"Today is a good day."

He began this way every time he addressed them. It was a mantra that he hoped would seep in and tend the wounds they were ignoring. He saw some nodding their heads and the occasional smile. They had faith in him. More than he had in himself.

"We live in fear of the Terrors' return, as you know," he said. Murmurs of assent. Shifting of feet at the mention of their biggest fear. "We never know when they'll return."

The children looked at each other. He could see the tears well eyes and gave them a few seconds to feel afraid. He wanted them to know the fear so release from it would have more impact.

"But," he continued, "I have a plan. We're going to use these two to end the Terror's reign of... terror, for good!"

There it was. The light of hope. Their eyes grew wide. He heard their sharp intakes of breath. Even with his stumble over the script he'd practiced, they were now verging on actually feeling a sliver of happiness.

"She's waking up!" hissed Eva. She raised her spear and held it against Dorothy's chest as the older girl stirred and moaned softly.

"Let her," said James. "She can hear how she's going to help us. She won't escape this time."

Brie had been responsible for tying the girl to the chair and, as such, her subsequent attempt to break free. James, himself, had checked the knots this time. There wouldn't be a repeat occurrence. He turned back to the group.

"It's been too long since the Terrors came. We know they'll come back at some point. With these, we can make sure it's the last time. And with this!"

He brought out a syringe from the pocket of his coat. It was filled with a bright green liquid. He held it high, letting it be the symbol of liberty they needed.

They all recognised the contents. They were immediately nervous of them, but with the thrill of anticipation.

It was the poison.

19

Edward was conflicted.

He had taken the life of the farmer. He'd killed him when Stephen Decker, husband and father and monster, was on his way home to the family that loved him. More importantly, Edward had taken his leg.

A leg that was firm and well-muscled

And too short.

It was only a fraction of an inch, but it was enough to cause him to limp. He couldn't run with the ease and speed he was used to. When he crouched in waiting for his next quarry, his balance would be off, meaning his strike might be too.

It shouldn't have happened. The Tinkerer, for all his failings, had given his creation a brain that could compute calculations at a blinding speed. The eyes could magnify an object many times over and were able to see great distances, though colour tended to fade and blend if Edward attempted too great a view. They could zoom in to see the individual pores in human skin, though doing so gave him a headache.

So, the leg he took should have been exactly the correct size.

He wished he could have taken the other one. Both at once would have been perfect. They would have served him well and Stephen would have paid double recompense for his atrocities. Unfortunately, Edward could only replace one part of himself at a time. His own body would not accept more than a single new addition to its structure at once. As advanced as his clockwork brain was, it could not compute the intricacies required to connect to multiple new organic appendages or organs.

It needed time. It needed to, perhaps, become used to the change. To adapt and learn how to use it. If such a thing was not required, Edward could have harvested much of Stephen's corpse. It was in fine shape and there was plenty to choose from. The legs, arms and internals could have been swapped over and would have brought Edward closer to the perfect being he had been created to be.

It would have also hastened his final goal of killing the Tinkerer.

It was not to be, however. Time took its leave of hope and danced upon the desires of mortal people. And of immortal machines that *wanted* to be mortal. Edward had to take his time. He had to allow his metal body to acclimatise. By the time, short though it would be, he was able to upgrade himself again, the body he had reaped would be decaying. The transfer needed to be done rapidly, with minimal time for putrefaction to take place. If not – and Edward had discovered this to his detriment – the new limb would begin to fail. Once decomposition had begun, however slightly, it could not be stopped.

An intestine served little purpose when one did not eat, but the old woman who had beaten her children and grandchildren daily to teach them how not to treat people, had not hesitated to donate hers for a grander purpose. She had even smiled as the axe came down to split her head. Edward had taken the time to bury the woman who had willingly given her life so the Tinkerer's could be snuffed out. It was her apology, once the need for one had been explained to her, for the way she had treated others. She was sincere in her sorrow. She had died with an apology resting on her lips in the hoarse whisper of someone who had aged badly and lived worse.

By the time Edward had exchanged the entrails for his own internal tubes and pipes, they were already perishing. If he had not realised soon enough and swapped them back, Stephen might still have lived. His wife and children might not have.

So. Edward was conflicted. He knew he was imperfect. He knew he was a failure and was failing being even that. But he was trying. He was. And h was rebuilding himself in his creator's image, more or less. The Tinkerer was abnormally tall and thin. Not slender, because that implied a certain grace to the form. No. The Tinkerer was skinny. Edward did not believe that a person should appear to be less than their shadow. With his father, the silhouette appeared to be bulkier than he really was, as if it balked at having to be almost skeletal.

Edward chose victims, at least for outward use, who had substance to their frame. For his innards, his kidneys and spleen so far, he didn't mind the age or the weight of the owner. He was not particularly proud. One would work as well as another.

He had a dilemma. The leg was too short. He didn't want to remove it and put his back. The transition was markedly more difficult than for an organ, for example. He had to soldier on. He would find another of the same size and then he would feel more complete.

But, how had it happened?

It shouldn't. It couldn't. Yet it *had!*

If he were a human, full of blood, bones and beautiful organs that were desperate to be transplanted, he would have said he was ill. It was a fever. A virus. But he wasn't. He was mechanical and so could not possibly become ill, yet he was not working as he should. Something was wrong and Edward needed to find out what it was before he could no longer function.

He would rebuild himself faster. It was a risk, but one he was willing to take. Eventually, he would be complete and he could take care of his father. He would embrace him and he would give him the only kiss deserved from his son.

That of an axe.

20

Beauty is in the eye of the beholder.

When that beauty is shattered, a sliver punctures the beholder's eye and renders it blind to all that comes after.

James had been told that by his father. The conversation had taken place only days before the Terrors came. Such a short time from the words being spoken to them being fulfilled. They were discussing the way the world was turning. James, being a young boy and wanting to see that things were good and bright, was having his ideals dashed by a father who wanted his son to be realistic. Fatalistic.

The world his son was so optimistic about was damaged. It was injured. It was dying. The open wounds were evident everywhere one looked. The seasons could never decide which order they should appear in. This caused crops to fail and food to be in short supply. A disease was spreading that was turning ordinary, caring people into monsters. The water had to be siphoned and treated to be drinkable. Fields were once covered in glorious colour from the vast variety of flora that had always taken immense pleasure in blossoming. They were now either bare or covered in the strange red flowers that had begun to grow everywhere. Red flowers that reduced those who came into contact with them to seemingly sleepwalking corpses. They walked with their eyes open but were unseeing. Nothing could rouse them from their waking slumber.

The beauty the boy saw was shattered by the father who had seen the decay eat away at his happiness. Though he would never tell his son so, his wife's infidelity had driven him to drink and self-destruction. Though she would never tell her son this, her husband's alcohol abuse, which was on the verge of being domestic abuse, had turned her to the arms of another man.

James had believed his father. His view changed. Darkened. When the Terrors came and proved his father right, James' opinion took another shift. He would prove his father wrong. He would do what he could to rebuild the ruin that everything had become.

James was a young boy. An adolescent on whom adulthood had been violently thrust. Grown up decisions had to be made, no matter how painful they might be.

So, he was the first to leave the cellars after the attack. He had to be. Others volunteered, but they were younger. They were afraid of the dark or of spiders or of keeping their leg out of the covers in case something hid under the bed. James' upbringing ensured any such fears irrational were quashed. Spiders were purely small creatures that spun webs and had more legs than they knew what to do with. The dark was only the light gone to sleep. There were no monsters under the bed. They were all already loose outside.

He had surveyed the ravaged town from the windows of the very classroom he'd kept the girl in. When the Terror entered and went to attack him, he grabbed the nearest thing to him. It was a simple, ineffective weapon. The narrow, tapered cane the teacher used to point to things on the chalkboard and slap across the backs of misbehaving hands. James didn't think about how easily it might snap or how strong the Terror could be. He thought of the town and the people and his parents and his wards. And the ongoing decline of everything that should have been good.

As the Terror roared at him, he raised the cane and ran at the beast. It sank down, prepared to greet the oncoming child with his clawed hands and blood-soaked teeth. At the last moment, James thrust the sharp end of the cane forward. It hit the bridge of the Terror's nose and bent. James was suddenly worried it could snap, but the tip slid across and plunged into the eye socket. The red rimmed orb popped audibly and the Terror's roar turned to a gravely growl where pain and anger sought control of the voice and neither won.

James' force was strong enough for the cane to continue its journey into the creature's skull, travelling through the brain tissue and only stopping when it hit the bone at the back of the head. That's when the cane snapped. The boy's momentum carried him into the arms of the Terror, but those arms could no longer grab him or tear him apart. The open maw could no longer take chunks out of his neck. The Terror fell back, James' weight knocking it over.

They landed together with James on top. He froze, waiting for his rash decision to result in the creature sinking claws and teeth into him. When that didn't happen, James pushed himself back up. The Terror was staring at the ceiling. Its mouth was opening and closing in sharp, short movements. The whole body was twitching. It was still breathing and still moving, but...

James smiled. His father, if he had still been alive, would have told him that he was being foolish. No good came from hoping. The spark it ignited in him should be extinguished.

No, father, he thought. *You're wrong.*

He removed the cane from the socket and wiped it on the torn clothes the thing wore. He took the legs and pulled. There was a large storage room further along the corridor. The key was always left in the lock, but the room was never really used. It had old boxes of pupil records and faded homework books in it. No one noticed the room any more. It had become a part of the corridor. James dragged the Terror in and locked the door. It was a slow process, but the corridors had smooth floors that were always slippery whenever it rained outside, the wet footprints giving a slick, slow drying coating to the surface. The weather was fine so the floor was dry, but its condition was good enough to make the effort easier than it might otherwise have been.

The Terror didn't move, apart from the rise and fall of its chest and the odd spasms. James left the room, taking the key with him. He returned to the classroom and looked out of the window. It offered one of the best views of the town in the school. The long bank of windows faced the main thoroughfare. On a normal day, it would be filled with people. On this abnormal day, it was empty. There were no people and there were no monsters.

James went back to the cellar and told the other children they would have to wait for a while longer. There were still Terrors about. It wasn't safe. He said that he would continue to explore each day until he was sure that the monsters had gone. He had to make sure. He was doing it for them.

They looked at him with pride and adulation lighting their faces. Even Brie swelled at the knowledge that her brother was the bravest person she had ever known.

James couldn't return their gaze. He didn't like lying. He hated the deceit, but it was necessary. He had the chance to fight back. They had a chance to survive.

He thought of the Terror locked in the store room and smiled. He would enjoy testing it.

21

The next day, and each day after that, James ventured out. He returned hours later, telling them that the Terrors remained.

It wasn't a lie. It was a half-truth. A plural rather than the singular.

He did go out into the town and look for himself, rather than trusting what the view from the classroom window told him. The Terrors had, indeed, left. Apart from the one he held prisoner, at least. He saw the strewn, discarded bodies of his parents. He saw the remains of the other adults. He cried, once. The tears flooded his face, a tsunami washing away the last of his innocence. When they dried, so did his heart.

His mood was grim as he walked back to the school. The tears were gone and his sorrow was spent but a shadow had settled upon him. His prisoner bore the brunt of his anger. James discovered that they didn't bruise. They also didn't bleed, other than a small amount of leakage. It was as if their internal circulation had stopped with their humanity.

A week later, James discovered the locked strongbox of the science teacher. The school was progressive in that it accepted science and magic could work together rather than each being exclusive to the other. So many people still regarded science with distrust and, though magic was rare, it was something they either had experience of or knew someone who had. The school had argued for months to allow science to be taught. It had always been aberrant to question the workings of nature. Life was a miracle that should be seen as a blessing and a privilege. Those who wanted to take it apart to understand it were deviant.

More recently, science was gaining momentum. In certain circles, the practitioners and teachers were viewed as visionary. In others, they were scoffed at and looked down upon.

The Tinkerer excelled in his field. His devices were not seen as science, however. They were novelties. Distractions. His investigations into other things, such as creating life, were carried out in secret.

The science teacher at the school was a young man with enough enthusiasm to excite the entire staff. Even those who were initially reticent fell under his non-magical spell. The pupils were hesitant – some being prohibited to take part by their parents – but those that could mirrored the faculty in their response.

The lock was fairly lightweight and broke easily. Inside was a variety of tools and vials. Labels were fixed to glass jars, with handwritten names that James didn't recognise. He took them all and the syringes that accompanied them.

During the following weeks, he injected the Terror with various combinations of the chemicals. He had to cut its tongue out to stifle the cries it made. Even with the damage to its brain in addition to whatever changes being turned made, it reacted – sometimes violently – to the injections.

James took a calm pleasure in his work, especially when the Terror started to shudder so much it was shaking across the floor. He put his foot on it to keep it in place and watched as it trembled. When the effects had calmed, he moved it back into place and chose his next concoction.

The Terror survived each attempt. Until, one day, it didn't.

James was careful with his notes. He kept track of how much of what liquid he mixed together. When the newest one made the monster froth at the mouth and its eyes turn white before it gave a jolt and stopped moving at all, he was almost disappointed. His experiments had been something he had looked forward to. He had taken pleasure in administering his creations and watching the results.

But, he had what he needed. He had a way to kill them.

They were children, he and the others. They had no real hope of engaging in a fight, if the Terrors returned. Now, they didn't have to.

He only needed the opportunity.

22

"What's happening?" Dorothy mumbled.

Her head was throbbing and there was a sharp pain in her temple when she moved. She blinked to clear her eyes and tried to rub them clear. She couldn't move her hands and could feel the ropes keeping them tied behind her. There was something hard at her back, holding her up. She tried to focus and looked around.

"You!" she said angrily, staring at James.

"Me," he said smiling. He hid the syringe from her view. She would have the pleasure of seeing it soon enough.

Dorothy looked around her. She saw that she was secured to the stake by ropes around her wrist, ankles and waist. She knew there was little point in trying to free herself. Maybe the boy would listen to reason and finally bring an adult.

She looked past him and saw the other children gathered. There were so many! They were so *young!* Where were their parents?

"What's going on?" she asked, trying to keep calm. She wanted to shout at them. Insist they released her. She knew that would be fruitless. She had to use persuasion. "Where are your parents? Can I speak to them?"

"Don't you remember our conversation from before?" asked James. "I did tell you. Weren't you listening?"

"Listening?"

Dorothy tried to think back. What had he said? It was all so confusing!

She'd asked him to speak to his parents. He'd said…

"They're dead?"

"Very good. You were listening. I'm impressed. Anything else?"

Dorothy frowned. There *was* something more. It was then that she saw the man next to her. He was unconscious still, hanging in his bindings. He was the man who had attacked her!

"Who is he?" she asked. "Is he with you?"

"With us?" James responded, surprised. "We thought he was with you!"

"I've never seen him before! He attacked me!"

"Interesting. It doesn't matter. You're both going to help us."

"Help you?"

Dorothy gasped. Of course! He said he needed her help! She'd be glad to help. More than happy. Anything to get out and get away and find her way home.

No. That's not what he meant. That's not what he wanted. He'd said something else. What was it…?

Then she remembered.

"Let me go!" she screamed. "Please, let me *go!*"

James could see the children becoming distressed. It was easy to forget they were all so young, including himself. The girl's hysterics were going to undo the delicate fabric of society he was working so hard to weave.

"Unless you want to be hit again, I suggest you stop crying."

Dorothy didn't need telling again. She closed her mouth, stifling the sobs that wouldn't entirely stop. She tried to stand, the ropes cutting into her wrists and her arms starting to ache from the weight they were carrying. Her legs felt weak and she struggled but she refused to give them the satisfaction of seeing her collapse.

"Excellent," said James.

He turned to the children. His sister moved to his side, wanting to bask in the glory that she could feel was forthcoming. James held her hand, taking support from the contact and passing some of his triumph on to her. Eva stood on his other side. He smiled at her and she felt a flutter in her stomach. That simple look would raise her stature and brought her a step closer to her goal.

"Today," he said, continuing the speech he had written for the occasion, "we give ourselves a future."

He raised the syringe again. The sun was getting low and he wanted the ceremony to be over before night fell. Everyone needed to be back in the cellar while it was still light. He had practised the entire routine over and over during the day while the stakes were erected and the prisoners moved and the town was checked for monsters. He wouldn't allow it not to go according to plan.

One of the children, an eight year old girl called Brayden, clapped her hands. James felt relieved. He hadn't lost them yet. He took a deep breath. The final act was approaching. It was one thing to torture and kill a Terror. He could do that with a complete lack of remorse. It was entirely another to condemn a normal person to a similar fate. Neither the man nor the girl had really done anything other than be there, be available. They were innocent.

But they were necessary.

Dorothy saw Julian standing nearby. He was watching the proceedings but not appearing to understand what was happening.

"*Julian!*" she shouted.

James spun back to her, ready to order her to be hit again. Silence the bitch! He saw the creature mouth something and could guess what it was. '*Dorthy.*' It was all he had said. All he could say. It was tiring. The other prisoner, the man, was starting to move. He, too, was waking up. James sighed. Control was slipping. He couldn't do with both of the captives interrupting or spoiling his moment. He had to hurry. He nodded to Brie who raised one of her blades to Dorothy's neck. It silenced her.

"In this syringe," he said to everyone including the girl, "is a serum that will run through the veins of these people. It will, no doubt, kill them – I don't know for sure – but it *will* kill anything that tries to eat them"

He pointed at Adam and Dorothy in turn. The excitement was building within him and he didn't know how much more he could contain it.

"How do you know?"

James was thrown. He hadn't expected to be questioned. It was Eva. He glowered at her and she realised her mistake. She shouldn't have asked, except… she wanted to know! If they were going to commit murder, she needed to know if was for the right reasons.

"Because I've tested it!" James exclaimed. "Because I captured one of them and worked until I found something that would work!"

A murmur rippled through the group, echoed by the stares from his sister and Eva. He had to move quickly to assert himself.

"One broke into the school. I injured it and then I experimented until I killed it!"

The children were shocked, but the pedestal James stood upon only grew higher. He had put himself in danger for them. He'd risked his life. Now, he was going to save them all!

James had more to say, but he had tired of the interruptions. He wanted it over. He brought the syringe up to the man's neck and drew back to stab the needle in.

"Please don't."

He turned quickly, startled, almost dropping the poison. When he saw who had spoken, his mouth was suddenly dry. His boldness had evaporated. His youth had returned.

Everyone knew her. Every girl wanted to be her and every boy, and man, wanted to just have her notice them. The air sparkled around her, a remnant of the magic that had brought her there. She held out her hand to James and, reluctantly, he passed her the syringe.

"Let them go," she said.

Brie looked to her brother for confirmation. She wouldn't dare to refuse one of the Circle, but her arrival was so unexpected, Brie couldn't help but have James' agreement. He nodded, his face showing the same shocked expression that had fixed itself to all the children. Brie swung her knives down, severing the ropes. Dorothy and Adam fell, one to her knees and the other onto his front. Dorothy could only stare at the witch, not knowing that's what she was. The woman had just appeared. One second there was no one there and the next, this beautiful woman was stopping her murder.

"You should get everyone inside, quickly."

"But, we haven't finished!" James protested. Brie and Eva exchanged a glance. Had his bravery become stupidity?

"You have, I'm afraid," said the witch. "Now, get inside, quickly."

"Are the Terrors coming?" He asked nervously.

"No," she said. "But there are other things you need to worry about."

As she finished her warning, a cloud drifted to the side revealing the large, glowing disc of the moon. The man they had found attacking the girl twisted unexpectedly. His eyes snapped open. They were bright yellow. His lips curled back in a snarl. Hair, coarse and wiry, pushed through his skin. His fingers elongated, the nails lengthening into claws.

"*Now!*"

23

Often, choosing a victim can be a time consuming combination of research, observation and timing. The suitable, deserving candidate is sought out from listening to conversations and watching the movements of the humans. The visual and auditory capabilities of the mechanical organs given to Edward enabled him to do this at great distances, letting him remain undetected.

From what he knew of feelings, he had thought people would react unfavourably to meeting him. From what he had experienced, he'd found this to be true.

Edward had been young when he came into contact with the first human other than his father. It wasn't youth in the human sense of the world. He didn't grow or age. It was youth in the sense of the passage of time since his birth. Four hours after he had been cast out by the Tinkerer.

The woman was a prostitute. Not a very good one, from what he overheard her previous customer say. The words 'dead fish,' 'thief' and 'harlot' implied that she was, perhaps, best suited to other work. Edward had the good sense to keep to alleyways and shadows, at least until he was more confident in traversing the world outside the workshop. He had held back when the irked customer had passed him, and the complaints made him curious of the woman. He knew what she was – his knowledge was quite comprehensive – but he was unsure of the reasons why a prostitute would be required. He had been taught about marriage and relationships and the issues inherent in both, nonetheless the concepts of such things escaped him. He thought he might talk to the woman. Learn from her.

She had seen him coming, a large, muscular looking figure. An easy mark and potentially a pleasurable one. But then, when she saw him in all his metal glory, she screamed. He silenced the scream with more force than he had intended and her crumpled body was found hours later by a drunkard on his way home from an all-day alcohol binge. He had thought her sleeping and wanted to wake her so he could spend his remaining change on ending the night with a smile. In his inebriated state, it took him some time to notice her broken neck. He had started to explore her body in the hope that the intimate contact might rouse her. When he felt the shattered bones in her neck and saw the bruising, he both sobered and threw up.

The man avoided all alcohol after that night, and only shared a bed with his wife.

Edward realised that his form was abnormal to them. *Humans*. It was then that the seeds of reinvention were planted.

He knew killing the woman was a mistake. He understood the difference between right and wrong. If he'd had the skills of his father, perhaps he could have given her some of the life he'd received. He didn't, though. Remorse was something he knew the definition of, but was unable to feel. He left her where she was and vowed to himself that he would be more vigilant in future. More careful. More selective.

Edward found that remaining unseen was easier than he expected. Perception was an oddity that intrigued him. People would look through or past him if they were entranced in their own thoughts and lost in their own lives. They saw what their minds told them to see and that was not always what was real. He took some clothes to disguise himself, clothes he shed later as his body started to change. A hat, though it was a tight fit and perched rather than sat on his head, added to the impression that he was not made entirely of metal. People did not expect to witness a man made from anything other than flesh and bone. As such, they didn't. Not unless they looked closely and this was something that they were wont not to do. Eye contact implied a stepping into personal space. An invasion of sorts. Edward used that to his advantage.

For a week and more he avoided detection. His plan to rebuild himself was fully formed in his mechanical mind and he had begun to seek out potential candidates.

When he saw the little girl, he was not sure how to proceed. The knowledge of human growth was something that he found difficult to grasp. Why would people not just be created fully grown and able to fend for themselves? Where was the efficiency in being born completely dependent on your parents? And the length of time between birth and independence was time completely wasted. It was a period of learning and experimentation and of making, stretching and destroying boundaries. The guardians of those young were prevented from enhancing their own lives by being tied to their children.

It seemed to be evolutionary insanity.

The girl, the first child he had encountered, could help him make sense of the madness.

With the prostitute reacting so unfavourably to his appearance, Edward chose to be more discreet in his dealings with the girl. He estimated her to be about eight years old. That was six years of wisdom gained in having every need served by an adult. She should have so much information to impart.

She was playing by a small stream created by a recent downpour. She had pulled a handful, of leaves from a low hanging branch and was letting them float on the running water. The leaves were becoming stuck in the shallow flow, but the girl gave them a nudge to shift them, persevering with her game.

Edward approached cautiously. He didn't want to startle her and have her alert anyone else. He kept under the cover of the tree she had been stripping.

"Why do you do that?"

The girl looked up, surprised, but she seemed unconcerned about either the man or the question.

"Do what?" she asked.

"Push them like that. Why do you persist when you know they'll become stuck? What is the purpose?"

"It's fun," said the girl.

She smiled at him and Edward realised he now knew what innocence looked like. His father and the prostitute wallowed in the muck of their misdeeds. The other people who busied themselves with their lives, in one form or another and in one measure or more, were guilty. The severity of that guilt differed with as many shades as there were strands of hair on the girl's head. In this younger version of the miscreant adults, guilt had yet to take a hold. She could tell a lie and she may shout at her mother, but it was without a real perception of the colours of sin. Life was black and white. The gradients in between were for adults.

"I don't understand," said Edward. "It appears to be tedious rather than fun."

"I like it," she said. "I'm making a marina. I like boats. My Grandpa has one. I go on it sometimes in summer."

Edward was keen to know what enjoying something was like.

"May I join you?"

The girl smiled again, concentrating on a leaf that was refusing to move despite her tapping the edge with her finger. She nodded without looking up.

"Sure," she said. "But you have to bring your own boats."

"I don't want to frighten you," Edward said.

"I'm not afraid," she told him. "As long as you don't steal my boats. I had to reach right up to get the right ones."

"I don't look like you.

"Everybody looks different," she laughed. "It would be boring otherwise. My mummy says that it's because we'd forget who we were." She looked up at where he was concealed. "I think it's because, if we looked the same, it would be like marrying yourself and that would be just weird."

A sound came from Edward's mouth that he hadn't heard himself make before. He hadn't realised he was able to do so. It was laughter.

He walked over to where the girl was crouching and held out his hand.

"I'm Edward," he said.

The girl looked up at him. Her eyes were a bright blue, the colour of, he thought, the untouched sun at the beginning of its journey to night time. When the day, itself, was laden with unspoilt innocence. When potential was born and had yet to be polluted.

"I'm Jessica," she said. "You look shiny."

"My father made me this way," Edward said. "I think it was so he could see himself in me."

"Mummy says I have her eyes."

"How is she able to see?"

Jessica laughed. It was a crisp sound, like splintering glass. He could feel it entering him and cutting through the restraints the Tinkerer had incorporated into his design. His creator had, when he'd chosen to discard his son, set specific rules. At six hours old, Edward had decided to kill his father. The laughter of the girl, over a week later, had severed the restrictions inherent in his programming. The intention was not the same as the ability. The rules prevented this. Edward felt the limitation fracture. It was a blossoming sensation within him.

"Are you alright?" Jessica asked.

"I am, thank you," he said quietly. "I think you may have just set me free."

"You're funny," she said, returning her attention to her leaves. "Come on," she said. "Our boats can have a race."

24

Adam woke to screams.

And pain.

And a terrible growling.

He was laying on his front and he could see people… no, children, running. The girl he'd seen in the school, who he'd tried to help, was backing away frantically. A woman scooped up a little boy, grabbed the arm of the girl and yanked her up. They, too ran.

The pain was increasing. He felt as if thousands of needles were piercing his skin, from the inside out. He could hear his the sound of bones cracking and realised they were his own. He looked at his hands and saw them stretching impossibly. He cried out in agony, and the voice that greeted him was the roar of a beast. His gaze was drawn upwards. He saw the moon. It was full and he was held by its power. He tried to look away, but couldn't.

He was hungry. Ravenous. He felt he could eat...

He could eat anything.

He sprang to his feet and howled up at the moon, consenting to its request. Feed, it was saying. Hunt, it was telling him.

He turned and saw the children fleeing to a large building. It looked familiar to him, but his memories were jumbled. They were fading as if he had been dreaming and was awake for the first time in his life. He fell down onto all fours, his hands now claws. With a snarl, he launched himself forward after the children. After his feast.

The last of the children disappeared into the school and the door was slammed shut. A lever was pushed as the last child ran past it and bolts slid and bars dropped. A series of clicks sounded as locks fastened.

The witch thrust the boy she was carrying into Dorothy's arms and pushed her down into the cellar.

"Come on!" she shouted to the three stragglers who were sprinting along the hallway.

The doors bowed with the impact of the beast slamming into them from outside. They held but the remaining children were given a boost of speed, fuelled by fear. Another crash as the doors were hit again. The splintering of wood. The hammering of small feet against the smooth stone floors.

"RUN!"

They were running. They were gasping for breath. They were tiring, but then they were on the steps, tumbling against each other, collapsing at the bottom.

The witch pulled the cellar doors closed and secured them. She held out her hand and muttered something. The locks glowed briefly. She turned and held her finger to her lips. *Shhhh!* James pushed his way to the front of the panting, huddled children.

"What the…?"

The witch moved her finger across to his mouth, touching his lips. He was suddenly silent, the words halted in his throat. He looked surprised and tried to protest but Brie moved to his side. She held his hand and shook her head.

No, she was saying. *We have to stay quiet.*

James looked angry at first, then realised they were right. His indignation was secondary to the safety of his group. He nodded and felt the spell stopping him speak release. He had the sense not to test it.

Dorothy, confusion whirling around her, held onto the child she had been given. The boy's head was buried against her chest and his arms were tight around her. She wasn't prepared to let him go. He was as much support for her as she was for him. She had no idea what was happening. In fact, none of it *could* be happening, yet it was. It was all impossible, yet all real. This was no dream, she knew. Reality had a taste to it that was lacking in dreams. And this lunacy was full flavoured!

They heard the doors surrender to the beating they were receiving and crash open. There was another roar, this time of jubilation, and the creature entered the school. They could hear it sniffing and prowling. It was heavy footed, each thump of movement drawing muted gasps from the children. The witch glared at them and held her finger to her lips again. They understood and held their hands over their mouths.

It moved overhead, the weight making the cellar door dip slightly. The sniffing increased, concentrated above them. After a while, it moved off, further along the corridor. A collective sigh of relief, exhaled almost in unison, came from the children and the one in Dorothy's arms began to cry softly.

Dorothy whispered to the boy, trying to comfort him and make him stop his sobbing. She could see the witch and James staring angrily and shook her head. What could she do?

The creature above stopped moving. Stopped its hunting. The children held their breath.

There was a thud from some distance away and then the cellar doors almost caved in from the sudden landing of the beast directly on them. It was snarling and clawing at the doors. Splinters began to rain down on the children as gaps appeared, filled with tearing claws.

Abruptly, the sound ceased. The slashing stopped. A deep, bone shaking growl shook the group to their core.

Dorothy's eyes grew wide as a voice she never thought she would be so thankful to hear said:

"*Dorthy!*"

25

Simple pleasures are invaluable in enabling one to appreciate the more major occurrences in life. If that life was artificially created in a laboratory, the appreciation is no less valid.

Edward found the game of making leaf boats race each other along a steam to be cathartic. What should have been moments wasted were actually moments spent enjoying the act of doing nothing constructive, something that, bizarrely, was constructive in itself.

Conversation with the girl was limited to a smattering of brief comments based on the prowess of each other's craft and the benefits of large leaves as opposed to more slim line ones. Edward was disappointed when she announced that it was time for her to go home.

"You don't have the ability to know the exact time," he said when she had stood and was preparing to leave. "How do you know what time it is?"

"I'm hungry," she answered. "I always get hungry at dinner time and that's when I have to be home."

Edward had not realised the human body could be conditioned to habits such as the correct time to imbibe a meal. He hadn't foreseen speaking to one of the very things he thought were illogical and pointless would teach him so much.

"I've learned much from you," he said.

"Was this a class?" Jessica asked, frowning. "I thought we were just playing."

"I think all of life is a class," he said.

"I think that's boring," she said, her frown deepening.

"Why do you say that?"

"You always need time to play," she said. "Otherwise everything is work. I don't like to work all the time. It'd be boring if every day was a class and I didn't get to play."

Edward thought about this. He was unaccustomed to the concept of 'play' and how valuable it might be.

"I suppose," he said, "Even in play you are able to learn."

"Sometimes," said Jessica before turning and running off, "a leaf boat is just a leaf."

Then she was gone. He watched her small figure disappear over a hill as she ran home. He didn't move until darkness came and went, bringing with it more of the rain that had caused the storm. As the hours passed and he remained in his crouch, he thought about the girl's words.

Sometimes, a leaf boat is just a leaf.

How could one so young be so wise? Edward saw that he had been viewing the world and those that inhabited it all wrong. He was searching for meaning in his existence. In his creation. In the differences between him and the humans who he was avoiding.

He realised he didn't need to.

Sometimes, things happen purely because they are leaves on a stream. Sometimes, he thought, meaning is something that is stepped over on the never ending journey to tomorrow. An obstacle to be walked around and ignored. Sometimes, reason is completely absent and 'just because' fills in the void left behind.

When he stood, his joints ground together, making a quiet but high pitched screeching sound. He had not even noticed the rain as it fell and only now was its presence, as evidenced by the puddles on the ground and the soaked clothes he was wearing, grasped. He needed to lubricate his body lest it seize and he find himself unable to move. He did so quickly, aware that he should not become so lost in epiphany that he lose sight of his goals.

He wished he could see Jessica again so he could thank her for her insights. He knew, however, that she wouldn't see them that way. She had not been imparting wisdom. She had been playing. Her innocence enabled her to see things simply. Her views were not corrupted by adulthood and so were shrewder because of it.

Since that day, Edward had contemplated her words many times. He tried to see things through her eyes and not try and see the multiple layers that existed beneath everything. *A leaf boat was just a leaf.* Just accept. The recognition gave him a greater sense of freedom and of purpose. He began his search for donors in earnest.

He had to, he knew, choose the right person and not take lives randomly. That wasn't right. Before Stephen Decker had given his leg, there had been six others.

Bremen was kind enough to give his arm. He would not be needing it as it was difficult to steal when you'd had an axe sever your skull.

Cariba's real name was actually Oswald but he played on the fact he appeared to have been born way off to the west where the sun was hotter and life was much more relaxed. He hadn't and, in reality, it wasn't. But the untruths had an exotic zest that was attractive to both woman and men. Oswald was not choosy who he seduced. He liked the challenge and the collected trophies of their tears when he ended the relationships immediately after they proclaimed their love for him. His kidneys were in place but had yet to be connected to anything other than that which was required to keep them healthy.

Anton took it upon himself to relieve families of their pet dogs. Like Decker, he had an appetite for killing. Unlike Decker, it was not going to extend anywhere beyond canine victims. He had been bitten by a dog when he was a child. The dog had been kicked to within an inch beyond its life by Anton's father based on the story the boy had told him. Anton neglected to mention the sharp stick that he'd been using to prod the dog with and the fact the dog only retaliated when that stick had been lit and the dog's fur set on fire. Anton gave his hair. It was thick and had curls that cascaded over his face like a dark waterfall. Edward didn't have to lose any of his own body parts for that. He only needed to find something to glue the peeled off scalp to his metal skull. An easy task.

The twins, Horatio and Harvey, were the first to fight back. They were also the last. Edward learned to be swifter in the enactment of his judgement and to not attempt to kill more than one candidate at once. The twins used their almost identical visages to murder an entire congregation of churchgoers. The original intention was to steal from them. When their subterfuge, a complicated dalliance with mistaken identities, was discovered, the parishioners wanted the pair to be punished. They imprisoned them in the church crypt until a suitable penalty could be decided on. The crypt, however, had long been a store room for anything that could or should not be kept anywhere else. This included items of excessive value, such as priceless jewellery donated by local gentry and explosives that were recovered from the nearby mine after the roof caved in, trapping and thereby killing the twenty workers who had been inside at the time.

Horatio and Harvey broke the lock to the crypt door. It was an ancient mechanism that was in dire need of replacement. A second exit to the church was close by, hidden by thick curtains. They took what valuables they could easily carry and let the explosion deal with the rest. They didn't know and didn't care that the congregation had gathered together again in the spirit of forgiveness. They had just decided to allow the twins to go free.

None survived.

Edward took Horatio's arm to be the left to Bremen's right. He allowed Harvey to supply his liver. Edward planned to rebuild the whole of his body for his father. The order in which he did so was unimportant. After he had attacked them, though injured they fought back. The outcome was obvious and their death was only prolonged. Edward's body, being metal, was untouched by their exertions. It could not dismiss the effects of having both of their donations implanted at the same time.

Edward almost died.

Once he had removed the offending and potentially fatal twins from himself and replaced his own arm and liver, it was another three weeks before he could leave the hayloft he'd taken refuge in. Daily he heard the farmer talking to his workforce and flirting with his wife's sister who worked the land for him. He was wearing her down, using both promises and threats to find his way beneath her clothing. Edward would have happily exercised his own brand of retribution but he could barely lift his head, let alone his axe.

By the time he had fully recovered, the sister had told the wife of her husband's actions and he had left, a bruised eye and scratched face the women's farewell letter.

The old woman and her intestines were next and then came Decker and his too short leg. Edward had to do better. He felt under pressure to complete his new self and visit his father, but he couldn't choose haphazardly. He had to stick to his morals. He had to. It kept him above those who he and his axe reprimanded. He would not fall into the trap of becoming like them. His father had taught him many things and not being in his image was one of them.

Edward's actions helped people. It gave meaning to his existence. He was not merely a plaything created on a whim to see if it could be done, then discarded when it was too successful. He was a metal angel of death that removed offenders and, so, aided the offended.

And he was a farmer himself, in a way. He was harvesting others to help himself grow.

He needed another. He had to find the next. His lapses in judgement were becoming too severe. It occurred to him that the human parts of him were fouling the portions that were original. He dismissed it. His mind was still working exactly as it should. The rest of his body would follow the instructions the brain supplied.

Except that it wasn't.

26

A chorus of screams sang in the face of that single, simple word.

"Dorthy."

The screams died down and the lack of movement from above kept those below still. They listened intently. Was the creature waiting for them? Was it trying to fool them into believing it had left? Dorothy doubted it. It had seemed too feral to think in such coherent terms. It certainly hadn't left, knowing they were so close.

And then there was Julian. His voice was unmistakable. He couldn't have subdued the beast. He could barely walk or talk, let alone do battle with that.

She hesitated to say the word 'werewolf.' She also hesitated to even think of the fact that the woman standing close to her had used some form of what appeared to be magic. And, of course, Julian. What had happened to him? She had to push these thoughts away. They were opening a doorway into places that she cared not to visit. These things did *not* exist. They did *not* happen.

Even though they did and were.

"I think it's gone," whispered James.

"I think so too," said the woman.

James filled with pride at the fact that she had acknowledged him and positively overflowed with her agreement. He stepped forward and started to climb the steps.

"James, no!"

Brie ran to her brother and grabbed his hand. Eva was behind her, but remembered her place rather than stepping into the exchange. This wasn't the time for lovelorn foolishness.

"I have to see what's up there and if it's gone." He was the leader. He had no choice.

"That's admirable, James," said the witch, "but not this time."

"Listen to her!" Brie said, not hiding the tears that were welling.

"I have to go and find out if it's gone. They depend on me."

"They do, which is why you have to stay here." The witch took Brie's elbow and together they pulled him back. "It's her turn."

The witch nodded towards Dorothy. James and Dorothy gasped. Brie and Eva smiled.

"Me? Why me? I don't even know where I am, let alone what's up there." Dorothy was shaking her head emphatically. "Besides, they kidnapped me. They were going to feed me to… *something!*"

"They were trying to protect themselves. They were, perhaps, misguided."

"*Misguided?*

"You're shouting. Please don't. You'll scare the children and alert it."

She smiled at Dorothy and the girl felt herself flush with a sudden warmth, as if the woman's very nature was infusing her.

"I can't. I just can't. What about this boy?"

"I'll take him," said Eva. She was pulling the young boy from Dorothy's arms before the other could protest.

"Why me?"

"Because your friend is up there. Because you're not from here. Because that might be the only thing that can save you. And us."

"*What?*"

"Just go."

Dorothy looked at the children filling the cellars. There were so many and they were all looking back at her. James was their leader but they were expecting her to do this. To sacrifice herself. She sighed.

"Fine," she said. "I'll go."

She started up the steps, having to force her feet to move. They felt heavy, resistant of the madness she was being dragged into. They wanted to stay. No, they wanted to run! But there was nowhere *to* run. She didn't look back. She didn't need to. They were all willing her on. None of them would be hoping she'd just stop and come back.

Besides, the woman was right. Julian was up there. She had to know what had happened to him. Dorothy gritted her teeth and raised her hand up.

"Wait," said the witch.

Dorothy froze. She hoped she'd be told to go back down. She was still, really, a child herself, though she often told her aunt and uncle the opposite. That wasn't the case, though. The witch raised her hand and spoke an incantation. There was the slightest of breezes over Dorothy's face and then the locks clicked as they were unlocking. There was no turning back. She reached up, took a hold of the cellar doors and pushed.

Rather than a rush of fur and teeth tearing her apart, the hallway appeared to be empty. Dorothy was going to say something to that effect when:

"Dorthy!"

She turned, almost losing her footing on the steps. Julian was standing just to the back of the cellar doors. Next to him, shaking on the floor, was the man.

The clothes on Julian's chest were torn. Claw marks sliced across the flesh. There was no blood. Barely a response to the wounds from Julian himself. But then, if the damage to his neck did not seem to concern him, a claw across the chest wouldn't faze him.

Dorothy pulled herself up, practically leaping upon Julian. Her school friend remained impassive, except for a slight softening of his eyes.

"Julian!" she said, a sob sending a shudder through the words.

"Dorthy." he responded.

She looked at the man. There was no sign of the beast he had become. His eyes were closed and he was trembling and moaning softly. She climbed up from the cellar, followed by the witch and James. Brie and Eva started up the steps too, but James held out his hand and shook his head.

Stay there.

They held back, but remained on the steps. Eva had moved up to stand beside her friend. They held each other's hand, gripping tightly.

"What happened?" asked James.

He circled around the Terror and stood near the man's head. His weapon was held ready. There would be no repeat of before. If the man moved, his skull would be crushed.

"This is your friend," said the witch. It was a statement rather than a question. Dorothy nodded. "Who are you?"

"Dorothy," she said.

"*Dorthy!*" said Julian.

"Who *is* Dorothy? Who is this creature?"

"He's a Terror," said James angrily. "And she's in it with him. They can't be trusted. And now *him!*"

"He's not a Terror," said the witch, putting her hand on Julian's shoulder. "If he was, you would all be dead already."

James' eyes widened and his face paled. He knew she was right, but it didn't explain what the thing was. If it wasn't a Terror, what was it? And what of the man?

"What's a Terror? Will someone just tell me what's going on?"

"What do you know?" asked the witch. Her voice was calm. Dorothy couldn't help but feel the tension seep from her.

"I was on a bus. I was going to the mall for some jeans. Julian was with me." She fought back the urge to cry, blinking to keep the tears at bay. "There was a storm. A tornado. It lifted the bus and... and dropped it here! That's all I know!"

"And your friend? Julian? What happened to him?"

"We were attacked by these creatures. We tried to escape. I managed to get out but Julian..."

Dorothy couldn't finish. She didn't need to. The evidence was standing in front of them. Julian didn't escape.

The witch nodded thoughtfully.

"I see," she said. "You're not from here, are you?"

Dorothy shook her head. *No*, she thought. *We're definitely not from here.*

"That's why your friend survived. That's how he beat the wolf in that man."

"I don't understand. Who are you? Where are we? Wolf? You mean he's...?"

"We shouldn't have this discussion here. We need to move." She turned to James. "Have your sister stay with the children. We should talk."

"No!" protested Brie, climbing up. "We're coming with you!"

"No," said the witch. "You're not. You need to stay with the children. They need you."

If anyone else had told her that, including her brother, Brie would have laughed in their face and ignored their advice. Brie was not going to contemplate arguing with the witch. Eva felt the same. You just *didn't!*

"Fine," she said indignantly. She descended again and Eva pulled the cellar doors shut, giving James a smile of support.

"Bring him," said the witch.

Dorothy and James stared at each other. She was clearly talking to both of them and obviously meaning the man. Their mutual mistrust had to be put aside to do as she instructed. James would because he knew not to argue with her. Dorothy had no choice, as she seemed to be the only one willing to give her any answers. Carefully, they lifted the man by his arms and pulled him into the classroom that Dorothy had been taken to.

"Does it have to be in here?" she asked.

"It's the only one big enough," said James. "And most of the others are kept locked. That way, we have the chance to trap a Terror."

"What is a *Terror?*"

"A Terror" interjected the witch, "is the result of someone playing with things they don't understand."

27

The man was tied to a chair. It was the only real option for incarceration that James had. He voiced his concerns to the witch.

"What if he turns again? Those ropes won't hold him."

"He won't," she said. "It's only to keep him in place. He'll be disorientated when he wakes up."

"Disorientated? He'll kill us!"

"No, James, he won't. He's not a killer."

"Not a killer?" James seemed to forget himself and stormed up to the witch. "Didn't you just see what he did?"

"I did," she said, ignoring his rant. "But still, it's not him. We'll be fine."

James huffed and backed away. He was seething.

"Please tell me what is going on," said Dorothy. She wanted to curl up in a ball in the corner and wait for everything to go back to normal. She no longer felt sensible. She felt frayed. She felt that she was on the verge of either breaking down or exploding and wanted neither to happen.

"Take a seat," the witch said. Dorothy was unsure. She felt vulnerable sitting in this room. Bad things happened. "You too, James."

James didn't argue. He nodded and sat. Dorothy followed. At least the boy couldn't get her if he was sitting too.

"We need your help, Dorothy."

James stared. Dorothy gasped.

"*My* help? With what? What can I do?"

The last time she had been told she would be aiding them, the boy was going to inject her with poison and feed her to the monsters.

The witch took a chair and placed it before them, sitting herself. She looked from one to another, wondering what to tell them. They would both hear things they wouldn't understand. They were both young. Too young. She had no choice, though. *They* had no choice.

"Dorothy, you're in Oz."

"Oz? Where's that? Is it in Europe?"

"I don't know where Europe is, I'm afraid, but I can assure you, Oz won't be there. Or anywhere else in your world."

"My world?"

"Her world?"

"Yes," said the witch. "It's a safe bet that you're not in Kansas anymore."

"I've never been to Kansas," said Dorothy.

"I have," said the witch. "Once."

"Where....?" James was confused. He didn't know the places they were talking about. How could this girl not be from their world?

"Look. The storm that brought you here. It wasn't natural, was it?"

"I don't know," said Dorothy, shaking her head. "It did seem to come out of nowhere and it did lift the bus up, but that happens, doesn't it?"

"I suppose it might," said the witch. "But it doesn't transport you to somewhere completely different, does it?"

Dorothy shook her head again. She would think not.

"You're in Oz. Your friend is now part Terror, but he's not going to turn fully, so he's not a danger. If anything, it's only going to be of benefit." She held up her hand as Dorothy and James both started to speak. They closed their mouths. "And this man has a wolf within him that is desperate to be unleashed during a full moon. He just doesn't know it."

"A werewolf? But they're only in movies!"

"Movies don't exist here," said the witch, "but I can assure you the 'werewolf,' as you call him, does."

"This is insane," said Dorothy, standing. "I'm not listening to this. I'm going!"

She turned to leave and Julian stepped in her way.

"Come on Julian," she said, moving to walk around him. "Let's go."

Julian stepped to intercept her and she stopped.

"Julian?"

"Dorthy."

"I think he wants you to stay," said the witch.

Dorothy stared at her friend and then stepped to the side. He matched her, staying in front of her and preventing her from leaving. She sighed and sat back down, avoiding her friend's gaze.

"OK," she said quietly. She'd listen. What choice did she have? "Who are you?"

"I'm Tamara," said the witch. "I'm a witch."

James couldn't help but smile. Her name was one that was always spoken with reverence. It was said when giving thanks and in times of hardship, as if just the mention of it held a power of its own. Tamara and her sisters were legendary. They kept the world in balance with their magic. They were naturally gifted, powerful witches who seemed always at hand in times of trouble.

Except recently. Recently, their absence had been noticed. The devastation that had ruined the town should have been stopped by her. James' parents should still have been alive, thanks to her.

But they weren't.

He wanted to say something. He needed to shout at her and ask where she had been. He craved to hit her and not stop until he had forgotten the reason he wanted to in the first place. He didn't. She was *Tamara.* She was one of The Three.

Dorothy's reaction was more one of derision. She suppressed a laugh, but couldn't hide her smile. A witch? Really! Where was the Sorting Hat when you needed one? Even with everything that was going on around her, this couldn't be real! Though she *had* made James stop talking. She *had* frozen the locks. She *had* appeared from nowhere.

"My sisters and I try to keep things in harmony. We use our gifts to help people. At least, we did. My youngest sister, Emily, was kidnapped. Clara, my other sister, has gone missing. She and her dog were searching for Emily. I've spent my time travelling, trying to right his wrongs."

She bowed her head and wiped her eyes, taking a moment to breathe deeply and slowly. When she looked up again, she looked as if nothing had happened. James felt bad. Though he hadn't voiced his thoughts, they had still been at the forefront of his mind. He was ashamed.

Tamara looked at him. She could see the guilt on his face and could imagine why.

"I'd be the same, if I were you," she said. He nodded briefly, though he didn't appear convinced.

"What does this have to do with me?" asked Dorothy. It was all so much to take in, much less believe. She felt no closer to real answers or solutions. Also, the longer those took to come, the more likely the man was to wake up.

"So what's a Terror. Why does he think Julian is one?"

"Have you heard of the Tinkerer?" Tamara asked, though she was sure of the answer.

"Who?"

"I thought not. James?"

"Yes," James nodded. "My father told me about him. He's some sort of inventor. He uses science. My father didn't trust him. He's in the capital, I think."

"Exactly that," Tamara said. "An inventor. He's more, though. He doesn't like to stop. He believes it's okay to delve into things that should not be investigated. He thinks that false starts are stepping stones to discovery. He doesn't see that some things should just not be discovered."

"But what does that mean? Who is he? Why does it *matter?!*"

"Questions are wonderful, but throw too many into the mix and the answers become jumbled. I'll tell you, just listen."

Dorothy felt she'd been reprimanded by her head teacher. Just as if he had, actually, spoken to her, she nodded and sat back in her seat.

"The Tinkerer did something a while ago that he shouldn't. He created life. It was a perfect life that could have been beautiful, but it shouldn't have been at all. Science and magic should have limitations. They should not be used to excess or irresponsibly. Unfortunately, the Tinkerer cast his creation out. We don't know what happened to it after that, but we do know that the Tinkerer moved on."

"What do you mean?"

"He thought he wanted to create something that wasn't there. He is misguided. He believes himself to be a good man, but he's mistaken."

"Maybe he is?"

"Perhaps, on some level, but… no. I'm no judge, but I don't need to be. His actions speak for him. The Terrors. The change in the world. It's all him. He unleashed a virus that is besieging all of Oz. He wanted to, he sincerely believes, eradicate disease. He didn't wait until he had the knowledge to do so. He didn't care if there were mistakes. To him, they weren't mistakes. They were tests. They didn't even fail, according to him. They were used for gathering information for the next time and the next."

"How do you know all this? Why haven't you stopped him?" Dorothy wanted to let her speak, but couldn't help interrupting. There was no time for stories!

"There is one answer to both questions."

"Yes?"

"He's my brother."

A leg.

Edward was looking for a specific candidate. He needed a certain body part. He had to find the right one. The exact, flawless, right one. He had been created to be an example of his father's expertise. The Tinkerer had the idea and carried it to fruition. He'd made something that was wondrous, and he had hated it. He cast it out and moved on to his next project.

Edward didn't see himself as a project. He was more than that. He was his father's son. He had been made perfect and he was making himself more perfect. He could then show his father, just before he killed him, what his creation could have been. Should have been. The Tinkerer would see the error of his ways. He'd apologised for his mistake. The axe would cleave his head. Edward could then be happy in the knowledge his father's work was complete and that no more 'Edwards' would be made.

For, though he knew himself to be unflawed, he could not wish his existence on another.

He had found, if he was searching for any of the other parts of himself to replace, multiple potential donors. Murderers. Thieves. A man who would beat his young child every evening for any reason he could think of and would then beat his wife for being too afraid to stop him. The woman who told her husband their baby had died. She didn't tell him she had become so frustrated with their baby, Meadow, crying that she shook her until she stopped. There were so many. It was as if they were appearing deliberately to muddy the waters of his search.

He wanted them. All of them. He could have harvested each in turn and replenished much of himself. He would have been nearing completion. Closer to seeing his father. Closer to…

But, no. They would have to wait. They would still be there, committing their atrocities, when he had found the one he needed.

He had visited a village. It was one of the most picturesque he had seen on his travels and he could see why people would build beauty into their homes. He could appreciate the aesthetics of the cottages and the grandiosity of the larger houses. For a village that was content with its medium size and did not aspire to be a town or city, there were a great number of parks. Each was filled with well cultured flower beds, neatly trimmed trees and imaginative topiary bushes. The residents spent many of their evenings either in the parks or walking along the river as the sun set and the moon arose.

Life cycles intrigued him. His discussion with the little girl, Jessica, had taught him the worth of youth and he was fascinated by the young of all species. On the river were cygnets. They were still the dark feathered babies that had yet to don the white of their parents. They followed their mother in an even line. Edward found this the most enthralling by far. They did not have to be told to do so. They didn't try to swim off and lead lives of their own. They followed and they grew and they were a family.

If Edward had a full grasp of feelings, rather than a clinical understanding of them, he would have realised he was feeling sadness. He wasn't given the chance to follow his father. He had done all of his growing on his own after being banished. No matter. He would be able to show his father the beautiful swan he had become.

Something terrible had happened in the village the night before. He had been drawn to there because of the screams that could be heard by his sensitive ears from miles away. He was too late to witness the murder or see the beast, but he knew he had to find it. From the descriptions of the missing man, he would be the match Edward so desired. Though the connection hadn't been made by the citizens, Edward knew the man and the beast were one and the same.

As much as life was so captivating to him, so was death. The sense of loss and the emotional devastation that accompanied it were something he knew he could never feel. He had experienced a similar feeling when his father had closed the door on their life together, but it paled next to the outpouring of grief that the dead girl's family and, indeed, the entire village, were showing.

He stayed for her funeral, watching the proceedings from closer than he would otherwise have dared to be, perhaps in the hope some of the anguish would seep into him so he could suffer along with them.

When the girl was in the ground, a bizarre ritual, he left the village behind. While the villagers searched for the abducted man, Edward would hunt for Melody's, the girl's, killer. They were both the same person.

His name was Adam.

29

"Your brother?" James was shocked and couldn't conceal the fact. "Your brother did all this?"

"He did."

Tamara had berated herself for her brother's actions so often, the expressions of James and Dorothy shouldn't have affected her, but they did. She clenched her fists, digging her nails into the palms of her hands. The pain reminded her that she was at fault. Though a very young girl, she hadn't stopped him when he told her what he was going to do with his spiders. She didn't tell him it wouldn't work. She didn't know, but could have guessed. Poison was something they all kept away from. Just because her brother was the only child in the family without magical ability didn't mean he had no talents, he just exhibited them in a different way. It had resulted in multiple deaths. It had meant his banishment.

She was younger than him. She looked up to him. She thought that everything he did was right. That was why she used her magic to make the sleeping potion a little stronger. Not much. She was still learning how to use and control her magic. It was more powerful than her body could contain and she was instructed by their parents to only use it when they were with her, just as with her sisters.

But it was just a little push, that was all.

She wasn't about to share that knowledge.

"That's not important now," she said, wanting to move on. "I can't stop him. If I had my sisters with me, perhaps. I think he may have been the one who kidnapped Emily. If that's true, then I can only assume he knows I'll try to find her. I don't know why, but if he's trying to get us there together…" She shook her head. "We have magic. He doesn't. But he's clever. Resourceful. It makes me nervous."

Dorothy nodded. She could understand the witch's dilemma. He was her brother. How could she bring herself to stop him? Dorothy wasn't sure she'd be able to herself. Family was… she thought of her aunt and uncle. She worried if they were missing her. Would they be out searching? Would they even know she was gone? This witch needed to find her sister. Maybe together they could…

Her sister.

Tamara had mentioned a dog.

Frank.

"What sort of dog did your sister have?" she asked nervously.

"It was a little thing. Lots of fur and a tail that didn't stop wagging." She smiled, reminiscing. "I don't know dog breeds, but it's a lovely little thing. She called it To…"

"It's dead," Dorothy said.

James' mouth fell open. He couldn't believe the girl had been so abrupt. Even as young as he was, he understood subtlety. If the dog was dead, did that mean…? From the look on the witch's face, she was thinking the same thing.

"What do you mean?" she asked.

Her voice was calm but her face was not. It had flushed a deep, angry red. Her eyes changed from silver to a matching crimson. She licked her lips and clenched her fists again.

Dorothy realised she should, perhaps, have been a little more sensitive rather than blurting it out like that. Death was something that she was cold to. The loss of her parents had numbed her, somewhat, to the delicacies of the related emotions. She fully understood and still felt them, but her reactions were delayed as if they had to remember what sadness was.

"Um… the dog. I think it might be dead."

The dog. There was more to tell. More to share. Dorothy couldn't bring herself to say the words to the witch. She knew she would have to, but maybe that could wait?

"What makes you say that?"

"The bus I was on. It landed here. The storm dropped it, or something."

"Yes?"

"Well… when I escaped and the things… Terrors? While they were attacking Julian, I managed to get away. The bus. It.. It landed… on…"

"It landed on my sister's dog?"

"I think so."

"You *think* so?"

"It did. It landed on the dog."

Tamara nodded slowly. She was breathing heavily, struggling to control herself. She knew it was an accident. The girl wasn't to blame. If anyone was, it was her brother and, by default, her.

"I'm sorry! I didn't mean it to happen!"

"It wasn't your fault. Don't worry. She'll be devastated, but it was an accident."

Dorothy couldn't keep quiet. She wanted to, but she couldn't. No, wait! There was something else!

"It came back," she said, not sure how insane she was about to sound.

"What did?"

"The dog. It came back. Or its ghost did."

James had remained silent during the exchange but he couldn't now. He knew there had been some stranger things recently, but ghosts? He had to draw the line somewhere. It was getting out of hand. He was sorry for the death of the dog, but not a ghost! Ghosts didn't exist!

"She's crazy! This is all crazy. Who cares about a dog? The Terrors could come back any minute! You should let me do what I planned! Feed them to the monsters!"

Before Dorothy could react to the boy's outburst, the witch was standing in front of him. The move was so fast, Dorothy barely saw her blur of movement. She seemed to grow, towering about him, her hands raised as if preparing to strike him.

"Who cares about a dog? Is that what you think? You should offer people to monsters to help yourself? Is *that* what you think?"

She leaned in close and James pulled back but had nowhere to go. He was terrified and was whimpering.

"I'm sorry! I just meant... I just..."

"You have a lot of growing up to do, boy. I suggest you do it quickly."

Tamara stood and slowly walked back to her seat. She smoothed down her dress and ran her fingers through her long, dark hair. She was breathing heavily, but appeared composed.

"Now," she continued. "I care about a dog. It was my sister's dog and they were never apart. Dorothy, please carry on."

Dorothy didn't want to carry on. At that moment, she would have been prepared to take James up on his offer. Perhaps she could divert the conversation. She could lead it elsewhere and not have to admit to the question she knew would be coming.

"The dog visited us, me and Julian, when we were in the forest. It followed us then, when we were captured by these," she nodded accusingly at James, "it disappeared."

Tamara shared Dorothy's look at the boy. He squirmed in his chair, wishing the Terrors *would* come. He was less afraid of them than he was the witch. She looked back at Dorothy and asked...

"What of my sister? Did you see her?"

Dorothy stared at the witch. She knew it was approaching, but still felt as if the question had slammed into her with the force of a car. She felt broken by the words and suddenly knew her detachment from death was only a facade to protect herself. The anticipation of the witch's feelings opened wide the doors of the prison she'd locked her own in. She started to cry. The tears spoke volumes and Tamara didn't need her to actually answer. Dorothy couldn't anyway. She had no words.

Tamara nodded, stood, and left the room. There was a loud crash and the sounds of splintered wood and shattered glass. James and Dorothy stared at each other, neither daring to speak. Eventually, the witch came back in. Her hands were glowing with a pulsing glow that shone a pale green. The light trailed from her fingertips as if the magic was dripping from them. She repeated her movements from moments before, sitting, smoothing her clothes and ruffling her hair.

She was calm once more, the news that her sister was dead seemingly dealt with and moved on from. Dorothy knew this wasn't the case. It would resurface at some point. From the sound of destruction in the hallway, Dorothy wanted to be elsewhere when that happened.

"She had a ring on her finger," said Tamara finally. "Did you see it?"

"A silver and red band?"

"The red is visible?"

Dorothy nodded, frowning.

"Yes," she said. "It was silver with these red veins all over it."

"Oh, goodness!" exclaimed the witch. Her eyes were closed and her hands were clasped together. She was beaming. "There's still hope!"

"Hope for what?" Dorothy asked. She wanted to say that dead was dead. Where was the hope in that?

Tamara could see what Dorothy was thinking. Dead was dead. Gone was gone. She tried to subdue the excitement bubbling in her that threatened to overflow in a very non-witch way. She was one of The Three. Composure was a part of their nature. It was required to face many of the horrors they had to deal with. She needed to keep a hold on hers. Dorothy was wrong.

"The ring," she said, "It's a talisman."

She held out her own hand. On the middle finger, the same as her sister's, was a plain silver ring. There were no red seams threading though the metal, but it was obviously the same otherwise.

"What does it do?"

"It protects us," Tamara said.

Dorothy kept her thoughts to herself. If it offered protection, it hadn't worked. Clara was dead. Her little dog too.

"You need to find the ring," said the witch. "Find it and we can bring my sister back!"

"Bring her *back?* You can bring back the *dead?*"

"In a way," said the witch. "In the only way that really matters."

Dorothy wanted to pry further, but chose not to. She didn't want the woman to confront her as she had with the boy. She sighed. The witch had said she wanted Dorothy to retrieve the ring. The guilt she felt was irrational, she knew, but she couldn't refuse. It would be simple, wouldn't it? Just go back to the bus and... take the ring off... the dead woman's hand...

Easy. It was easy. It *was.*

"OK," she said.

"You're trusting her? *Her?* You don't even know her!" James had jumped up again, forgetting himself. "How can you trust her? Let me feed her to the Terrors!"

Tamara slammed her hands together. The impact sent out a shockwave that threw James against the wall and made Dorothy and Adam fall back in their chairs. The witch hadn't moved or spoken. She just watched the boy get to his feet, ignoring Dorothy standing herself.

"You will *not* speak to me like that again," she said. Her voice was even, a monotone of menace. "If you do, I won't feed you to your precious Terrors. I'll eat you myself."

James sat on his chair heavily. Though his actions were petulant, his expression was that of a boy who had been reprimanded to within an inch of his short life. He knew better now. He already had known better, but the fight had been shocked out of him. He wouldn't dare to speak out or disagree again.

"I'm sorry," he said quietly.

"One more outburst, and you certainly will be." Tamara was taking no more nonsense. She would not pander to his youth. If he wanted to step up to be the leader of his group of survivors, he needed to know when to step up and when to step back.

It was a lesson learned from experience. James was lacking experience. She could forgive him his temper, but she had to ensure he knew the level of respect she commanded.

He nodded, not daring to speak. He was thankful his sister and the rest of his band were not there to see his humiliation. Let the girl go. They had survived the Terrors this long, they would continue to. Another chance would arise. The girl had been a gamble that had failed to pay off.

"Dorothy," the witch said. "Will you bring my sister back to me?"

When it was asked in that way, Dorothy could not refuse. If she had, though, what else could she do? She still had no idea where she was. Oz? She'd never heard of it. Another world? Ghosts and monsters? She needed some focus. Besides, returning to the bus, to where it all started, might give help her find a way home.

"Of course," she said.

She put the feelings of guilt to the back of her mind. She was only a passenger on the vehicle. She wasn't driving or directing it. The invisible hand that had lifted it from its course and dropped it here was not hers. Telling herself that and believing it were different things.

"Once you have it, you'll need to take it to my brother."

"What?"

She hadn't just heard that, surely. Take the talisman, something that clearly contained some power – and potentially the sister – to the very man who was causing it all? No. It couldn't be.

"You have to take my sister's ring to my brother. He created them. Only he can bring her back."

"But… You've already said… What makes you think he'll even do it?"

"I don't know if he will." Tamara shrugged. "I can only hope he's still our brother."

"But you said he'd kidnapped your other sister. Emma?"

"Emily."

"Emily."

To Dorothy, the name didn't matter. The fact that the witch wanted to give what was effectively her dead sister to the man who had kidnapped her other sister was unbelievable. Even though he was their brother, it was a ludicrous idea. The fact he was their brother only made it worse. He'd proven he couldn't be trusted. Why did she imagine he'd want to help?

What if, along with all his inventions, he had messed with weather control? What if the storm that brought Dorothy to Oz was something else he had created? If that were the case he'd essentially killed his own sister.

"OK," Dorothy heard herself saying.

Tamara stood up and embraced the girl. Dorothy was stunned, but returned the hug. She was going to save one of the witch's sisters and rescue the other one. She needed the morale boost. She needed a lot more, when she thought about it.

"I could do with some help," she said. She didn't know her way around the country. She wouldn't be able to find her way back to the bus without help. Finding the Tinkerer would be even more difficult, not to mention dangerous.

"Of course," said the witch. "James will stay here. He needs to care for his extended family. He's hot headed. Impetuous."

James fumed silently. On the one hand, he wouldn't want to go with the girl anyway. It was a fool's errand. On the other, the witch was talking about him – insulting him – as if he wasn't there. He thought about telling them he'd like to go too. He'd fight by their side. But, he didn't want to spend the time with Dorothy. He wanted to be as far from her as possible.

For Dorothy's part, she didn't want to be around him, either. She couldn't be sure he wouldn't kill her while she slept and carry out his plan to poison the Terrors using her.

"Give me the syringe," Tamara said.

With a deep sigh, James pulled it out and placed it in her hand. He had hoped she wouldn't notice and he'd be able to hold onto it, using it when the opportunity arose.

Tamara closed her hand around the syringe, followed by her eyes. She murmured an incantation. The hand glowed. The syringe glowed. The emerald liquid thickened until solid and then liquefied again, this time being a deep red colour. She handed it to Dorothy.

"Take this," she said.

"What is it?" Dorothy asked. She held the syringe carefully. The contents were poisonous when they were green. There was no telling what they would be or do now.

"It's hope," Tamara told her, smiling.

Hope.

Indeed.

"What do I do with it?"

"Just keep hold of it. Be careful with it." She touched Dorothy's cheek and looked at her gravely. "Be careful."

"I will," said Dorothy. "But what do I *do* with it?"

"I hope that will become self-evident when the time is right," said the witch.

"And my help?"

"Ah, yes." The witch looked thoughtful. She appeared to be wrestling with a decision. "You'll have your friend, of course."

Dorothy smiled, despite the circumstances. Julian was going with her. She needed him, she knew. He was her grounding. She needed to hold on to him, figuratively speaking. Still, she had to have someone else. Someone with reaction times in the milliseconds, rather than the million seconds. There was only one candidate.

"You can take the werewolf too."

31

The Tinkerer was under a cloud.

He was re-evaluating his choices and himself, and was not sure he liked what he saw. The pleasure that came with the pain he caused was leaving a sour taste in his mouth and he thought that the decent man he was meant to be was becoming a stranger.

Where did things go wrong? When did they change? He'd felt safe in the darkness, but it was starting to feel like a suffocating pillow over his face rather than the welcoming blanket it had been. He had wrapped it around him for so long, it had seeped into his bones, dimming the bright spark of life he had shared with his sisters.

He was not used to feeling regret. He wasn't sure, at first, what the sensation was. It crept up on him without his noticing and had settled over his head before he'd realised. When he did, he was surprised. He was the Tinkerer. He did what he needed to do and he did it without being constrained by the restrictive morals and standards that others felt compelled to live by.

It had to be her.

Emily.

His sister.

When he had abducted her, it was for reasons more nefarious than nurturing. He was aware that, potentially, some of his experiments had not quite provided the results he'd expected. It was part of the fun or discovery. You had to make mistakes to learn from them and improve yourself. If you succeeded every time, your ego wouldn't know humility. Humility was important. Or so he had been told. It was the only 'wisdom' his mother had ever tried to impart. Usually, she left the teaching of life lessons to her husband while she busied herself with her daughters.

The Tinkerer wasn't sure why it was important. Though he didn't always succeed, he also didn't see it as failure. Science was not and could not be exact. It held within its grasp the essence of possibility. The Tinkerer saw himself as an explorer of those possibilities. Often, the voyagers into the unknown would be waylaid or take routes that meandered off from their original course. It was an adventure.

He had worked his way into the lives of the Oz aristocracy. His inventions had ingratiated him into their homes and, even though their favour had faded due to his descent into the shadows, they could not free their desire to be associated with him. He was a guilty pleasure. A dark secret. They would all know they associated with him but none would admit to it.

Even the Prime Minister, ruler of all Oz, was in receipt of one of the Tinkerers contraptions. It was a spyglass. The inner workings were very similar to the eyes of the man-machine he had created. They had superior zoom and highly defined accuracy. The Prime Minister used the spyglass to *spy*. He would delve into the lives of his cabinet and of his opponents. The secrets he gleaned kept him in power. He could be gracious and in tune with the populace and rule with a tolerant but firm hand. He could do this because he knew what they wanted. If it agreed with his own needs or beliefs, or if it would benefit him, he would implement ideas before they were presented and be seen as visionary. If it did not, he could divert the attention. He could make compromises. He could remove the person and thus the problem.

The Prime Minister did not want anyone to know of his spyglass. It had been a gift from the Tinkerer. Things that are free always came with a cost. The Prime Minister had yet to discover what that price would be, but he was sure he would find it expensive – and not in a financial way.

When The Tinkerer had requested an audience, the Prime Minister thought that it might be time for him to find out. He accepted the request graciously. In addition, as asked, he invited a specific list of people. He was automatically suspicious of the inventor's intentions but was too intrigued not to play along.

The attendees were, though they didn't all know it, recipients of the Tinkerer's toys. They were each powerful people in their own right, though none matched the Prime Minister. The chancellor. The butcher from Evands Street, a man who had lived in the capital city for all of his extended life and had put food on the tables of almost every family. He knew secrets that not even the Prime Minister's spyglass could reveal. Three cabinet ministers. The sister of a fourth and the fourth herself. It was debateable who was the most influential of the two, and it was something that had not gone unargued.

The influence of all of them was something the Tinkerer had worked to be beholden to him. He had skirted around their fringes, creating the things they desired but wouldn't admit to, as well as playthings that they could.

The room was opulent. It was another example of the Prime Minister's guilty secrets. It housed massive sofas and deep pile carpets. A well stocked bar lubricated the throats of the guests therein. A large window, with mirrored glass that prevented anyone seeing in, covered an entire wall.

All those present had been in the room before that night. Its existence was closely guarded and the one person who *did* let slip had an unexpected fall and been unable to speak again. He also walked with a permanent limp and could no longer make a fist with his right hand.

The Prime Minister didn't tell them why they were there. He thought, quite rightly, that if he'd said that the Tinkerer had summoned them, their beds may be empty and their accounts closed.

"Why are we here?" Sidney, the butcher, asked. "The invitation was very mysterious."

"Yes," said Evilyn, the fourth cabinet minister. "I have to be in Phylisto by the day after tomorrow. Can't this wait?"

She was in charge of dealing with other countries. It meant she travelled a lot and her sister, Winifred, was jealous of the fact. Evilyn had made numerous allies in her travels abroad and had closeted away a substantial wealth. It left Winifred to build an empire at home. She did that easily and it spread throughout Oz. She was not as devious as her sister and she was seen to be honest. Trustworthy. The façade was extremely convincing.

"It can't," said the Prime Minister. "All will be revealed very soon, don't worry."

He hoped it would be, anyway. In reality, he had no idea if the Tinkerer would even turn up. He may have been playing a prank. He was trying to get everyone in one place so he could… He stopped thinking about it. It was destructive. The Tinkerer would be there. Whatever he wanted to talk about would be simple. He needed some help and wanted to ask Oz's most prominent people to aid him.

Nothing to be worried about.

Nothing at all.

There was a knock at the door. Everyone jumped, startled, and tried to pretend they hadn't. There was a ripple of embarrassed coughs. Sidney was the most imposing figure in the room and, by unspoken vote, walked over to the door. He glanced at the others and even he looked fearful. He couldn't understand why. Anyone could be on the other side of the door.

But the Prime Minister looked worried. That concerned the big man. He clearly knew who it was and had chosen not to share. There must be a reason for that.

Another knock sounded and Sidney gritted his teeth as he pulled the door open. He was ready for trouble.

But not that.

"Good evening!" exclaimed the Tinkerer, bowing low before entering the room with a painted on smile that thinly disguised his contempt.

"You!" Sidney said harshly. His mouth was suddenly dry.

Sidney, when the Tinkerer had not been around for very long, had asked for a knife that would cut through his meat smoother. His cleavers and saws were adequate, but he believed if he could cut the joints and slabs of meat faster and finer, he would bring in more custom and so become wealthier. Plus, if more people came to visit his shop and fell into easy conversation with a good listener, he would have more ammunition and so be more dominant. He could, perhaps, take over as Prime Minister if the current one stepped down.

Or was removed.

The blade he was given was a work of pure art. It was powered by tiny motors that charged themselves kinetically. The edges were coated in a sort of oil that had no reservoir but never seemed to run out. It kept the knife moving smoothly at enormous speed. It could cut through flesh and bone as easily as if they were nothing more than air.

He wished he had it there with him. The distrust he had for the painfully thin, brooding man burst to the surface like pus from a boil, painful and oozing and disgusting.

"Me!" said the Tinkerer, bowing again.

"What do *you* want?" asked Evilyn. "Why are we here?"

"Why Evilyn! How lovely to see you! It's so good of you to be able to make it." He danced over to her, his footsteps light on the floor as if the carpet's pile was hesitant to touch his toes. He took her hand and kissed it. "You're not off visiting your lover? I *mean*, visiting the rulers of Phylisto and Baumer!" He laughed. "My apologies!"

Evilyn scowled and avoided the angry look of the Prime Minister. Her dealings with the Tinkerer had been to supply her with listening devices. Four of them. They were controlled remotely and she could listen to what others were saying from almost anywhere. One was secreted in Phylisto, in the King's own chambers. Another was in Baumer. The ruler there was a small, rotund man with a jovial face and an ironclad will. He wore a peaked cap everywhere apart from in bed, and even then it was on his nightstand. In the inner rim was hidden one of the contraptions. The third was stowed away at her home. She used it to keep her eye, or her ear, on her husband. She wasn't afraid he might be doing something he shouldn't be. She wanted to make sure he didn't discover that *she* was.

The Tinkerer was correct. Evilyn visited those other countries only around half as many times as she said she did. The rest of the time she was with her lovers. She alternated between the three of them. None suspected her of having any others.

The final device was in the very room they occupied. It was hidden behind the large portrait of the Prime Minister.

Knowledge was the only currency that mattered between all the people who controlled Oz. She had to ensure she was the most knowledgeable.

"Enough of this," snapped the Prime Minister. "What do you want?"

The Tinkerer stopped his prancing and allowed his smile to fade. His mouth seemed thankful that it didn't have to pretend any longer. He stretched to his abnormally tall height and faced the Prime Minister.

"You," he said.

32

There was a fine line between confidence and arrogance. It appeared to the Prime Minister that the Tinkerer had stepped happily over into the latter. His attitude and comments were brash. Conceited. It needed to be slapped out of him. He had to be put in his place. There was something about him, however, that prevented any of them doing so. It wasn't his height, though he towered above all of them. It was *in* him. He was dark, and it was a darkness that made their childhood fears resurface uncomfortably.

"What do you mean?" the Prime Minister asked nervously.

He should have had the strange man removed after he had made use of him. The thought had occurred to him many times. He didn't like knowing there was someone out there who might have damaging information about him. But he hadn't. He didn't know if there might come a time when he'd have need of the Tinkerer's skills in the future. Enemies could be useful. Dangerously so.

He was regretting his reticence.

But, no. Nothing to worry about. Nothing at all.

The Tinkerer grinned. It made the Prime Minister feel queasy. He felt as if he had just bathed in oil and it had left him feeling greasy. Unclean.

"Why Horatio," the Tinkerer said. "Isn't it obvious?"

No-one called the man by his given name. He loathed it. The name had been the subject of constant ridicule as a child and poorly disguised sniggers when older. When he came to office, he made sure the name was not used again. He was 'Minister,' or 'Sir.' Even his late wife had called him 'Minnie.' It would make them both smile. He suddenly missed her, something he'd not felt for a long time. He was always too busy being official to notice the gap her passing had left. The disease had been savage and swift. Thankfully, *so* swift.

"Please," he said. "Let's not have any games. You've asked for this, so just tell us what you want."

"I did," said the Tinkerer. "I want you."

Sidney stormed towards him, his hand coming up in anger. Horatio stopped him.

"No, he'll want that. Let's hear him out."

"That's very good of you," the Tinkerer said. "And you're mistaken. I would really rather not be on the end of a butcher's fist."

He laid his hand on the Prime Minister's shoulder. It was a gesture that both implied kinship and concern, but meant something much more sinister. He resisted the urge to recoil or to throw a punch himself. Violence wasn't his way, though. At least, not inflicted by him. He had lackeys to carry out his orders. He had mercenaries to tie up loose ends. Here was an end that was becoming looser by the second.

"Tinkerer, whatever your real name is, just talk to us and then let us go." It was Winifred speaking. She had a headache and she wanted to just be at home, in bed with her curtains closed.

"Wini!" laughed the Tinkerer, spinning around twice before facing the woman. "I'm going to do just that! Oh don't you worry!"

Winifred backed away, any bravado being replaced by a cold chill. She had asked the Tinkerer for tools to help her listen too. But she wanted to listen in on her sister. She wanted to use what she found out too expand and build on her own authority. She was merely the sister of a minister. She was a forgettable nobody who most would not have heard of. She wasn't going to be obscured by her sibling's shadow or be dragged along by her coattails. She was shocked to learn of her sister's infidelity and had told her brother-in-law about it some time ago. They'd entered into an affair themselves and now the Tinkerer could potentially expose everything!

He appeared to disregard her, however, turning back to the Prime Minister.

"Horatio," he said, advancing forward. "I want you. Or rather, I want your position."

He took his tall hat from his head and turned to the room, spreading his arms out wide. He looked to be offering the upturned hat for donations. Spare change. Souls for sale – except he already had those.

"You are all going to make me the ruler of Oz," he said. He spoke so matter-of-factly, it seemed to be only a formality and not something they would think of denying him.

The Prime Minister spluttered. He then laughed. He then regretted it when the Tinkerer turned to him, the dark eyes boring into him.

"I wasn't under the impression I was joking."

Everyone started to speak at once, to him, the Prime Minister, each other and the room itself. Anything to be heard or simply voice their astonishment. The Tinkerer let them. He walked away silently and poured himself a drink. He wasn't one to often turn to alcohol, but he felt that he should celebrate.

He was going to change the world.

Finally, he became bored with the babbling. He took a small disc from his pocket and pressed the slight indentation on its top. A shrill whistle blasted into the room, silencing everyone immediately.

"What the...?" Horatio's hands were on his ears. He wasn't the only one.

"Are you going to step down?" asked the Tinkerer.

"Of course not! You've finally gone insane" It's all that science. It was bound to happen sooner or later."

"Oh, I'm sure I'm quite mad," said the Tinkerer. "But I am not insane. And please do not blame science!"

Lima, the minister for crops and forests stepped forward. He had yet to speak, preferring to allow others to voice their opinions first. He would then pilfer the parts he found useful and make them his own. It made him appear to be a good listener and highly insightful. He was far from either. He was the stealer of ideas and the forger of falsehoods. But, it worked in his favour, so he cared little.

"Science is to blame for all the world's ills," he said, pushing the Tinkerer back.

He didn't care if the man told his peers about his toy. It was small. Easily portable. He had hardly used it and, when the person was dead, there was no evidence of it ever being there. They were all guilty of immoral behaviour. Let them discover his. They would each be equally deep in blame.

"He's right," agreed the Prime Minister, taking strength from the others audacity. "Science isn't magic. It can't be relied upon."

"Again, you are mistaken." The Tinkerer moved over to the window, standing next to the Prime Minister's spyglass. The long tube was on top of an ornate stand the Tinkerer had been kind enough to make for no extra charge. He was so giving. "Science *is* magic! It's more magic than magic itself!"

"You're not making sense!" Evilyn yelled.

"Woman, keep your voice down!" The Tinkerer glared at the woman and she closed her mouth. At any other time, he might reprimand her but he had more important things to deal with. "Magic can make things appear and disappear. It can cause things to grow. To die. To be any manner of opposites, as night is to day. But, it's unpredictable. It's difficult to properly control."

He rested his hand on the spyglass, running his finger along the cold golden surface.

"With science, I can do almost all of those things," he said thoughtfully. "But I *can* control them! Each of you has had some form of contraption from me. Not one has been used for the good of others. They have all had their power taken for granted and misused."

The protestations began in earnest until he held up his hand.

"Don't. You only lie to yourself. I'm not judging you and you shouldn't judge each other. That's not why we are here." He looked at the Prime Minister. "Horatio, do I have your consent?"

"Never," said the Prime Minister. "You are completely insane."

"Perhaps, on reflection, I am. But, come see my magic. Look through your spyglass. See the wonders it reveals."

"I know what it does," said the Prime Minister. "I use it every day."

"Humour me, please."

Horatio sighed. If this was the only way to be rid of the man, then so be it. He walked over to the window. He looked at the Tinkerer and shook his head, but bent down anyway. He moved the spyglass to the side and adjusted the zoom. There was nothing interesting to see, but he went through the motions.

He didn't hear the sound of the many tiny metal feet scuttling. The brief obscuration of his view was simply a bird flying across the front of the building. It happened often. The spider's sting was out of the lens and into his eye before he could react. He didn't have time to cry out or to fall back. He dropped, instantly.

He was dead.

33

Evilyn and Winifred screamed. The Tinkerer thought it amusing that their screams sounded the same. Equally shrill and piercing. Lima fainted. The other two ministers, Karyn and Katherine, ran for the door but the loud click of it being locked remotely stopped them from trying to open it. They stood, staring at each other so as not to look at the Prime Minister's corpse.

Sidney dropped the glass he had been filling. It smashed on the side of the cabinet as it fell, shattering. A large piece stabbed into his leg and he cried out. He pulled it free and held it up, advancing on the Tinkerer.

"Stop!" yelled the inventor.

Everyone did. Sidney froze, still prepared to attack but unmoving. The sisters stopped screaming and held each other tightly. The ministers at the door held hands and stood, quivering.

"Now. Let's sit down and discuss, shall we?"

Sidney roared and ran at the Tinkerer, who sidestepped neatly out of the way. The butcher tripped over the dead Prime Minister and stumbled, knocking the spyglass over. It snapped in half and a tiny metal spider dashed across to the Tinkerer. It ran up, inside his trouser leg and reappeared from the collar of his shirt. It settled in place on his shoulder. Its sting was out, pointing at Sidney.

There was a faint rustling that increased in volume quickly. Suddenly, from under the door, hundreds of mechanical spiders surged into the room. They surrounded the sisters and ministers and butcher, becoming an undulating mass of menace. All movement and sound from the aristocrats ceased. They were barely breathing.

"Sit," instructed the Tinkerer. "Please."

They sat, dropping to the floor like a dead Prime Minister. They were watching the spiders, trying to squeeze themselves into the smallest space in the hope they'd be a harder target.

"Excellent. Now, it looks like you're in the market for a new ruler."

"Never!" shouted Sidney. The spiders circling him moved closer. He squealed.

"Let's not be hasty," said the Tinkerer. "You misunderstand me. I just want to help people."

"Help them? How can you help them?" Evilyn asked. She was shaking visibly, the vibrations causing her sister to tremble too, though she needed no assistance.

"I'm going to save the world!" The Tinkerer laughed and clapped his hands together, applauding himself.

He moved to the middle of the room, the spiders parting to let him pass. He sat down, his long, bony legs crossing.

"So, here it is, and I would prefer no interruptions" he said, his jubilation vanishing.

He was now sombre and his eyes were sad, as if a switch had been flicked and the brief light had been extinguished. The others nodded. They would stay quiet. They dare do nothing else.

"I once made a man. I created him. He was perfect and he was flawed. I had to cast him out." He interlocked his fingers and stared at them as he spoke. "I once killed my friends. They were meant to sleep, and they did. They just didn't wake up again. As people we are defective. We have diseases that consume us. We grow old. We die. I want to improve things. So, I'm going to eradicate the diseases that eat us alive. I'm going to remove one of our biggest mistakes so we can work on the others."

"Disease isn't our mistake," said Winifred. "It just... *is!*"

"Perhaps it's not ours, but it *is* a mistake. It's something that can take people of all ages. Rich or poor. I can stop it."

"How?" Winifred asked. She was unsure if he could actually do as he claimed. He was talented but he was also a lunatic.

"I have a cure." He brought out a vial of deep red, thick liquid. "This will prevent all disease. People will just not be ill again. Physical and mental, this can resolve it."

"And how will you administer it? That won't go around the whole population."

"It doesn't have to." The smile was back. "In the depths of this very building is the spring that feeds all the rivers of Oz."

"There's what?" Sidney asked.

For a large man, he felt very small. He was not normally afraid of spiders, but the vast numbers and the knowledge they were some sort of machine and poisonous into the bargain was forcing his to reassess his phobias. He had never heard of any such spring. He looked at the others. They either shook their head or shrugged. They hadn't either.

"Oh yes. For all your endeavours in seeking out information that you can use to increase your influence, you miss the most important things." The Tinkerer leaned forward. "This building is very old, and it's built on the foundations of a much older one. There's a cellar, filled with some of the most expensive wine Oz has to offer. Not one bottle in that cellar has ever been opened."

He pushed himself to his feet and began to pace, the spiders scattering at each footstep and rushing to fill in the gaps afterwards.

"There's a doorway concealed by one of the wine racks. Beyond that door, is a staircase. There's three hundred and twenty seven steps leading down. At the bottom is a spring that comes up from a massive underground ocean. That spring is the source of the Aren Rush. As I'm sure you're aware, tributaries from there feed all the rivers of Oz."

The sisters did know this. Lima, if he had been conscious would have too. Sidney had heard of the fact, but thought it was a myth. The rest were ignorant of such things. It was knowledge they couldn't use so didn't want.

"How do you know all this?" asked Evilyn. "How can you possibly know any of this?"

The Tinkerer stroked the spider on his shoulder. It moved slightly to push itself against his finger, as if enjoying the contact.

"My friends told me."

"How can we trust you? You killed the Prime Minister!" Winifred cried.

"We all know, if I hadn't, one of you would have done. I was saving you the work. And, regarding him, I will be your new ruler. You can thank me later."

"Thank you?"

"You're welcome." The Tinkerer giggled to himself.

"You can't be ruler. The people will never accept you."

"That's why you're all going to pledge your allegiance to me."

Evilyn shook her head.

"And if we don't?"

The spiders rustled loudly. The sound of metal on metal answered the question for her. The threat was clear.

"It won't work," she insisted. "They won't accept you. They won't accept the science."

"I've told you," he said. "Science *is* magic. Tell them I'm a wizard. It'll be wonderful!"

He waited for a response. One that didn't come.

"Well?"

After a pause, Sidney nodded.

"Okay," he said. "I'll agree."

"Perfect," said the Tinkerer. "That's one who I don't have to kill. Any more?"

The spiders and the word 'kill' were the prompt they all needed. They each nodded, eyes downcast and mouths firmly closed.

"You've made the right choice. For all of us."

They were unconvinced but they wanted to live. Irrespective of the effect it might have on the country they loved, they cherished living more.

The Tinkerer turned and moved to the door. There was a click as the lock disengaged. He opened it and walked though. The spiders followed, keeping to the sides of the corridor so the others could walk without the danger of being stepped on. Knowing exactly where he was going, the Tinkerer turned along hallways and went through doors without breaking his pace. The others followed hurriedly, not wanting to be left with the spiders.

They arrived in the wine cellar. There was a mutual appreciation of the collection that was shared by the Tinkerer, but he kept his feelings to himself.

He would not ingratiate himself with them. He didn't need to, they belonged to him now. The spiders skittered across the stone floor, the sound filling the room. They filled the space beneath one of the tall racks. The first ones to enter the gap stopped moving and flattened down. Their bodies became thin discs. Others moved in and rested on top of the first, doing the same. A third advance mounted the two before, then the compacted ones expanded back to their original size. The rack lifted and the spiders moved to the side, taking the wine rack with it.

A door – the door – was revealed.

One of the spiders ran up to the large, rusted lock. It slipped in. There was the sound of metal scraping and parts moving then a liquid started oozing out of the hole. It was oil, lubricating the lock. A click, loud and echoing.

"Please?"

The Tinkerer motioned to Sidney, who took the hint and pushed the door. It was heavy and stiff on hinges that had not moved in decades or longer. Inside, it was totally black. Again, the spiders surged forwards. They started to rub against each other until a faint glow, brightening steadily, illuminated the promised stairs. The Tinkerer led the way down.

When they reached the bottom, red faces and breathlessness evidenced the effort of climbing down. None wanted to think about the return journey.

In the centre of the rough-hewn cave was a small circular wall. Within that wall, water bubbled. It was coming up from a long crack in the rocky floor. Crystal clear, it seemed to be inviting them to taste it. They declined the invitation. Off to one side was a channel, deepened over time, that led out of the room. Within the channel, the water flowed easily.

They were at the source.

The Tinkerer held the vial over the flow of water. It was unstoppered.

"Wait!" shouted Winifred. "What if you're wrong?"

"I'm not always right," he said, "but I'm never wrong."

He turned his hand and the viscous liquid poured out. The river ran blood red, then cleared. There was no trace of the supposed 'cure.'

The Tinkerer smiled. The others did not.

34

Adam's head throbbed.

When he opened his eyes, his vision was blurred and he struggled to focus. He could hear voices but they were indistinct, as if the words were blurring along with his sight. Slowly, his senses cleared.

He was tied to a chair. Beside him was the girl he'd followed and the boy who had taken her. In front of him was a woman. She was tall, elegant and beautiful. For a second, his heart forgot about his beloved Melody and quickened its pace, but he berated himself quickly. There was only one woman for him.

They were talking about a syringe and hope and… a werewolf?

He was suddenly wide awake, the fog that had clouded his mind, ears and eyes vanishing. He looked around, trying to free his hands and legs to distance himself from the mythical beast. He had thought they were only creatures of fiction. How could they be real? But the way the woman spoke was too sure. Too honest. It wasn't just belief that was soaked into her words. It was truth.

"You're awake," said Tamara.

"Where is the beast?"

"Don't worry about that. It's not here. Not now."

"The way you said it. I thought they were imaginary. They're not, are they? It was in your voice."

"I do not lie," said Tamara. "I am forbidden to. If I say something is so, then it is."

This, in itself, wasn't quite the truth. The Three were not directly untruthful, but they *would* bend their words around a lie to achieve their goal. They'd omit facts to paint a different picture. They actually had made a vow of truth, and had intended to uphold it. Tamara and her sisters wanted to be paragons of virtue. They believed they had been born to keep the good that had always been inherent in Oz alive. Their task had become much more difficult in recent times, so they had taken to interpreting their vow in different ways, as it suited the situation.

In this case, she was certainly not lying. Werewolves *were* real. The one they were referring to *wasn't* there. Not at that particular time. Not as a werewolf, at least.

"But…" James began. How could she say the beast wasn't there? It was the man she was talking to!

"James, you will be quiet," she said. Her tone was calm but had a sharp edge he might cut himself on should he chose to continue.

James chose not to. Dorothy chose to follow suit.

"Where am I? Why am I tied up? Let me go!"

"Why does everyone insist on throwing so many questions at me in one go? It's very difficult to keep up with what I'm meant to be answering." Tamara was smiling, though she knew she would be the only one who found anything about it amusing. She didn't herself, not really, but if she showed her real trepidation, they would fall apart.

Adam was silent for a moment. He was thinking about how to phrase his myriad questions.

"Who are you?" he asked her.

"I'm Tamara. I am a witch and I'm one of The Three. You may not have heard of us."

"I would be surprised if anyone in Oz hadn't heard of you and your sisters," Adam said, awestruck.

"That's kind of you to say, but there are many. It means they are resistant to our aid. We offer it anyway."

Adam nodded, then repeated another question.

"Where am I?"

"You're tied up in a school," Tamara said. "I would prefer not to say where in case you choose to return and exact revenge on those who tied you to that chair and wanted to offer you as sacrifice."

"Sacrifice? What?"

"Don't worry, it's not an issue now. They were misguided and have learned the error of their ways, haven't you, James?"

James nodded but didn't say anything. He wished she hadn't pointed that fact out to the man or beast or whatever he might be. He wished she hadn't planted the idea of coming back and retaliating.

"The boy? Where are the adults?"

"They're *dead!*" James yelled, unable to stop himself.

"And there you have the reason for your potential sacrifice. So let's not dwell, shall we?"

Adam thought about it. He had no idea what the sacrifice had entailed. He didn't know how the boy's parents had died or what his part was in it. The witch had a tone to her voice that was persuasive, however, so he nodded.

"Why am I tied up?" Adam asked.

"We don't know you. We had to make sure you were… safe."

"Safe? I just wanted to help the girl, that's all."

"Help me? You attacked me!" Dorothy shouted.

"I was trying to free you!" Adam returned. "You were tied to a chair! Like this!"

He pulled at his bindings angrily. He shouldn't be there. He should be back with Melody watching the cygnets grow and perhaps having some of his own.

"Oh…" said Dorothy sheepishly. "I thought you were attacking me."

"I can assure you that looks can be very deceptive," said Tamara. "In Oz, now, nothing is as it seems."

She stood and paced in front of the trio.

"Who are you?" she asked. She hadn't directed the question at the man, but its aim was obvious.

"Adam," he said. "I'm nobody."

"Everyone is somebody," the witch said. "There are no nobodies. So, who *are* you?"

"I told you, I'm Adam. I'm a baker. There's not much else to tell."

"You missed out the fact that you're…"

"James! Hush! Now! Or you won't be able to speak at all!"

James was quiet but the nervous energy was bubbling inside of him, ready to explode. His leg was shaking and the tremble was threatening to spread throughout the rest of him. Tamara knew she should speed things along, before the boy gave her a situation she would struggle to contain.

"What's he saying? I'm a what? Has something happened?"

"A great many things have happened," said Tamara, taking her seat again. "All of the adults in this town have been consumed by the Terrors." She indicated Dorothy: "This girl is from another land." She sighed and averted her eyes. "And my brother is the ruler of Oz."

"Another land? Ruler?"

It was too much to take in for Adam. He just wanted to get home and be with his Melody. He didn't understand why he was tied and couldn't think of a way out. He knew who the woman was. A witch. One who used and abused magic. He distrusted her kind. They should let nature and her subjects find their own way, not interfere with their conjurings.

"That's correct."

"Your brother is the Prime Minister?

"No. The Prime Minister is dead. It's my brother now."

"Your brother. Did he...?"

"He did. He needs to be stopped. He's unwell and has done things that he wouldn't do if he was thinking straight."

"Are you sure it's not all intentional?"

"No" Tamara said sadly. "I'm not. I'm trying to think the best of him. He has always had a darkness about him. He needs someone to give him some light."

"And that's us?" asked Dorothy. She knew where this was leading and didn't like it. Why should she be dragged into their problems?

"I'm afraid so," said the witch. "It has to be."

"*Why?* Why us?"

"Dorothy, you're not from here. Your friend is proof that you have some resilience to my brother's creations. And Adam here can get the help he needs."

"What help do I need?" asked Adam. "I just want to get home."

"You have no home now, I'm afraid," she said. "You... It has... It's gone."

"Gone? How? What about my Melody?" Adam fought against his ropes, trying to escape, but they held.

"She's gone too, Adam. There's nothing that you can do. Except, perhaps, help us."

"Gone? What are you talking about? Are you saying..? What..? What happened?"

He stopped struggling. The fight had left him with the revelation of Melody's death.

"She was killed by... She was killed by a beast. It's gone now. *For* now, anyway."

"And this was your brother's doing?" Adam asked, failing to hold back his tears.

"It was," Tamara said.

She could have said otherwise. She could have told them it was a mysterious disease and her brother was trying to stop it, but they'd discover the truth sooner or later and then they know she had lied. They had to go into it with both eyes open and unencumbered by the blinkers of deceit.

"I'll kill him," Adam said calmly. He was staring straight ahead, playing out the various ways he would make the Tinkerer suffer.

"Are you a killer, Adam?" Tamara asked.

Adam hesitated. She knew the answer before she'd asked the question. He wasn't. He didn't know if he could hurt anyone. He was just a baker. He did his best to not offend anyone, just enjoying peace and a chilled happiness.

That could change if he came face to face with his beloved's killer. He could become an executioner himself. But, could he? Was an eye worth an eye? Did murder justify murder?

"No," he said finally. "I don't think I am."

"And that's why we need your help. You'll do what's right."

"Okay," he said quietly. "I'll help."

"We are in agreement," said Tamara. "Dorothy and Adam will retrieve my sister's ring and take it to my brother. The syringe I've given you... it's a cure. Find a way to use it."

"We'll try," said Dorothy. She felt immensely unprepared for such a task, but she could think of nothing else to do."

"Thank you," Tamara said. "And, if you can, find my sister and free her?"

Dorothy nodded. Adam did, too, though he had no idea what was meant by that. He felt he should just agree with the witch. What was the point in doing anything else? He had lost his only love. He had nothing else. Doing as the witch asked would bring him face to face with Melody's killer. He would see if his usual pacifism remained intact.

"James," Tamara said, "your people need you. Go to them."

James stood and left, not speaking. He felt small in the shadow of the older people in the room. His protestations had been shouted down by the witch and even the girl seemed to be more important and useful than he was.

And the *creature!* Even that *thing* was being treated with respect! He didn't miss the fact that the man had killed his wife or whoever she was, and didn't actually know. He was torn between pity and loathing.

And now he was being dismissed.

"James," Tamara called. He turned, trying not to look sullen but not succeeding. "Thank you. They'd be lost without you."

He smiled, feeling a rush of pride that dissolved his anger. He *did* have a part to play. He was the leader of his band of survivors, and he'd ensure they continued to survive.

"You should leave," said Tamara. "Things are progressing swiftly and we do not want to delay too long."

"I don't know where I'm going," said Dorothy. "I don't know how to get to the bus, let alone your brother."

"Don't worry," said Tamara. "I can direct you to this 'bus' of yours. Just... if you can be respectful of my sister, perhaps bury her?"

Dorothy shook her head. A burial, unfortunately, would be out of the question.

"I'm sorry," she said, hesitating as she thought what to say. Suddenly, she changed her mind. The witch didn't need to know what had really happened to her sister. "No, of course. I'll do what I can."

"Thank you. As for my brother, finding him is easy. All roads and rivers lead to the Emerald City. Head into the morning sun and you'll not lose your way."

Preparations were made swiftly. James and his sister gave them provisions to keep them fed for the journey. There was an atmosphere between the siblings and it was clear Brie disagreed with her brother's aiding the two travellers but she, too, wouldn't cross the witch.

Tamara embraced them before they set off.

"Please don't think too harshly of my brother," she said. "He's different. Special. It's not all his fault."

Dorothy nodded. Adam remained impassive.

"Safe journey," the witch said.

She embraced them. Adam stood, his arms to his side as she held him. Dorothy returned the hug, taking from it the support she would have received from her aunt. Adam, feeling uncomfortable, moved away, giving them their moment.

"Why didn't you tell him?" Dorothy whispered.

"I can't tell him he killed her," Tamara answered quietly. "It wasn't him, not really."

"What if he turns again? Attacks me?"

"It's not the full moon. You have a month."

"A month?"

Tamara nodded.

Dorothy broke her hold on the witch. A month. She didn't know if that was too short a time or far too long to be still searching. Either way, she felt she was suddenly drowning under burden of the knowledge and the fear.

"And you have your friend."

Julian was standing close by. Dorothy looked at him and smiled. She did, indeed, have her friend. He had already, somehow, saved them from the beast within Adam. She had thought him to be something of a hindrance but now had to rethink her opinion. Julian had always been someone she loved to hate, in case she forgot herself and hated herself for loving him. His mischievous nature had had its throat ripped out and he had lost that which so irritated her. She tried not to feel sorry for him, knowing pity was wasted. Instead, she concentrated on just accepting him and his predicament. He could have wandered off. He could have died. He didn't. He stayed by her side. He stopped a monster.

They left the town, following the directions the witch had given them. Tamara watched them going, her heart sinking. She had defended her brother, but were his actions defensible? She wasn't sure, knowing her heart was ruling her decision.

Her hand went to her mouth and her breath caught in her throat with an audible gasp as a small figure materialised and bounded after Dorothy. Its tail was wagging happily. She recognised it immediately.

It was her sister's dog.

Toto.

35

At first, the Tinkerer enjoyed his newfound power.

He was no longer secondary to sisters who were adept in magic. He wasn't inferior in the eyes of his parents or, if he was, it no longer mattered. He ruled all of Oz. No-one dared challenge him. The cabinet ministers were in his thrall and word was beginning to spread of his rise to dominance. There were the expected protestations. People reacted badly to change and, when the Tinkerer's past was revealed – the fact that his school friends had died when he was young – the dissenters were more vocal.

The Tinkerer had his ways, however, to silence that opposition. If persuasion failed, it would be bolstered by his eight-legged little friends.

His familial connections helped his cause. Being brother to The Three was taken as a good thing. Most knew of the witches and the boundless work they did. That there was a male sibling was a shock but, if he was kin to them, he couldn't be all bad. Besides, it was well known that the Prime Minister was concerned with self-interest more than the well-being of the country he ran. Essentially, he was a bad man with good intentions. He fell into the habits of the former while attempting to fulfil the requirements of the latter.

The people of Oz were happy, friendly folk. They were respectful of each other and, naturally, were content.

They *were*.

Then the Tinkerer took control. Then the Tinkerer gave his gift to the populace. He would eradicate disease. He would make, barring accidents, Death the only taker of lives.

Unless, of course, he had to step in and take Death's mantle temporarily.

He didn't like killing. He felt it just seemed to happen around him. The school friends. The Prime Minister. Those in between and those after. They were necessary. He did what was necessary.

He had enjoyed himself. He felt as if he had achieved his destiny. He'd tried to give life by creating Edward when he should have been enhancing life by making it pain free. The good of the all came at the cost of the few. The Tinkerer had no illusions and no qualms in paying that price or asking others to. The requests were not always verbal, of course. They were often more forceful in nature. But the price would be paid. It had to be.

Something was off. It was faulty. He tried to think what could have gone wrong, but was at a loss. He tried to look around his ego, which was positioning itself firmly in the way of his investigation, but struggled. It *should* have worked! How could he have failed?

No. Stop! He hadn't failed. He had simply not quite succeeded.

Reports of strange creatures roaming the land were met with derision at first. Such things didn't happen in Oz. They didn't exist. They were just stories, made up to scare young children into sleeping at night and not answering back their elders. The reports increased, though. Sightings. Deaths. A town wiped out. They couldn't be ignored and nor could their cause.

The Tinkerer knew it had been his own cure. He supposed he should have tested it, somehow, rather than just believing in his own abilities. Those skills must be lacking for it to happen, but he couldn't see why or how. The science was absolute. There was no margin for error.

Yet an error had occurred.

He had poured his cure into the waters of the Aren Rush. It had spread far and it had spread wide. He had meant for it to cure infection yet it had, instead, infected. He tried to tell himself it was just a trial. A run through and he would, based on the findings of the experiment, perfect it.

Unfortunately, it wasn't a test. It was meant to be the one and only attempt. He was so confident. He was the Tinkerer. He knew what he was doing and he didn't make mistakes.

He just didn't.

He had only one option. Or, rather, three.

The Three.

Even though he'd been banished from his home, leaving his parents behind, he had never totally lost touch with his sisters. They had kept in contact, though conversations and secretive visits under the cover of night and magic had grown more infrequent. He didn't blame them for his exile. Yes, they all were skilled witches and had exercised fine control of their powers from an early age, but they didn't treat him any different to each other. He was talented in other ways. He could build. He could modify. He could improve and enhance.

It was a skill he presented from an early age and one his sisters insisted was on a par with their magic. It was still magic, just in a different form, they told him.

But it needed *real* magic to solve the problems he encountered.

Magic abounded in Oz.

There were the *Fae*, who lived in the vast forest to the east. Aloof and proud as a race, they had a playful side to them that occasionally showed itself in the random and bizarre configurations of the trees in their home. Magic would be used to form odd tunnels and assault courses using the trunks of the largest trees, warping them into shapes that they could never, normally grow in. They were generally avoided, their detached nature making them seem indifferent to the ways of others. In reality, they welcomed all, but resisted getting too close to non-Fae races.

Fae bloodlines were pure and it was from this sanctity that they derived their magic. Mixing that with a non-Fae lineage would be fatal to them. Their magic gave them power but also gave them life. The Fae were woven from the intricate threads of enchantment that unified all life. Purity was essential or the web would be broken and they would unravel.

The *Auki* were mountain creatures that came from the Pelican Ridge, the series of mountain peaks the split the left shoulder of Oz off at the collar bone. They were legendary and rarely seen. Only supposed shaman could call them down for their healing powers and only then with a perfectly toned whistle.

Various other magical creatures roamed throughout the land. Magic was almost commonplace, so those that possessed it were thought, to a certain extent, ordinary. But the powers of those were limited. The ability to help a crop grow in arid earth. The gift of healing, though only as much as to salve a wound or reduce a disease to a mild discomfort. The occasional person was born with the skill. It was usually mild. A novelty. Sparks from the fingertips. Water in a drought.

When the Tinkerer's parents gave birth to three, very gifted daughters, it was seen as a blessing. The girls grew to be beautiful, graceful and generous. They were happy to travel to wherever their craft was required.

Their brother should have been magical too. He should have shone with their light. He wasn't, however, and he didn't. The lack of both only served to darken him.

But, he needed them. He had intended on changing the people of Oz. In that, he was successful. The changes, though, were not what he had wished for or imagined. So, he needed his sisters.

He had reached out to them, but they'd resisted. He was taciturn in his explanation of the difficulties and they, it seemed, had larger issues to deal with.

The Tinkerer knew those problems were his doing. He neglected to tell them that but assumed they would realise. When they didn't come, he had only one course of action to follow. He would, whether it was agreed with or not, do what was necessary.

So he had kidnapped his sister, Emily.

He hadn't harmed her. He wouldn't. She was his sister. He *couldn't.*

He had instructed Sidney to capture her. At first the butcher had refused, but the promise of his wife and children being given new pet spiders had given him the stimulus he needed. It had been relatively easy for the large man. He had asked for her help and she had given it easily, without questioning the motives that might have been abundantly clear. By the time she realised and retaliated, his club was swinging and her hand was moving. Her body slumped in his arms.

There was only a small bruise on the side of her head. It would be barely noticeable. The spell that she had conjured had hit his chest rather than his face where it would be absorbed and enter him cleanly. He stumbled and dropped her, accidentally stepping on her hand. The bones had crunched underfoot.

The Tinkerer was displeased. It was only the fact that Sidney was too useful to him that stayed the execution. His sister's hand would heal. The scorched stump Sidney found himself with would, probably, not.

When Emily awoke, she tried her very best to escape. The Tinkerer had, by way of numerous locks that were so complex that Emily couldn't use her powers on them, prevented her leaving. She had then gone from a wild beast wanting to tear its captor to pieces to a complacent and accommodating young lady who wished to help her brother in any way that she could.

The Tinkerer wasn't fooled. He saw through her subterfuge. She *couldn't* trick the ruler of all Oz!

So, she stayed where she was, in captivity. Recently, though, she was getting under his skin. She was changing his mood. She was casting a dark cloud of uncertainty over him.

Was he doing the right thing? Were the deaths required? Why were his experiments inconsistent? His conscience was calling out to him. At first it was an itch at the far back of his mind but, gradually, it became a whisper and then a shout. He started to feel remorse for some of the things he had done.

Some of them.

Turning his back on his creation. The Tinkerer hadn't just built the man, he had *named* him. He couldn't pretend that there was no connection to the mass of leads, springs, cogs and limbs if he had given him a *name*. That made it personal. That made him a father and his automaton a son.

Killing his school friends. It was an accident, surely, but he knew a part of him had deliberately put them into the most permanent of sleeps.

The Prime Minister. The Tinkerer didn't doubt that the man had to be removed from office, but he wondered if he should have been the one to do it. Should he have been the one to step into the breach he had created?

There were so many more. He could feel guilt chipping away at his unblemished self-image, revealing the cracked surface beneath.

Emily was working her empathic way into his mind and he could see and feel the changes she was making. He built a mechanical arm for Sidney. He should have had his spiders eat their way through his flesh and bone to reduce it to a shank similar to his other one. But he didn't. He gave the butcher a hand so much better than the one he had lost. It was more dexterous. Stronger. Faster in its fluidity.

Why? Why was he doing this? He was losing his way. His sister was buttering the crust of his comportment and, in doing so, was making him more palatable.

He was losing himself. The Tinkerer was a man of decision. Of innovation. Of cold science and impassioned wonders. *Im*passion, not *com*passion.

The cure he created was designed to wipe out disease. He should have been seen as a phenomenon. He should have been equal to his sisters in stature if not power. And even then, power depended on one's definition. They had their magic. He had called science 'magic.' So, perhaps, they were equals.

He, of course, was more equal. Events would snowball, he was sure, if he did not take back the crown he felt Emily was causing to slip. He had her. He needed Tamara and Clara too.

For that, Emily would be bait.

36

Those bound together by terrible circumstance can find a common thread of desperation that ties them to one another. They cling to it lest it fray and unravel, leaving them adrift on the ocean of despair that surrounds them. They swim through its waters, ever vigilant of the fierce creatures that swim beneath the surface, waiting for them to tire or waver or surrender.

Those bound together by circumstances so terrible, they cannot even be spoken of, scrabble for that thread. They grasp frantically, only to see it come apart and leave them vulnerable and prey.

Dorothy, Adam and Julian were undecided as to which they were. Could they bond and become a single unit, doing battle against monsters and madmen? Or would they eventually break apart and lose their way, leaving the ocean to swallow them up?

They walked in silence. Even though Julian's gait was little more than a shuffle, he kept pace with Dorothy and Adam without the need for them to slow or wait impatiently for him to catch up. They hadn't noticed the ghost dog scampering along behind them. Every so often it would stop to smell a flower or mark its territory. It seemed to be content with remaining unnoticed while they continued on their taciturn way.

For her part, Dorothy was struggling to think of what to say to the man she had thought was attacking her, who then went on to actually do so before joining her in a quest she wasn't sure she could complete. She also wasn't sure how she had ended up agreeing to so much. How had retrieving a ring morphed into rescuing a kidnapped sister and stopping a maniacal brother?

Werewolf. The word kept whirling around her mind. Whenever her thoughts would finally start to settle, there would be a roar and the glint of red eyes slashing them apart. Tamara had eased her fears, but that had been short lived. When they left the town and the witch behind, her influence faded. Dorothy was all too aware of what the man was capable of.

She wished she could tell him. No. That's not quite accurate. She wished the witch had told him.

"You're a werewolf and you ripped your beloved Melody apart, before devouring her innards."

If it was said quickly enough, perhaps it wouldn't sound so bad. A blur of words would soften the blow. Perhaps not. Maybe, he would embark on a murderous rampage, slaughtering everyone in sight and then move on to those who hid in cellars. Tamara had insisted he was fine. They had a month, an exceptionally long time to just grab a ring and… do something with it. A month until the wolf inside of him decided to break out.

She shuddered at the thought, picturing the ease with which it shredded the thick wooden entrance to the school cellars. If that were her chest…

Adam felt lost. The fear that night imposed on him was making him tremble as he walked. The knowledge that his betrothed had been murdered was a frozen ball of disgust in the pit of his stomach. It weighed heavily, turning his heart to ice. The fires of revenge did their best to melt its wintry hold on him, but they could not burn hard or hot enough.

The witch had spoken of her brother in the way that a parent might about a child who required special care and a touch more love to avoid falling under the bedevilment of pity. He wasn't one to be blamed. He should be sympathised with. He had not effectively destroyed Oz deliberately. He had stepped on a path strewn with potholes and pitfalls. He had stumbled along the way.

Poor him.

As with Dorothy, though Adam didn't know it because they had yet to converse, the effects of Tamara's sway were dissipating. He had felt a pang of sorrow and the tinge of empathy for the Tinkerer. That was no longer. He could only see that the man was responsible for whatever nightmarish hellion had taken Melody from him. Recompense must be made. For him, there was only one person to blame. That person should not be sympathised or empathised with. Only stopped.

Adam wasn't a killer, he knew. There was no point in pretending otherwise. But that didn't mean he wouldn't make the Tinkerer suffer. There were ways. He felt, with Melody's death, a beast was inside of him, rattling the bars of a cage that in no way could adequately contain it.

Then there was the girl. She was an enigma. The witch had said she was from 'another land.' She didn't make it sound as if that was just another country. Her manner of speaking and her dress sense were too different from that of Oz and its surrounding territories. The materials and machining of her clothes were of a kind he had yet to see anywhere else. She used terms he didn't recognise. 'Bus.' What was a 'bus' and how could it crush the witch's sister and her pet?

The girl's friend. Adam didn't trust him. He, at least, shared some of the foreboding voiced by the boy. Julian had only partly turned into a Terror. That didn't mean the transformation couldn't still continue. He might still rip their throats out while they slept.

Something Julian had some experience of.

Julian shuffled along. His head bounced on his shoulder, the tendons and sinews keeping a hold, albeit not a tight one, on the neck remnants to ensure it remained connected to the torso. If he could speak, he would mention the dog that was following them. He could tell Dorothy that a month was really too long to be in the company of a man like Adam, moon or not. He would tell her that he was sorry that he couldn't stop the creatures that attacked the bus, ate the survivors and savaged the dead. He'd explain how the Terrors that ripped at his throat were once like all of them and were not entirely in control of what they did.

But he couldn't talk. He couldn't think. The thoughts that had once spun in his head were gone, leaving the decaying murmur of coherency. He followed Dorothy because she was Dorothy. Somewhere lost inside of him, wandering the corridors of his brain, was the knowledge that they had a connection. Whether it was one of family, friendship or love didn't matter. It wasn't anything corporeal. It was more instinct. It was an echo that fell flat against the deadened walls of his mind.

The trio were thrown together. They would have to work together and be together and they would have to help and guard each other. None would survive if not, and that didn't just refer to them.

"What is a bus" Adam asked.

He *had* to break the virtual sheet of ice that stood between himself and Dorothy. It was allowing them to see each other but with mutual suspicion in the way they would never build anything remotely resembling trust. He didn't trust her, but he didn't know her. It was obvious she thought the same.

Dorothy didn't answer straight away. She had no concept of what passed for transportation in Oz. She'd yet to see anything that wasn't horse or hand pulled so a diesel or petrol fuelled vehicle would feel out of place with their simpler lifestyle. No mobile phones. No television. No WiFi. Would the man even understand such concepts?

"It's… It's a form of transport," she said.

"Where were you going?"

"To the mall. I needed some jeans."

"Mall? Jeans?"

Dorothy sighed. This was going to be somewhat painful.

"A mall is a collection of shops, but quite a big one. Jeans are denim trousers."

Adam shook his head. She might as well have been speaking the language of the *Ipsos*, the mainly silent but deafening when they did speak people who were resident along the lower banks of the Aren Rush. Their language was a cacophonous mash of noise that no one outside of their clan could comprehend. Adam had once spent a month trying to understand them and only succeeded in giving himself a headache that refused to give him a reprieve for days.

"Don't worry," Dorothy said. "It doesn't matter anymore. They'll be closed now, anyway."

Adam was struggling to think of something to say. He wanted to start a dialogue. He should learn something about the girl and her friend. It would, if nothing else, divert his attention from things he really didn't want to think about. He couldn't think of any common ground to work with, though. They were thrown together but they were worlds apart.

Dorothy had a similar dilemma. At home, she could enjoy the silence. She would read. She would go for long walks. Often, she would be listening to music, but not always. Birds would sing, passersby would be chatting, cars would beep warning horns. Even without the ambient noise, she felt she would be fine.

Now, there was birdsong, but that was all. There were no cars and she didn't want to encounter the sort of passersby that might roam around Oz. The void between them grew wider as time went on and the silence seemed to become more deafening in proportion.

Dorothy wanted to ask Adam about his life, but didn't know where to start. Anything she might say would eventually come round to Melody, she was sure. That was a subject she wanted to shy away from. It would be painful for him, certainly, but she wouldn't be able to hide what she knew.

No. This was ridiculous. There was no way they could travel all the way to the Emerald City without speaking. It wasn't possible. Their distrust would become antagonism. They *had* to find something that they could both associate with.

The directions the witch had given them were clear. They would be back at the bus fairly soon. Perhaps Dorothy should tell him what to expect. She should prepare him for the carnage. It wasn't going to be a pleasant discussion, but it would still require an exchange.

"Tamara's sister was..."

A high pitched screech pierced through the feeble attempt at conversation, popping it like a soap bubble hanging in the air. Adam and Dorothy stopped. Julian took a few more steps and then halted too. From the trees, ran two Terrors. Dorothy couldn't be sure, but she thought they were the same ones that had attacked the bus. She cried and automatically moved to Adam for protection. He might think he was just a man, but she knew better. Suddenly, it occurred to her that Julian had saved them from the very thing she hoped Adam could bring forth. It was too late to change her mind.

The Terrors eyes were wide and she could see an unceasing hunger burning in them. They neared the trio and raised their hands, ready to tear into the flesh and sever the limbs.

A howl from behind Dorothy made her spin around. An attack from both sides?

There was a flash of white and an animal lunged forwards towards the Terrors. They skidded, falling to the ground, then scrambling upwards and backing away. The animal was growing, its bulk increasing rapidly as it moved towards them. It howled again, larger than all of them and with a mouth that could easily swallow the Terrors whole. The brute's teeth were stretching and curving.

But...

How...?

It was...

Dead?

The witch's ghost dog had metamorphosed into a massive, savage creature. It swept up one of the Terrors in its mouth. There was a sickening crunch of bones and a spray of blood and the dog threw the body away. The second Terror had regained its feet properly and was running back to the tree line. The dog leapt into the air, covering the distance in a single jump. It landed on the creature. Its head dipped and ripped, chewing and swallowing the head. The decapitated body twitched once and was still.

The dog turned and ran back to Dorothy, Adam and Julian, shrinking back down as it moved. By the time it was sitting at the girl's feet, its tail wagging happily, it was its normal size once more.

"Don't touch it!" Adam said, swinging his leg to kick at it. His foot passed through and he staggered to prevent himself from falling over.

Dorothy crouched and went to stroke the dog. Her hand, too, and as she had expected, sank into it, with no resistance.

"He's okay," she said, smiling. "Adam, meet Frank."

"*Dorthy*," said Julian.

"I know," said Dorothy. "I know."

37

"What just happened?" Adam asked.

He was staring at the dog, not sure if he was seeing what he thought he was seeing. The dog had just been a massive beast that had torn the attacking Terrors apart. But it was a dog! Except…

Except it wasn't. It was… imaginary? Dorothy's hand was passing through it. It wasn't really there, yet they could both see it. Even Julian, the Terror who wasn't a Terror could see it.

His head hurt. Was it a symptom of something more serious? Had one of the blows to his head caused more damage than he thought? He's woken up in the forest with no knowledge how he had arrived there. He had been attacked by the children when he was just trying to help the girl. He'd been about to be sacrificed. Then…!

The witch. She'd set them on this path. Adam was meant to be protecting Dorothy, but who would protect him? The girl had shown herself to be very capable, but the boy was a hindrance and the addition of an imaginary dog was only confusing the situation even more. They must all be under the influence of whatever the Tinkerer had done. The disease he had unleashed was affecting their minds and, he had to believe, would work its way into the rest of their bodies. They would eventually become Terrors themselves, or worse.

If there was anything worse.

The boy, Julian would finish his transformation and they would all be lost. Adam imagined that the terrible creatures did not suffer from delusions such as dogs that weren't there, which was something. They only fed and killed. Such a simple life. It had its good points. Perhaps he should surrender to the inevitable and let them take him. The others would be forced to give themselves too, of course. There was no refusing the bite of a Terror.

He thought about speaking out, telling them of his decision. Not that he'd actually make the choice. He felt that he was accepting the lesser of a multitude of evils. Become one willingly or wait for the inevitable to happen. What was the point in continuing a quest into the heart of failure? The blood would be pumping around you anyway. Wasn't it better to be in its flow voluntarily?

If they fought, they could end up dead. Really dead. The sort of dead where you didn't rise again. The kind where you found out whether there really was a spirit world where everyone lived in happiness and your loved ones were waiting for you.

Wait!

If that were the case, then... Melody?

But it was all a big *IF!* What if none of it existed. Maybe there was only darkness, light and darkness. No afterlife. No resurrection. Just an eternity of cold, lonely *nothing.* Adam couldn't think about that. He couldn't bear to believe that he would never see his Melody again.

Besides. The dog!

Dorothy's hands were passing through it, so it wasn't there, but it had killed the Terrors so it clearly *was.* He knew they weren't under the influence of the Tinkerer's tinkerings. They were fine. Even Julian, whose head was desperately trying to stay attached by the remains of his neck. He was fine.

No. He couldn't do it. He couldn't offer up his throat as a sacrifice to his future. Thoughts of Melody and the reality of the canine spirit were too much to ignore. He was letting his fear get the better of him. He had always been its victim, being bullied into decisions all his life by the anxiety that followed him like the ghost of a dog, except this one bit at his ankles and threatened his jugular.

He was afraid, but he would use it to give him courage. He would spit in the eye of his fear and hope that it didn't, in return, open its maw and devour him.

"He saved us," said Dorothy.

"Dorthy!" agreed Julian.

"He did that," said Adam. "Though I have no idea how."

He crouched by Dorothy and went to try and stroke the animal himself. It hunkered down and growled at him, baring its teeth. He snatched his hand back. He didn't want to lose it.

"Hey, Frank," said Dorothy soothingly. "Come on, good dog. He's a friend. He's with us. Good dog."

"Frank?"

"It's from a movie," she said. "It made me always want a dog called Frank, though he's no Pug."

"Movie? What's a movie?"

Dorothy frowned. What sort of place was this?

"A movie is like a play, but on a screen. Moving pictures."

"Is it magic?" Adam asked.

"Erm... kind of."

Adam nodded. That was something he could understand. She spoke of strange things, but magic was, at least something normal.

Dorothy was frustrated. These people seemed advanced enough, but she was beginning to feel like an explorer discovering a new tribe in the Amazon. They had no televisions or cinemas. No smartphones. No WiFi. Probably no flushable toilets. No cars. They didn't even know what a *bus* was! It wasn't somewhere that she fancied being stranded, even without the monsters. If she couldn't find a way home, maybe she should just give in and become one of them. It might be better than running or having to fight. She was neither a decent runner and fighting was something she generally left to others. She kept out of trouble. This place was a whole world of trouble.

And they had magic. How could that be possible?

She felt something warm and wet run along her hand and squealed in fright. Frank's tongue was hanging out and his tail was wagging happily.

"He licked you," said Adam. "And it made contact."

Dorothy smiled. Well, maybe monsters and magic weren't so bad, after all.

Who was she kidding? They were as bad as it could possibly be, but she had a dog called Frank and she had friends. Ignoring the fact that one was on his way to being a zombie and the other was a werewolf, she knew she had no choice but to accept the way things were.

"Just call me 'Van Helsing'" she said to herself.

"Van Helsing? I thought your name was Dorothy."

Dorothy sighed. It wasn't worth the effort to explain.

"Don't worry about it," she said.

She ruffled the back of Frank's head, just holding her hand in place and shaking it to give the effect of him being petted. Adam reached out again and, though the dog tensed and bristled, it allowed the semblance of contact.

"See," Dorothy said. "He likes you. He just needed to get to know you."

Adam wasn't so sure. He had a feeling that the dog was behaving for the sake of the girl and, at any when she wasn't looking, it might attack. Monster or mutt. Not much of a choice.

"We should go," he said. "There might be more of them."

Dorothy pushed herself up. She wasn't feeling as afraid as she might, or potentially should, otherwise have been. Both Julian and Frank had come to her rescue when she'd been attacked. If, between them, they could do battle with the creatures they had already encountered. She felt a sliver of confidence working its way into her concern. Dorothy had no doubt that there were things in Oz she had yet to see. Her experience of the country was minimal and even that had been terrifying. She couldn't let that worry her. She had a job to do and she needed to take off her head, give it a good shake and put it back on, free of the cotton wool fogginess that was muffling her thoughts.

"Come on," she said. "This way."

They walked around the remains of the Terrors. Adam would have like to have avoided them completely but, unfortunately, they needed to enter the woods the creatures had exited. Dorothy stepped over one rather than circumvent it. Adam looked at her, horrified.

"It's dead," she said when she saw his expression. "It's just meat and blood now. And it's in my way."

Adam nodded, the queasiness causing a tightness of his throat and a bubbling in his stomach. Who were the real monsters? The corpse wasn't really in her way. A single step either way would have avoided it completely. She had deliberately stepped over it. She was announcing her dominion over the Terrors, those dead, undead and personal.

Part of him warmed to her. Another part shuddered.

38

In the trees, every sound seemed amplified. Moving slowly and keeping watch for any other Terrors, the slightest noise made the travellers jump. They kept their breathing tight and muffled with their steps light and slow to ensure they made minimal disturbance to the overall silence of the forest.

The sounds came from birdcalls. The screech of some animal scurrying through the undergrowth. The leaves whispering warnings as the breeze tickled their surfaces. *Turn back! Go no further! Deeeaaathhhhhh!*

"Can you hear that?" whispered Adam.

"What?" Dorothy asked. She stopped moving, poised to defend herself but to run if necessary.

"The forest." Adam took her arm, his nerves tightening his grip. "It's taunting us."

Dorothy pulled her arm sharply, dislodging his hold. Taunting? Hardly!

"It's just the wind and the animals. Get a grip."

Adam looked doubtful but nodded slowly, his eyes darting around for the slightest sign of movement.

"Can we get out of here?"

"That's what I'm trying to do!" hissed Dorothy.

He was meant to be protecting her, not the other way around. He had a monster prowling inside of him. How could he be so twitchy? This was his world, as twisted as it was. She was a fish floundering out of water and felt as if she couldn't breathe. She had enough to handle with Julian being... not Julian. She couldn't cope with her knight in battered armour using her as a shield.

She motioned to Julian to follow. Her friend followed silently, appearing to understand not to utter the only word he seemed capable of. Frank looked to be oblivious to their peril. He scampered around them, passing through tree trunks and bushes as if they didn't exist.

Adam followed too. He knew how he appeared. Weak. Afraid. It was exactly how he felt and he was ashamed of the fact. He only hoped, when it came to it – if it did – he could redeem himself. He could step up and defend the girl.

Melody would have wanted it.

But still, trepidation ran down his spine, vaulting from vertebra to vertebra and making him shiver. He could feel his legs shaking. He could feel the urge to flee. He fought with himself to stay put, not sure he would win that fight.

Dorothy was hoping that something would seem familiar. She'd been here before when she had escaped the bus and been taken by the children, but she couldn't help thinking they were going around in circles. One tree looked much like the next, as if they had all worn the same outfit to the summer festival and were standing around wondering what to do about it. Should they go change, so oaks resembled oaks and elms looked like elms? Or should they just stay where they were and enjoy themselves, soaking up the sun and chucking out some oxygen for the world to breathe? She wished they would make up their minds. The longer they roamed the woods, the more chance they had of being discovered.

Frank ran on ahead a little way and turned to them. He spun around in a circle, chasing his ghostly tail then stopped, barking at them silently. He ran away and came back over and over, his tail frantically waving.

"Do you think...?" began Adam, stopping because it sounded ludicrous.

Dorothy knew what he meant, though. It sounded equally preposterous to her, but the dog's meaning was clear.

"He wants us to follow him," she said.

She thought that only happened in movies but didn't bother to say as much. Frank was becoming more enthusiastic with each return, his soundless barking more energetic. As they walked towards him, he ran over to Dorothy and nuzzled her hand. It was like touching fog, and she knew she wouldn't feel him, but she couldn't help a tingle of sensation. Not quite as much as when he licked her, but *something*. Frank ran off again and sat, waiting for them.

"Come on," she said.

The dog led and they followed. The witch's guidance was comprehensive but it didn't cover being deep in the woods. If they had kept straight ahead, they'd have been fine, but they didn't. They crept and fretted. Their sense of direction became skewed and they were lost. Following a dog that wasn't there was better than wandering aimlessly.

Wasn't it?

It turned out it was. After an hour of walking, if stealthy stumbling could be called walking, they broke out from the cover of the trees. It felt as if they were waking from a long sleep, the leafy canopy being the quilt covering them while stepping out into the open air was that quilt being pulled from their bodies. They felt bleary eyed and exposed. This made Dorothy's resolve tighten. The feeling that, at any moment, an attack might come, steeled her to their predicament. She was ready. Adam's resolve dissolved. He stepped closer to the girl, hoping he would look as if he had moved to protect rather than be protected.

Julian shambled to their side with Frank by his side. Both were effectively Dorothy's pets, waiting to be told to fetch, sit or roll over.

Lying on its side nearby, a shattered shadow of its former self, was the bus.

Dorothy kept the determination wrapped around her, a shield to the stalking panic that circled like a tiger around an injured antelope.

"That is a bus," she said confidently.

"What does it do?" asked Adam.

It looked to be a long, metal, rectangular tube. Odd appendages ran along the side closest to them and wheels were attached close to the corners. He assumed it was on its side, but couldn't be sure.

"It takes you places. It's a vehicle."

"How does it move?"

"Wheels, of course!" snapped Dorothy

They weren't there for a lesson in the vehicular habits of her world. It didn't matter what the bus *was*, it only mattered why they were there. She did, however, wish it was still standing the right way up. Perhaps it would still have been possible to drive it. They could get to the Tinkerer much sooner.

But, it was full of corpses.

Half eaten. Partially devoured. Which sounded better? Which one was easier to… digest? There could, no *would*, be more on board like Julian. Not necessarily the undead dead, zombies in the making, not knowing if they would become Terrors or gain the taste for brains. Terrors may even *like* brains already. No. Not still, somehow, walking and doing their best to be talking. Victims. Necks torn out. Possibly limbs ripped from torsos.

Even if the bus was settled nicely on its four wheels, dropped with consideration by the raging storm, she wasn't sure she could go back on. The boy who had died in her arms would haunt her. He wouldn't be a ghost, though it was only recently that she'd had her opinion of ghosts changed, so it was beyond the realms of possibility. He wouldn't, hopefully be a Terror or part Terror. He would haunt her because she had been holding him when his life left for the great white light in the sky.

It wasn't his spirit. It was his memory.

He was haunting her already.

They didn't need to go on it. She didn't need to see him or any of the other passengers. Or what was left of them. They were here for the ring.

"Can I look inside?" Adam asked. "I want to look inside."

"*No!*" Dorothy snapped. "You can't!"

"Why not? I've never seen one before. I'm curious."

"Just… just leave it. It's just a bus. A bus filled with dead bodies."

Adam shuddered. His curiosity wasn't strong enough to have him face that. He had yet to come to terms with the death of his beloved. There *were* no other dead. There couldn't be. Not ever. Not yet, anyway. Others would detract from the… strength of her loss. From the essence of her passing. She would be diminished. He could not allow that to happen.

"Of course," he said sadly. "I understand."

Dorothy didn't know about the inner turmoil that boiled within him. She only saw a dangerous man trapped in a coward. She might as well have been following the witch's instructions by herself.

The witch. Yes. The *witch*.

Dorothy pointed. Adam looked to where she was indicating. Ah. They walked forward slowly, neither wanting to hurry their macabre discovery. Adam told himself this was different. The bus covered the majority of her body. She was one of The Three. It wasn't like she was a real dead body. She didn't count.

Frank was in front of them. His pace matched theirs in its sombre approach and his tail hung low. He sniffed at his owners' hand, nudging the fingers and, probably, whimpering. After a moment, he moved over to his leg that had been twitching but was now still. He sat down next to his paw, looking sad. Dorothy's heart went out to him. He had been a boisterous, and ferocious when needed, dog. Now he was a ghost that had just encountered its dead self.

But she had a task. She smiled supportively at Frank and moved to the witch. Here arm and leg hadn't moved, but how could it? The weight of the bus and the lack of a life prevented any movement. The red veins in the ring glistened like fresh blood, which would normally repulse Dorothy. With this, though, she was drawn to it. Her hand was reaching and she watched it move as if it belonged to someone else, detached from her.

The ring was warm, though the hand that wore it was cold and clammy. Dorothy pulled and it slipped off easily. She paused before putting it on her own finger, thinking that wearing it would be the safest way to keep a hold of it. But, it had just been on the hand of… No. Don't think about it. Just do it.

She didn't need to push. The ring was already in place.

Dorothy gasped as the warmth in the ring became a heat in her body. The veins in the metal grew suddenly brighter, a fiery river across its surface. Then, just as suddenly, it stopped. It was just a ring. The red had faded to a faint pink. The warmth came only from herself.

Frank barked and, for the first time, Dorothy, Adam and Julian heard it. They turned to look at the dog just in time to see him dissolve to a light mist that floated away. Looking back at the witch, there was a vague hissing and the arm and leg melted leaving, in just a few seconds, a damp area in the grass.

39

It was dark.

Always.

His eyes felt as if they were being pushed back into their sockets and would pop if the pressure wasn't lifted soon. His mouth was dry. Dusty, as if every inhalation of air was taken while walking through a sandstorm. The gritty sensation ran down his throat, making him feel that he had somehow swallowed a million tiny splinters of glass. He couldn't concentrate either. He would run after his thoughts, and they would scatter before him like children playing Tig in the school playground.

And the darkness had a voice.

It whispered to him. It enticed him. It offered so much, if he would just listen. But he couldn't. The whispers were lies, he knew. He could feel it. Taste it. The bitterness hid beneath the sweet flavour of promise. He thought that his resistance was failing. The whispers wove their way into his mind, knitting a blanket of persuasion that smothered his resolve. But he held on. To what, he didn't know, but whatever it was, he wasn't letting go.

There was a light in the darkness. It filtered through into his mind every so often, lifting his spirits and giving him brief moments of clarity. They were short lived, however. They would slip away, dissolving into vague memories before he could properly focus on them.

He could remember when it happened. When the darkness fell. It was after the storm. After the crash. He had been helping her, his beam of light. He could remember the screams and the pain and the frantic, frenzied attempt to escape. Then he was pulled from behind. He hit his head on something hard and cold. Then there was pain.

So much pain.

They stopped trying to consume him, and vomited violently. Something about him, he thought, didn't taste right. Or maybe he was mouldy. He'd showered that day, hadn't he? So he should have been fresh. He couldn't really recall. But, whatever the reason, the creatures couldn't stomach his flesh and puked it back up.

But, it was then that things started to blur. It was then the darkness intruded on his senses. And it was then that the voice started.

His vision cleared, but the fog in his mind was too thick to wade through. Invisible hands seemed to grab at him and slow him down to the point he was barely, mentally, moving. He could feel himself changing. He was becoming something different. It was the bite of the monsters. It had poisoned him.

If it wasn't for her, perhaps he would have gone completely over to whatever it was they were. He thought not, though. Their… disease, for what else could it be, couldn't properly take a hold. It was in turmoil within him and his own body's defences were fighting back. They were unable to defeat the disease, but could, at least, hold back its advancement. While the battle raged, he was powerless to do anything except stand on the sidelines and watch. And hope.

The voice seemed to come to him in waves. It would be, one moment, barely audible. A whisper's whisper. An irritation on the edge of hearing that may not even have been there. Then it would build to a sudden rush of sound that was gone almost as soon as it had arrived, but that left him unsteady and disorientated. He felt as if he was standing on a shore of a vast ocean, being pulled by the tides and currents that were hungry to pull him under and drown him.

But, then there was *her*. At first, he struggled to remember her name. His own eluded him too, but hers was more important. She was something to look to and to reach for to pull him from the mire he was sinking into.

The creatures left. They had vomit splattered on their chests and stuck to their chins. They roared in his face and he could smell their fetid breath. The next he knew, he was standing on the ground outside. He heard movement close by and walked towards it. His legs weren't working properly. They were too heavy and he could only seem to move them with a great deal of effort. His view of the world was off too. His head was crooked, resting on his shoulder and he didn't seem to have the strength to lift it.

Then, there she was!

She was staring at something, stooping to touch... *something.* He couldn't focus on the words he needed. The miasma was thickening and he was losing the battle. He tried to speak and the words wouldn't form.

"D... D..."

She turned suddenly, scooting back, fearful.

No! It's me! It's...

What was his name? Hers had surfaced and he just needed to say it. SAY IT!

"D... D..."

"Julian, are you...?"

Julian! That was his name! He clung to it, repeating the word over and over though his mind fumbled with the sound and almost let it go.

"Julian?"

Yes! he thought. *I'm Julian!*

He tried to say it, but his mouth couldn't move in the right way. But hers, he could try hers.

"D..."

The frustration faded as he started to be sucked under by the poison that was flooding through him from the bites. She, and everything around her, was changing. He could feel the heat from the heart beating in her chest. He could smell the blood pulsing within her. He started to salivate, a hunger building.

"Dorothy," she said quietly. "I'm Dorothy."

I know!

But, her voice... it had a pure, sharp tone that cut through the fog and gave him a path through. He tried to follow the sound and escape, but he wasn't strong enough. The opening remained, however, and he could, at least...

He could...

Julian, the boy who had used his cheek and his charm to pave his path to success, was losing himself. His thoughts were puddling about his feet and seeping into the ground. He needed her to anchor him, knowing she could keep him from fading more even if he couldn't extricate himself.

"D…"

"Dorothy!"

"D… Dor…

"Dorthy!"

Was that right? Was that what she'd said, what he knew her name to be? He wasn't sure. It was close.

The darkness had closed around him and the voice had become deafening. It was no longer making promises. It had ceased the caress of his mind and was now shouting at him. Taunting him. Mocking him. It was a pounding presence that was intent on filling him until there was nothing of Julian left. It was filling him with appetites that sickened him. He shunned them, ignoring the twist of his stomach as her heartbeat drove hunger pangs into him like swords of wrath.

He clung on to her. On to the thought of her. It wasn't because of love. He knew he didn't love her. Not even close. But she was there. She was his friend, even though his jibes gave an edge to their friendship. In his befuddled state, she was a point of clarity that ensured he wasn't sucked completely under the spell of the Terror's bite.

She ran and he followed. Even though she was faster than he, he knew where she was. Her heart was a beacon that called to him. He wouldn't answer that call, he couldn't, though the temptation was so strong. But the beacon connected them. It meant they wouldn't be separated.

Soon, there was no conscious thought. There was only hunger, darkness and one single point of light. A light he followed, regardless of ghost dogs and orphaned children.

When the beast attacked at the school, the darkness receded momentarily. She was in danger. Terrible danger. Julian didn't know what the monster was, he just knew teeth and he knew claws.

Rage. It wasn't something he was familiar with. Julian, the boy from a world that didn't have monsters, was a person who thought fun and smiles would take him through life. He avoided fights and anger. Rage was a boiling mass of emotion that would build to an uncontrollable explosion, potentially decimating anything within its blast radius.

Yet rage built in him. The shadows fell back in its wake and the tear made from Dorothy's voice was ripped wide. His thoughts were still incoherent, but his intent was clear. Julian embraced the Terror inside and brought it forth, launching himself at the creature.

When it was over, the darkness flooded back and the fury subsided. The Terror was pushed back down, held by Julian's unsteady resolve. The beast was unconscious on the floor, now a man, but Julian didn't know this. He only knew that she was safe, and even then, it wasn't something he *knew*. She just was.

When the Terrors attacked and the ghost dog savaged them, Julian had felt the storm build again, but the Frank's intervention stopped its rise. He had become a shell, able to utter only one word while trailing after a girl he no longer, really, recognised.

But, when they finally reached the bus, something changed.

40

Edward had a problem.

Well, it was more than just one. He needed to find his other leg and also to find the man. Adam. Perhaps the one answer would feed the other? He would benefit from the full belly of resolution and be, once more, on the road to emotional and physical completeness.

Of course, the other leg he was searching for wasn't 'his'. Not yet. Once he had taken it – rehomed it, if you will – it would belong to him. There was the possibility that his hunt for Adam would bring him into contact with someone else who had the correct dimensions to suit replacing his own. There was a certain satisfaction, though, in killing someone and swapping their limbs or innards with his, if that person was one he was looking for rather than one whom he'd simply chanced upon.

Edward had discovered many of his victims on his travels. Hearing stories. Sensing a darkness on the air. Tasting the bitterness of sorrow or hate. But this – Adam – was a first. He was, now, prey. And, Edward thought, the man should pray. Not for forgiveness. Not for redemption. No. For a quick and painless death.

Edward was not sure such prayers would be answered.

Melody, he knew from the tears and the eulogies, was a woman of simple pleasures and bright disposition. She brought joy into people's lives just by being in the same room as them. No interaction was necessary. It was as if she flavoured the air with sincerity and congeniality.

There was not only one victim in Adam's attack and Melody's death. There were a multitude of wrecked lives and broken hearts.

But, how did you track someone you didn't know?

Edward didn't know. Adam had fled, but in which direction, there were no clues. He listened, as he would, to as many conversations as his mechanical ears could hear. His eyes scanned as far as they could reach and as close as he could focus. The werewolf was a beast of immense savagery, more so, in many ways, than any of the Terrors. He should have left a trail of devastation that cut a swath through the countryside for anyone to follow.

Yet, there was none.

He had no choice. All he could do was wander. Oz was a large country, but Edward didn't sleep. He rested, occasionally, to allow his human parts to recuperate, but otherwise he could spend every hour tracking down his quarry.

He pledged to himself that he'd do exactly that. Not, of course, at the expense of other deserving victims, but they would not hold his attention and nor would they claim his energy. If he chanced upon someone beating their children or forsaking their vows of marriage, he would deal with them accordingly. He would not, however, choose only those who might help him in the replacement of his body. If someone warranted murder, then that card would be dealt, but the deed would be done and he would move on to continue his search.

Murder. He wasn't a murderer. He was, at worst, a vigilante. At best, Edward was the righter of wrongs. A saviour to those who could not save themselves. The fact that he was fulfilling his own destiny in the process was a bonus. Those that died at his hand weren't really victims. The ones who suffered at their hands were the victims. Edward was balancing the scales of justice with the swing of his axe.

He moved quickly, his odd legs causing his gait to be awkward but, once he was accustomed to it, no less rapid. He chose a direction and continued on a meandering but still defined route that would eventually find him criss-crossing the entire land. If Adam still lived and hadn't already been slain by a hunter thinking he was killing a bear or other wild animal, Edward would find him. He would come across a clue or a victim or the man himself. He had to.

So, he hunted. Keeping away from the sight of the ordinary people that went about their day, oblivious to the semi-metal man in their midst, he searched. The weather had turned inclement fairly recently, and the sun didn't always win the war over the rainclouds and would be hidden behind them as they wept their tears of success. The hooded coat he had taken from the remains of a man he hadn't killed himself kept his face obscured, with his hands deep in his pockets. He had the occasional second glance but that was more for the fact that he limped than him not being entirely made from flesh and bone and blood.

The dead man, gifter of the coat, had been torn apart. His neck was completely missing and only the partially severed spine kept the head attached to the torso. Deep gouges ripped through the chest, exposing the guts on which flies were bussing and maggots were dining. At first, Edward wondered – or hoped – that the man had been on the receiving end of the werewolf's claws, but a closer inspection showed otherwise. He had seen Melody posthumously. He knew the way the talons cut through her flesh. He saw the pattern of teeth from the fatal bite marks. This man had different wounds.

Terrors.

Edward knew what the Terrors were. He was amazed that, with that knowledge being widespread across the country, people still went about their business as if nothing was amiss. Days passed quietly or manically as they would do had the monsters not appeared. It was as if ignorance was a wall that reality was unable to surmount. If you don't think about it, it isn't real. It can't hurt you. It's happened, if it actually *did* and it wasn't just a bucket full of nonsense, to someone else.

He had an idea of where the creatures had come from. He was aware of his father's other experiments, if not his intentions. Given the anomalies

Edward was finding in himself, he would not have been surprised if one of those experiments had gone awry. The Terrors and other mutations had appeared only in recent times. Prior to that, such beasts were only the domain of storytellers and legends. It could not be coincidence that the Tinkerer tinkered and the Terrors terrorised.

Edward left the man's corpse to the maggots and flies. He would have, perhaps, taken something from it. Not the leg, but maybe the pancreas or spleen or nostrils. But, for all he knew, the man had been a good person. Kind. Giving. Generous. A doting father and an attentive husband. There was no way of knowing otherwise so Edward chose to let him keep his dignity by keeping his body intact.

Apart from what had been damaged by the Terrors and eaten by the maggots.

He was a discerning and caring killer. He had a heart, even if one didn't actually beat in his chest.

41

"We should go," said Adam.

Dorothy looked up. She felt odd, leaving the crash scene again. The first time, she was fleeing. She was afraid and panicked. Now, she was much calmer though, probably, no less afraid. She felt as if she had been wading through a thick smog of fear that clung to her ankles and seeped into her skin, making her wet with its damp, clingy, touch.

She nodded. He was right. They had a job to do. A task to complete. Wasn't this sort of thing reserved for Lara Croft or Nathan Drake? Weren't they the ones to tackle quests? There were no tombs – as far as she knew – to wander through, but there were unbelievable creatures and things stranger than she'd ever scene. Oz was like an Upside Down, but without the floating ash.

Dorothy had neither the physique nor the tenacity to be either of the video game stars, and didn't want it. She wanted to go home. She missed her aunt and uncle. She missed being an outsider even with her friends. She wanted her bed and her quilt and her music. There was no place like it.

Certainly not in Oz.

"D..."

She looked at Julian. His head was not as lopsided as it had been. Perhaps he was becoming used to the lack of flesh around it and the tendons were strengthening. She hoped so. Even with the sight of dangling scraps of meat and the flashes of spine when he moved, having his head upright would make it easier to look at him. It wasn't that it horrified her, though it did. She just didn't like to see her friend as the poor victim of a savage attack. It was a reminder to her that she'd abandoned him to the monsters.

"I know," she said, interpreting his meaning. "We're going."

"D..." Julian mumbled.

Dorothy turned to Adam, letting Julian battle with his inability to speak properly. She wondered at the fog in his mind that prevented it. How deeply were the Terrors' bites affecting him? How far was he from turning completely? Would she have to…?

Adam. Concentrate on Adam. Concentrate on…

They were wrong together. Frank was a ghost of some sort that didn't seem to know it was dead. Adam was a werewolf but was oblivious to the fact. Julian had no idea of, well, anything. What if there was something wrong with her? Something she didn't know? Something that made her as dangerous as any and each of the others? What if, like Frank and Adam and, as she now thought of him, dear Julian, she was… changed?

Dorothy had a sudden fear of, rather than for, herself. If something hid inside of her, waiting to erupt in a devastating way, she could be responsible for all the things that she was trying to stop. Who knew what manner of beast prowled deep within her blackened heart?

But she felt fine! She felt herself! She felt normal!

Dorothy's sense of normality was wavering, however. Ghosts and monsters and witches were so far removed from 'normal' that she questioned whether the life she knew was reality or this bizarre world. Were her aunt and uncle just figments of a tinkered imagination?

No!

She *was* herself. She *was* 'normal.' She was just afraid and allowing it to eat away at her resolve. It was to be expected in such a situation. Wasn't it? She had no idea. Who had ever been in circumstances like these? Nobody. All her friends, all the people she passed without noticing them whilst going about her mundane, daily life. They'd think they were dreaming. A nightmare of epic proportions.

She was sensible. *Sensible!* She needed to grab a hold of that and not let it go. In a surreal world, it was all she had that she knew was real. As abstract and mercurial as the concept was, Dorothy felt she had little else when she was so far away from her home.

"D…"

"Yes Julian," she said, still not looking at him, "We're going."

Adam was growing rapidly impatient. The boy was holding them back. The girl was weak. The dog was probably not even there. He should take the ring and do as the witch asked on his own. He could do it. He wasn't a brave man, but he could be resourceful. He knew he could. If he had to be.

But he couldn't do it. He couldn't tackle her. He had to stay with them. If he left, with or without the ring, he would be on his own. Now Melody was gone, they were his only companionship. They distracted him from his mourning and, without them, he felt he would drown in his own tears.

"Can we please…"

"D… D… *Dorothy!*"

Adam's mouth remained open but the words were as stunned as he was. Dorothy's mouth hung open in sympathy. Both stared at the boy, with neither knowing what to say.

Frank scampered over and ran around him, yapping silently, tail wagging happily. The dog went up on his hind legs and leaned against Julian who tried to look down at him but couldn't quite move his head far enough.

"D... Dorothy?"

"Yes," she whispered. "I'm Dorothy."

She took his hand and held it tied, tears welling in her eyes.

"You're Julian," she said. "Do you remember?"

"Dorothy," he repeated.

Her heart began to sink, swelled momentarily by his proper pronunciation of her name. Its decent was halted, though, by the edge of a smile on his lips. One that was reflected in his blank eyes. There was a definite, unmistakable, sparkle in them.

He was coming back!

Adam smiled too. Perhaps there was hope for them. For him. Maybe he didn't have to leave them, or even be afraid of them.

Could they, he asked himself, actually succeed?

42

An echo is a sound with friends. It's one that, once uttered, dances around you, partying with those friends until they're too exhausted to carry on and just disappear off into the night. Or is it that your ears are too tired to keep up with the reverberating noise and, so, tune it out to the point you can no longer hear it? Maybe they want to join in the fun and refuse to listen in a fit of pique?

An echo is a sound with friends.

It can bounce from wall to rock to tree to the point where you can no longer discern its origin. It spins around you, taking your senses by the hand and whirling them in a jive of disorientation.

With some sounds, that's fine. A shout. A laugh. The tinkling of coins or the crackle of footsteps on fresh fallen leaves on an autumn day.

You don't mind those.

A shriek. A howl. A scream to curdle your blood as it rushes through your veins or arteries, from your heart to your organs and back again, keeping you alive in the process. Those, you have a problem with. Those, you do mind. Those chill that blood as it curdles. They stop your heart and they freeze your limbs. Those sounds are not partying. They're hunting. Killing. Searching.

"We should..."

The cry stopped Adam mid-sentence. It flooded the area with noise, leaping from every surface, as if it alone was staging an assault on their position. Adam squealed. Dorothy gasped. Julian was silent and Frank growled noiselessly.

"We're going," Dorothy said.

She felt bad. The witch had dissolved, yet Tamara had asked that they bury her sister. How they might have pulled her from beneath the bus, Dorothy didn't know, but she could have tried. Now there were just some dampened clothes and a shoe. She picked up the shoe and stood it straight against the bus. It seemed the right thing to do, rather than just leave it on its side as if discarded by the wearer on their way home, running from a royal ball at the stroke of midnight.

She didn't wait for the others to follow, she knew they would, and she couldn't wait to figure out where the shriek came from. If they encountered the Terrors, she hoped Frank would come to their rescue again. She'd even accept Adam taking on his other form, though she'd be running as fast as she could and dragging Julian along with her. As for her friend, she didn't know how he had bested the werewolf and she didn't want to. She wanted him safe, particularly now he seemed to be recovering somehow.

It might not be, exactly, him getting better. It might have been an aberration. A flashback to the friend she knew. But she'd hang on to the hope that he was coming back from the brink of zombie-hood and she'd have to put up with his inane jokes once more.

She started off, back the way they had come. She was sure she could find her way back to the river again, and then she'd do as the witch had asked – follow it to the Tinkerer. She looked back to make sure her group remained together. They were still with her. Julian's shamble was becoming steadier and he was managing the semblance of a run. Adam looked as if he could bolt at any moment. From the look of Frank's tail, he was as happy as if he was playing fetch and was waiting for the ball to be thrown.

As they entered the cover of the trees and she turned back, she caught a glimpse of movement near the far side of the bus. She didn't wait to see what it was. She didn't need to. Spurred on, Dorothy led the way deeper into the forest.

She slowed, but didn't stop. Panting from the exertion, she couldn't keep her pace up and the others were lagging behind but the threat of being followed by the creatures gave her enough energy to continue.

"Stop," said Adam breathlessly. "I can't... can't carry on!"

"We need to keep going!"

"We're far enough in!" he stammered, his breath and his words fighting for supremacy over his mouth. "We at least need to know if they're still coming after us!"

Dorothy stopped suddenly. It was partly because she knew he was right, partly because, in reality, she couldn't keep going anyway, and partly because she heard the rush of the river. Frank's momentum carried him forward, his body running straight through hers. Had she felt it? Something a little more substantial than air? Like a wind blowing into her? Julian slowed and stopped. He was breathing evenly and could have had a casual walk for all the effect their flight had on him. Adam was taken by surprise by the abrupt halt and tried to side-step to avoid running into her. His legs tangled and his stumbled, just missing her. He rolled, banging his head against the trunk of a tree and fell to the ground. His eyes were closed tightly and he held his head, moaning. His temple was bleeding.

Dorothy rushed to his side. She didn't trust him and wasn't sure if she liked him. She knew what lay dormant within him and thought that waiting for the phase of the moon was like sticking a wet finger up to the wind. You'd feel the cold draft against your skin but you didn't know if that signified that the day would be fairly fine or a storm was going to rip your roof off. Or throw your bus into another world.

She had to put her reservations aside. He seemed so jumpy that she felt she was almost protecting him rather than the other way around. Sensible head on, she moved him to a more comfortable position and used the hem of her top to wipe away the blood. It wasn't a bad wound. Little more than a graze. He'd be fine. She doubted there'd be much in the way of brain damage.

Dorothy berated herself. Such thoughts were the domain of the school elite, not her. She was never one to really judge or pass comment. Even under the stresses she'd faced since coming here, she wasn't willing to become one of the people she despised, even if it had been only a stupid mental joke. Adam, regardless of what he might, at some point, become, had agreed to go with them. He could have refused or left them at any point, but he didn't. She had to thank him for that. Even if he was a nerve perpetually on the edge of snapping, he was there.

"Are you ok?"

Adam moaned. His head throbbed, pounding a heavy beat through his skull. What was he doing? He should be crying for his beloved, not traipsing around the country searching for magic and that science rubbish! And this just proved it! They weren't even being attacked and he had already been hurt. They were just running. Yes, it was from the Terrors, but they were nowhere to be seen. He'd tripped over his own feet. How could he protect anyone else when he failed dismally to prevent himself being injured? If they were set upon by Terrors or worse, he wouldn't have a hope and nor would the others.

"Yes," he said, though his groans said otherwise. "I'm fine."

He could milk it, draining the last drop of sympathy from the girl, but he didn't. He wanted to run, but he couldn't. He needed to stay, but he couldn't. He wished he had another Adam hidden inside of him that he could let out when he needed a helping hand.

But he didn't.

Dorothy helped him to his feet. He was unsteady, but managed to stay standing. She held onto him, more for balance than support. After a few moments, he nodded, mumbled a thanks and let go of her.

"Right," she said. "Let's take it a bit steadier, ok?"

Adam nodded again. It was only a slight movement of his head to show agreement. Any more of a nod would have made the world spin and the darkness wash over him. Dorothy looked to Julian, not expecting any response but hoping his improvement was improving.

"Jul…?"

She stopped talking. Julian was staring at Adam or, more precisely, the wound on his head. The boy's eyes were bulging and red-rimmed. His arms were slowly lifting, with the fingers of each hand pulling back into claws.

He was licking his lips, a low growl rumbling deep in his stomach.

43

The bones of indecision crunched beneath his feet as he strode through the building.

He walked quickly, with purpose snapping at his heels. His sister's hold on him, filling his head with doubts, was broken. His resolve had tightened and would soon, if she didn't cooperate, become a noose about her neck.

Not literally, of course. He had no qualms about killing, as the Prime Minister had discovered, but she was his *sister*. He couldn't. The Tinkerer resented his family ties because of that. He was linked to the witch in ways that no magic or science would tear apart. It wasn't fair. He needed to use her. To manipulate her. To force her to do his bidding.

But, she knew him. She knew he'd not carry out his threats against her and she used that knowledge against him. Or she *did*.

He didn't have to hurt her. He only had to hurt someone else. Anyone else. *Everyone* else!

She would bring the remaining members of The Three to him. They would help him stop making the mistakes that plagued him. He would succeed in being the wonderful ruler Oz needed and deserved. He would be adored. And nobody would stand in his way. Not even his siblings.

Blood was thicker than the Emerald River. As much as he hated that fact, he couldn't avoid its truth. He knew others might scoff at his loyalty and turn their blade to family or foe without regard. The sisters and brother had been close at one point, however. They'd supported him when his lack of magic could have set him apart. They'd comforted him when derision had filled his eyes with tears and ripped at his heart with tears.

She, he would not hurt them. Imprison, starve, manipulate and scare perhaps, but not cause them harm or physical pain.

Mental and emotional pain was different. He had suffered it, but had endured. He was unchanged. He was still the same well balanced, thoughtful individual who had eaten his sisters' vegetables when they didn't like them, so they wouldn't be reprimanded by their parents. He was still the same compassionate person who worried for the welfare of others, except now he could remove those who tried to prevent him carrying out his dream of making the world a better place.

He had a dream. A vision. If he had to have his spiders help him achieve it…

Death was nothing.

Not the 'nothing' that came with an absence of life. Not the 'nothing' of the last breath taken and the lungs unable to carry another into the body. Not the nothing of a heart done beating, its quota of chest-filling thuds spent.

No, death was just another day. A night that falls after day has expired. The Tinkerer was as unafraid of it as he was of the sun rising or the moon chasing it from the sky.

Still, people seemed to be afraid of it. They cried at its mention. They fell apart, becoming self-destructive, at its impending arrival. They didn't seem to realise it was simply another state of being. If that state was an eternal darkness where sense, feeling and thought were frozen in the millisecond that you died, then so be it. If it were a light filled, wondrous place that was filled with all those you'd ever loved, fine. If eternity was spent in the confines of a copper lined tube in the Tinkerer's…

He had arrived.

He knocked. It was polite. He liked to be polite. Manners cost nothing, his parents told him. Particularly his father. Manners maketh the man was another saying drummed into him. Well, the Tinkerer wasn't so sure. With Edward, metal and tubes and cogs made the man. Manners had little to do with it.

There was no answer. He knocked again. With anyone else, he would barge in rather than be kept waiting. He would remain the epitome of politeness, apologising for any intrusion while severing the carotid artery of the person who had delayed him but not responding. With his sister, it was automatic. Knock and wait.

She didn't answer. She wouldn't, of course. Why would she want to speak to the man who had kidnapped her and was holding her captive? Her brother! The Tinkerer tried to picture her beyond the door. What was she doing? Sitting at the table where her meals were always left uneaten? Standing by the fire that was never lit in case she was tempted to either use it as a weapon or to harm herself? Hiding behind the door, waiting to leap at him or knock him out with the broken leg of the aforementioned table, broken away by her in order to make good her escape?

He held out his hand and a spider ran from under the collar of his jacket and along the sleeve. It settled in his palm, its metal legs moving silently on their tiny gears. He held out his other hand and another spider copied the movements of the first.

He set on down on the floor and lifted the other to his face. It spun around and rolled onto its back. Its legs folded in and there was a very faint whirring sound as the pointed tips worked on its stomach. There was a click and the legs sprang back out. The Tinkerer moved his hand closer, positioning the spider over his eye. The legs moved and then jabbed at his face. He winced slightly as they made contact with tiny, hidden insets just under his skin. Again, there was a click as the legs locked in place.

The Tinkerer lowered his hand and blinked twice. The iris of the covered right eye paled and went white. The pupil dilated, opening like a camera lens. From the stomach of the spider, a thin tube extended, entering the pupil.

Another click.

The spider on the floor moved quickly forward towards the door, slipping under it easily. The Tinkerer, now able to see through his creation's eyes, directed it over to one corner. It climbed up the wall and skittered along an empty book shelf.

Emily was standing against the table. She wasn't sitting on it, but was allowing it to take her weight. She was staring at the door with her arms folded. Waiting.

The spider moved forward and zoomed in on her face. She was impassive. Anger, fear and despair were absent. An emotionless mask, devoid of intent, seemed to smother her emotions, leaving her breathless of feeling.

Suddenly, her head spun around, tearing her gaze from the door and slapping it down hard on the spider. The mask dropped, her features morphing into a snarl. She brought her hands together, clapping loudly. The noise echoed in the room, sounding like a hard edged ripple.

The spider started to shake, as if each leg was dancing to a beat none of the others heard. The trembling increased until the mechanical creature was practically bouncing on the wooden shelf.

Then it stopped.

Then it was still. As unmoving as the witch's face had been.

There was a high pitched whine, increasing in volume. That, too, ceased. The spider shook one last time and fell apart, becoming a pile of component pieces that could no longer serve their master. As much as a stamped foot could crush the life from a living spider, the spy that the Tinkerer had sent into the room had been extinguished.

The Tinkerer tapped the back of the one covering his eye. It twisted, the legs unlocking from their connections. It dropped to his palm, rolled a little to right itself, then ran up his arm to take shelter beneath his collar. He wondered if it would mourn the loss of its brother, much in the way nobody mourned him.

He smiled.

Until that point, his sister had failed to give any demonstration of her powers. She had been a victim. A prisoner. Now, she had shown that she was still the feisty, temperamental Emily he had always known.

Good. He would have need of that.

The Tinkerer turned and walked away. The conversation he'd planned would wait for a little while longer. He'd allow her to stew for a few more hours. Or maybe days. She would be more amenable to persuasion then.

No, not persuasion.

Reason.

44

Zombie films had moved from horror to hokum. Gone were the days, really, that dead eyed monsters lumbering towards the screen would strike fear into the heart they wanted to feast upon. Did fear alter the taste of a person's body? To the dark creatures that roamed the screens or pages of entertainment, was it like a peppercorn sauce on a steak? The condiment to their bloody lunch? A little light seasoning to tantalise the palate as the victim is devoured?

Either way, zombies, along with vampires and werewolves, had become humdrum. Shows like The Walking Dead and Z Nation showed that a well-aimed bullet or spike-spangled club would have you free of the oncoming hordes by dinner time, and other tales exchanged gore for glitter. Streaming services allowed binge watching of programmes that, years ago, would have viewers hiding behind cushions and shrieking. The thrill was gone. The chill had warmed.

Why?

Because such things were not real. Because, when you are fed a repeated menu of the same food day after day, it loses its taste. The flavour that once kept you returning for just one more episode had become bland. You didn't mind having the occasional meal, didn't find it displeasing, but it didn't quite excite you anymore.

But...

Oz.

Oz was... Oz was an altogether different restaurant and Dorothy was discovering that, perhaps, not everything on the menu was imagined.

There was a typical expression in the shows. A classic posture.

All Julian needed to do to complete the image was, in a long, drawn out voice, say "*Braaaiiiinnnssss!*"

His arms were reaching. His mouth was already chewing even though it hadn't made contact with the man's flesh. He was moaning. His body, with the rumbling in his stomach, was displaying just how hungry he was. And his preferred dish of the day was clearly Adam.

Adam's eyes grew wide and he stumbled back into a tree. He was wavering, looking as if he might collapse again at any moment. Julian shuffled towards him, his movements showing that the progress he'd been making was taking a step back with every step forward. Any hint of the boy they knew had gone. Only bloodlust remained.

Adam was trapped. Not by the confines of obstacles around him, but by the trappings of fright. He could see the hunger in the boy. He could feel the stare burrowing deep within him, exposing his innards. The Terror had risen to the surface and Adam could not escape its clutches. The knots of the tree trunk held him in place just as effectively as if they were hands gripping his body. If he couldn't, himself, flee, his strength had no such qualms. It left him and he started to slowly sink to the ground.

To the man, the boy was towering over him. The youngster's stature had grown in direct proportion to him slipping to the floor. In reality, Julian's size was unchanged. His manner, however, certainly was. Cheeky boy had become docile follower had become monster.

"Julian!"

Dorothy had recovered from her initial shock, Miss Sensible taking up residence in her mind again. It had to happen sooner or later, she assumed. A person can only fight a poison for so long before its effects consumed them. Such it was with her friend. His battle had been valiant, but it had been in vain. He was becoming the very thing she would watch while sitting in the cinema, eating popcorn and drinking bottles sneaked in rather than paying the extortionate prices in house. Was that what the Terrors were? They were generally much more animated than Julian has shown himself to be, but perhaps they'd been interrupted while attacking him. Their bite hadn't been enough to take a proper hold immediately and the fact that they weren't from Oz meant the change was struggling to impose itself on his physique.

She hoped there was enough of friend left inside to listen to her.

"Julian! Stop!"

He didn't. He acted as if he hadn't heard her, moving in on the man. Nothing else existed. Nothing else mattered. He could smell the blood in the head wound. He could feel the pulse of the other's heart running through his own veins. His entire body was craving sustenance.

He continued his advance.

"Julian, *stop!*"

As she spoke, she held up her hand. She avoided his outstretched arms and tried to push him back. Her hand touched his chest.

Dorothy gasped.

A rush of emotion made her body unsure if it wanted to vomit or faint. Her hand grew warm, then hot, except… It wasn't her hand. It was the ring. The *witch's* ring. It was glowing, the red veins pulsing with her heartbeat.

Julian stopped. His body froze as if he'd been caught in that moment between the heartbeats that throbbed on Dorothy's finger. He staggered back, his arms dropping to his sides. He looked confused.

"D... Dorth... Dorothy?"

"Yes, Julian!" She exclaimed.

He'd stumbled for a moment, but had then spoken her name fully. His eyes had cleared, the familiar sparkle from before this nightmare began had returned. The shadow on his face had faded. Dorothy, for a second, thought that he was back to himself. Perhaps he almost had been, but then the rising sun of an awakening was quickly obliterated by a new cloud. His mouth dropped open, except this time it wasn't with hunger. It was with shock. The glint of humour became a blackened scar of realisation.

"*No!*" he whispered.

Dorothy reached for him, but he pushed her away. Adam stared at him, stunned at what had clearly been about to happen, any chance of reaction eaten by the threat of the boy's attack. Julian turned and ran. His feet were swift, the shambling that the Terrors' wounds and poison had weighted him with, gone. The trees swallowed him as effectively as he might have Adam.

"Julian!" Dorothy shouted.

"Let him go," Adam said quietly.

He was relieved that the boy had gone. He had expected his condition to have deteriorated to the point he would succumb to the appetites that festered within him long before now. The beast would be unleashed at some point, that much was inevitable. The fact that it had taken so long was likely only down to luck. Adam had shared that luck in his narrow escape. He didn't want to invite the boy to make another attempt.

Dorothy looked at him, briefly considering his words, but she shook her head. She couldn't. Regardless of what he was changing into, Julian was still her friend. He was her anchor to the world she'd come from. The 'real' world. There was no real way that she couldn't go after him. She'd seen the boy she knew, albeit it a fleeting glimpse. But he was still in there. He'd been fighting whatever was happening to him and was winning.

Until... What?

She looked again at the man who was still a stranger to her. Adam seemed pleasant enough, if he could grow a backbone and if you ignored his dark half. She didn't know him, though. Not really. She should be more fearful of him than her friend. What was it about him that had made Julian change?

Ah.

Of course.

The cut on his head. The blood. The 'zombie' label was given another layer of reality. Is that what the Terrors were? Dorothy shook her head again. She had to be dreaming, surely. These things just didn't exist! They *couldn't!* It didn't matter, either way. Julian, whatever he was, was her friend.

"Come on," she said.

She ran into the trees, following her friend. Frank scampered alongside her, running through the trunks that Dorothy was avoiding. She didn't look back to see if Adam was coming too. She wasn't really bothered either way. Eventually, though, he did. She heard him crashing through the forest after her. She smiled to herself. She should have known he wouldn't stay on his own.

Julian could have gone in any direction, but he was obviously fleeing. She guessed direction, or the changing of, wasn't something he'd be thinking about. She could see trampled grass and broke twigs to show the passing of someone or something. She hoped it was the former – and she hoped it was Julian.

There was a sudden, strangled cry from behind her and she slowed. Adam? What had he done now? Then she knew. The loud, bestial roar that followed was familiar. Too familiar. With the sound of the monster filling her with a terrified energy, she leaned in and ran as fast as she had ever done in her life. She knew that howl. She'd heard it before.

Adam.

He had changed.

45

Perception is a personal matter. One's opinion of a subject can widely differ from that of another. Akin to beauty being in the eye of the beholder, so perception is in the mind of the perceiver. It can be little more than a shade apart from that of the next person or it can be as mismatched as night and day or brother and sister. A busy desk can imply a busy person but, in reality, it can also show a lazy sloth who shuffles papers around to give the impression of hard work. Tears can come from an explosion of happiness or the deepest of emotional cuts. An onlooker has only the evidence before them and cannot see into the heart of the other.

Take a throne room, for example.

Picture one. What do you see? A cavernous room, ornate with gilded columns and a long carpet, plush and red? Do you imagine guards positioned at the doors and evenly along the walk up to the throne? Do they cast imposing figures of grandeur, welcoming visitors with the knowledge that the slightest wrong move could result in impalement upon a not entirely ceremonial pike?

And the throne itself. It would be massive, would it not? A seat mirroring the stature of the person seated. Intricately carved, thickly padded, and positively glowing with self-importance.

The Tinkerer was in his throne room. He was sitting on his throne.

The room was once occupied by an overweight bumbler who called himself Prime Minister. It had housed a large desk, unread books and a spyglass. The Tinkerer had liked that spyglass. He'd worked hard to instill in it a view that would be both unsurpassed and breathtaking. The Prime Minister had been suitably astounded when he took ownership of the contraption and it had served him well. As the Tinkerer had succeeded rulership of the country by virtue of a death, the Prime Minister's office would obviously become that of the Tinkerer.

He had cleaned the room out. He'd emptied it of almost its entire contents. Having had no use or interest in the drinks bar or books that were there to make the occupant look intelligent, he had ensured they were removed. They could have been passed on to others, piled in a store room or set fire to. He didn't care. Even the large desk was disposed of. The only item of furniture he kept was a tall lamp that had gathered dust in a corner. It was plain. A single, slender column of chrome topped by an uplighting bowl of translucent white.

The lamp was out of place in the office and that was partly why the Tinkerer retained it. He felt an affinity to its lonely existence, living out its days tucked away and hardly used. It was a poor outsider in a room of affluence. He felt its pain, though he would not admit to being pained.

He spent a little time on the lamp. He cleaned it, making the long stem shine with a polished glow that couldn't dim. The uplighter was dusted and made to add a sparkle to the emitted light that appeared as if the room was filled with millions of stars that you could never actually see, no matter how hard you looked. When the lamp was lit, it was as if the night sky was reflected on the backs of your eyes. If you closed them, the universe was there for you to explore, perhaps while you slept. If your eyes were open, there'd always be a hint of glitter just at the periphery of your vision.

The lamp was no longer drifting alone on a sea of opulence. The room had lost its embellishments, being stripped of everything that the Tinkerer found offensive. He sneered at thick, velvet drapes hanging at the windows. The desk that was far too large to be useful and only served to mirror the ego of the man who had been seated behind it had been reduced to firewood and burned on the hearth.

The Tinkerer enjoyed a roaring fire. The flames would speak to him of endings and, if not new beginnings, of transformation. Devastation and design. As with the lamp, he would stare into the fire and feel he was becoming one with it, to the point he thought he could understand the song that the crackling sparks would sing.

In one corner was a long table. Not a desk, a table. A desk was for papers that were never moved and pictures that were never looked at. A pen to be played with absentmindedly. A small plaque with a name engraved – the name of the person sitting behind it who the visitor would already know, making it redundant. Perhaps a plant that was only watered when the leaves wilted to the point of desiccated ugliness, but was forgotten for the rest of the time. A table was required. A table served a purpose. A table had a destiny that was fulfilled constantly.

On the table were drawings. Plans. Screwdrivers and cogs and ribbons of foil thin metal. A small hammer. A large magnifying glass with a tiny thumb activated lever that increased the magnification to the point of queasiness. A workplace other than his workshop. The table was where he would stand and tinker. It was his *pen* for the times he needed to think. Or those that he simply didn't want to.

A picture frame hung on the opposite wall. It was empty. There had once been a painting in its simple wooden confines. The portrait of a family. It was now ash, but not made so in a fit of pique. The Tinkerer looked at the empty frame and mentally filled it with new images each time. It was sometimes the original picture, except with his image having the slightly more rounded eyes and marginally lower forehead that he saw himself as having. At other times it could be his parents. His sisters, laughing. Their laughter was a crystal waterfall of sound, one that could calm or agitate him depending on the phase of the moon, the lilt of the sun or the day of the week. Himself, looking proud and stern, but with a mildly amused look on his face to show he knew he was superior and, eventually, everyone else would realise too.

A chair. Bare, unvarnished wood, little more than four legs and a back. Minimal padding to protect him from the numbness he might otherwise have suffered from. Into each leg was carved an letter. Nothing ornate or overly fancy. Just a simple, angular font. One initial for each of his sisters and one for him.

That was his throne. The room was his throne room.

To the uninitiated, it was a shell that was awaiting someone to come along and fill it. Or the discarded habitat of a hermit crab. To the Tinkerer it was filled with his memories and his dreams. His intentions stood proudly against a wall. To his right hand were his achievements and at his left were his failures. Those that he perceived as such, anyway. Any other furniture would disrupt the vision, so he kept it empty. It was cluttered, to a point, with imagination and this held a grandeur entirely of its own.

He held out his hand and a spider emerged from beneath his collar. It ran along his arm to settle in his palm. He looked at it and smiled, then turned his hand over. The spider dropped to the floor on a non-existent thread of silk. His creations could hover and fly, albeit it only a short, not very controlled distance, but he still preferred them to act like the creature they resembled.

The tapping of tiny metal feet could be heard and the spider was joined by hundreds, if not thousands, more. The ability to self-replicate was his greatest gift to his children, and they did seem to enjoy the task.

He moved to the window and opened it wide, allowing the spiders to exit. When the last one had left, he returned to his throne.

And waited.

46

Would you like to know what goes through the mind of a tree?

Did you even know they have minds? That they are capable of actual thought? Or did you believe they were nothing more than wooden stumps, though they might be standing tall and appearing proud with their crowns of leaves?

You would be surprised.

Their thoughts are drawn out, as if being stitched together over an extended period of time by unseen needles, knitting one, purling one until a coherent idea is formed. Perhaps it's the density of the bark that slows them down, the thoughts having to be pushed through the wood to be finally voiced and carried upon the whisper of a breeze. Such tapestries can take an age to construct, and our lives can come and go long before the wind takes the thought and transports it to its recipient.

Dorothy ran through the forest at a speed she had never achieved on any school sports day, when her only medal had been in the high jump and she'd given herself a bloody nose from bringing her knee up to sharply at the same time her face was moving down. She was struggling to control her panic. She was fleeing from a creature that should only exist in the seven-screen multiplex of her home town, and was chasing one that should have shared the credits when the movie was over.

The former was a stranger but the latter was her *friend!* Regardless of his sudden hunger, he was still that and, if she lost him, she would lose herself too.

Should she just veer off and leave them behind? No! Julian might just need her as much as she needed him and, besides, the werewolf would surely not be confused by a change of direction.

To the trees, Dorothy was a blur. At first, they didn't even notice her passing. She could have been one of the animals that lived, fed and died within their midst. The trees generally ignored them. Apart from the odd one that might make a home in their trunks, they were gone before the forest could really appreciate their presence. The trees realised something, however. Dorothy was unlike the others. As she fled and pushed the branches that hung in her way aside, she had a different flavour. She tasted sweet, as if she moved with sap flowing through her.

At the drop of a leaf, a forest, as a whole, can snap into the frantic timestream of those that have blood and breath. Such a change can be a painful experience, causing trunk twisting spasms, and is something that is only performed on exceptional occasions.

The only previous time this had happened had been the fire. To the forest, it was a recent memory that still burned through them but, in reality –

or, at least, the reality of people – it was a century or more before. They would never know what caused the flames that licked at them as if they were ice covered windows in winter. They would never discover that a small group of yet smaller boys had finally learned how to use a flint stone and only wanted to build a campfire like the big boys. It was an accident. The children ran as the flames spread.

Trees were just lumps of wood stuck in the ground. The children weren't hurting anyone. The rabbits and deer would escape. Birds would fly. It was just an *accident.*

The forest had grown for a thousand years and more. With the spark of a stone struck by a boy, the millennia had been reduced to glowing embers that only a rain cloud, generous enough to drift by, could prevent from becoming simply ash. It had realised that time, at times, it needed to flow in line with these mortal beings. The forest thought on the matter for three decades and, finally, slipped into the accelerated timestream of the rest of the world.

It was draining. Tiresome. Far too frantic. But it was also a reminder that not everything was as eternal as they were. The trees could only manage to live at speed for a short time before being forced to slow back down. When warranted, they would do so again but, in the main, they preferred their usual, ageless existence.

There had not been a reason to do so since. They'd grown back from the scorched remains with fresh saplings becoming tall and strong over the years. Once more, the forest was proud. Once more, it appeared untouched and untouchable.

Yes, there was now a girl running through it who tasted... different.

A ripple ran across the forest with a shimmer of leaves. A gasp could be heard as the air was expelled from knot holes and the trees exhaled a breath held for a dozen decades. Branches creaked and trunks twisted. The forest was a single mind that still held each individual tree as an entity when it was required. With Dorothy's flight, the mind fragmented into the component parts, each wanted to taste her themselves. But only the lucky few could as she pushed leaves and twigs away to pass.

Now able to see what was happening, the forest could tell the girl was in peril. She was being chased by a creature that should not exist. The forest had lived for long enough, and more, to know when something unnatural passed through it. The creature that chased her was just such an animal. It shouldn't be. It was an aberration.

Roots pushed through the earth, tangling feet. Branches reached down, gripping wrists, torso and ankles. A vine snaked around her head to cover the mouth and all, as one, lifted Dorothy up high. More branches moved together, interweaving to hide the girl as the beast ran on past where she hung.

Dorothy struggled against her bindings, but stopped when she heard the crashing of the werewolf beneath her. Adam halted, though she was certain the man was not in control of the monster. He – it – sniffed around the ground, trying to find the lost scent. It howled and, with a roar, ran off.

The forest let the werewolf go, then lowered the girl slowly. It released her, the branches drawing back gently as if reluctant to stop touching her skin.

Dorothy looked around bewildered. Had the trees just saved her? She still had to find Julian and, though she hated to admit it, Adam. She needed them both.

"Where is my friend?" she asked aloud.

Her voice sounded foolish as she spoke. Who was she asking? They were just trees, weren't they?

One of the roots that had tripped her lifted up, a cobra without its charmer. It raised until it was level with her eyes and was sure she was watching it, then it bent forward and turned to point along a path that was opening before her.

"Down there?" she asked.

In response, the leaves rustled excitedly. She nodded and said her thanks, though she wasn't sure it could be heard.

"And Adam?"

There was no response. The forest was still, devoid of any movement, including wildlife.

"The werewolf?"

Again, no response.

"Please? I need him. It's not his fault."

There was a pause and the root turned again to point in a different direction.

"Thank you," she said.

There was no rustling of leaves this time. The forest was accepting of her decision but wasn't about to agree with it. Dorothy could understand. She would be the same herself. It didn't occur to her to question the fact that she was talking to trees and they had moved to help her. It just seemed fitting with the madness that had surrounded her. She started off in the direction of Julian, but kept the way Adam had gone in her mind. She would find him afterwards.

The gentle movement of leaves and branches that was the heartbeat of the trees slowed and, once more, the forest returned to its natural speed. It had encountered and tasted what it needed to. Something not of this world was loose in Oz. The girl was only a part of that.

The forest was eternal. By the time it had thought through what that invasion might mean, the events that followed its aid to Dorothy had already happened.

And one of the band was no more.

47

Sanctuary can be found in the most unexpected of places.

A mother's arms, or an aunt's, during a particularly scary film. A doorway in the rain. A dark room when a severe headache makes you want to rip your head from your torso. A sofa with your favourite Gregory Peck black and white movie, a thick blanket and a large tub of cookie dough ice cream.

A tall, yet crumbling building, with one wall lost to time and elements. Windows had forgotten what glass was in the years since they were filled. The door had opened only three times in the last decade. Since then, it was stuck shut on hinges that were rusted and cracked. Any attempt to pull it open would result in the hinges breaking and the door dropping and sticking in its frame.

Once upon a time, the building wanted to be a castle. The builder of the building, Francis Oberon, also wanted it to be a castle. Funds and materials had other ideas, however. By the time the beginnings had begun and were progressing to the middle of the project, the grand designs had to be made less so.

Francis lived alone in his home, telling himself daily that he was still happy with the finished product. He hoped that repetition would result in conviction. By the time that, alone, he passed away, it hadn't. He still longed for the extended boundaries that would give him the room to feel the echo of his loneliness. The more compact living situation, though still extensive, didn't allow him to enjoy his empty life. Though others would be sad at such a state, he wasn't. He found solitude to be a generous companion. It gave him time to think. Time to sing and dance. Time to be alone with himself and his collection of alternate personalities.

He knew they weren't real. He knew they were, perhaps, aberrations of his mind. He didn't mind. The castle would have given each of them a room to themselves. They had to double up when the original plans went awry. The man, without his imaginary other identities, died in the only chair he owned. It was, apart from a single bed, the only furniture he had, or felt he needed. Imaginary friends required only imaginary belongings.

When Julian took shelter in the tall, crumbling building, the remains of the man still sat in the chair. The upholstery had faded. Various birds and rats had made nests and lairs in its stuffing. His bones were mostly intact. A fox had made off with a femur and most of the toes had fallen off and rolled off along the slight slope inherent in the floor.

Julian stood in front of the man.

Or his remains.

The boy, or *his* remains, looked down. A part of him wished he could swap places. He didn't want to be who he had become. He wanted free of the curse the Terrors' bites had inflicted on him. He would rather be bones than beast. But he wasn't and he had to deal with the conflict that was creating in him. And what else it was creating.

A hunger.

A lust.

For blood and brains.

He wanted to vomit. He could feel the darkness fading, taking the voice with it. He was swimming to the surface of the deepest pool and felt as if his breath was burning in his lungs, desperate to be free.

He would stay there, in the building. He'd keep the man company. There was one person he would not be inclined to attack or feed on. How long he would stay, he didn't know. It didn't matter as long as it was for long enough. Time for Dorothy to forget about him. Time for the other man to leave. Time for everything to make sense.

He looked around. He could feel his body changing, or at least his neck. He could hear, more in his head than through his ears, the sinews, tendons and skin rebuilding themselves. The damage done by the creatures that attacked him on the bus was reversing itself, and rapidly. Something had certainly changed and his body was feeling the benefits of that.

But inside, though externally he was improving, he felt that he was drowning. His lungs were bursting. The surface of the pool or lake or ocean he was lost in was too far away. He couldn't make it. He was going to lose himself completely.

So, he'd remain there. Whether in hiding or haven or penance, he couldn't say. The thoughts were still striving to form completely but he could sense the meaning trying to hold the jumble together. It was indistinct but *there.* He *would* prevail. He couldn't vocalise the intent, but it shoved a gag into the mouth that whispered to him.

The dead man became a focus. Using the bare ribcage as a loom, Julian's mind began to weave itself a new blanket of awareness. Though Francis had not succeeded in achieving his dream of rehousing his mind, his presence in the ruins was enabling another mind to build its own home. Julian wavered where he stood, as if the rhythm of the weave was having a direct effect on his body. As his thoughts reached out frail fingers to grasp at each other and become more coherent, his throat was slowly being wrapped in flesh.

Julian began to shudder rather than sway. The changes were increasing in speed and if his body was struggling to accommodate them, his mind was finding it even more challenging. He eyes, the spark in them dulling, became white orbs, the pupils and irises disappearing under a milky film. His head straightened, the muscles tightening and now able to hold the weight up. His hands were clenching and unclenching. His spine cracked as tension popped along its length. Foam leaked from the corners of his mouth and a thin trickle of blood left a trail from his right nostril down, over his lips and into his mouth.

When the blood entered his mouth and touched his tongue, Julian swallowed. His body spasmed. He gasped, a croaky rasp of air being dragged over a dry throat. He saw the man's skeletal frame suddenly be filled with organs and intestines. Rivers of veins ran around the bones, clinging to them in the absence of anything more.

None of it was real. Julian's brain was trying to imagine what the boy should look like by casting a mental image onto the corpse, but the damage caused by the Terrors was making it impossible to have a fully formed impression. His hunger growled at the sight of the brains that pulsed within the broken skull, unable to differentiate between what was real and what was purely a mental template of what should be.

He knew, though! He knew!

Fight it!

The shaking intensified and Julian moaned. His moan swelled into a cry and the cry gave birth to a Terror inspired shriek.

The shriek, however, was not that of hunger. It wasn't filled with the desire to devour or maim or kill. It was a mixture of anguish and promise.

And knowledge,

And thought.

Real, lucid, rational thought.

Julian fell to his knees. His head was bowed against his chest. His neck showed no sign of being partially eaten by monsters. He was… He was...

He was…

"Julian?"

48

"I'm going," said James.

He was adamant. The protestations of his sister were not going to shake his resolve. So what if the witch told him to stay and protect the other children? So what if he was more afraid of her than anything the monster that man had turned into could do? She was no longer around. She'd gone and, again, he was in charge. He'd made a decision and he was not going to let anyone change his mind.

Eva had told him he was being foolish. How dare she? He was the leader and she needed to show him respect. His sister seemed to forget her place. He would leave the care of the others in the joint hands of her and Brie. It would either force them to play nice or it would tear them apart.

If the former happened, then their petty squabbles would finally be put to rest. The cause of many headaches would be removed. If it was the latter, then, effectively, the same would be the case. One would be victorious and the other would be silenced. If that was in spirit or in more permanently, James didn't mind. He needed to be ruthless. The torturing of the Terror had affected him in ways far subtler than might be apparent to the others. He had acquired a slightly bitter appetite. He wouldn't admit it to himself, but the thought of Eva and Brie fighting each other, and one potentially dying, sent to cold shiver along his spine. An involuntary smile played across his lips and he licked them to disguise it.

"What are you smiling about?" asked Eva. She knew her brother's expressions too well.

"I wasn't," said James

He hadn't entirely known he was. The move to hide his pleasure was mostly an automatic response to guilt and the fact that his sister had noticed it made the guilt sharper. He was momentarily ashamed at the realisation that he'd have taken pleasure in the death of one of the girls. When had that spiteful streak woven itself into him? He wasn't sure, but it didn't matter. He was over it almost as soon as it happened. He answered to no-one – at least while Tamara was gone. He could enjoy whatever he wanted.

"You were," insisted his sister. "I wouldn't have thought that this was reason to be pleased!"

"I'm not pleased," he said tersely. "I'm resigned. This has to be done, and I'm going to do it."

"It *doesn't,* though!" she argued. "You're wrong!"

James turned from the window he'd been looking out of and stormed to face his sister. He was nose to nose with her and his eyes were narrow and angry. She flinched.

"Do *not* tell me I'm wrong!" he scowled. "I've kept you all safe since our parents were murdered. You can't deny that"

"I'm not!" Eva said angrily. "I just don't want *you* to die too!"

"I can handle myself," he said.

Her words dulled his anger. She wasn't meant to care for him. She was his sister. They were meant to be jealous of each other and throw insults like javelins to pierce the heart of the other. He was the leader of their group. Feelings were a luxury that had been ruined by the Terror's attack. He did his best to bury his own beneath the bravado of leadership.

"I know you can," said Eva.

He could, she was sure. James kept them safe for so long, he had certainly proved himself. But this plan of his was madness. And futile. He had been told by the witch to stay and keep protect his group. It was something her brother had done very well since all the adults had been killed. Why change that now? The girl, her strange, half-eaten friend and the man who had some sort of monster prowling around inside of him were gone. Let them venture out into the world and suffer whatever fate they might encounter. It was of no concern. Things could return to normal – or the version of 'normal' they now lived with. They had everything they needed.

So just leave it all be and stay alive!

But James was proud. His abilities had been tested and, in certain ways, had been shown to be inadequate. If it hadn't been for the witch, they might all have been dead. Actually, that wasn't quite true. Before Tamara had arrived, James had been about to put into place a bold new plan. It might well have worked too, even if it was as insane as his current one. Sacrificing people, whoever they were was…

It opened a doorway to a much darker place. One that was inhabited by monsters and not the kind with teeth and talons. Eva was still a child, but their situation had forced a maturity on her that she'd have preferred to have grown into. It wasn't often apparent, particularly in her interactions with Brie, but it managed to slip out occasionally. This was such an occasion.

"James," she said, choosing her words carefully so as not to offend his bravado. "We need you here. You're our leader. Me and Brie will just fight, even if we don't mean to. You've kept us safe. *You.*"

"You're right," he said and her spirits lifted, only to be dashed again. "But I need to go."

"*Why?*"

"Because they might come back."

It was obvious, wasn't it? Surely she could see that! He had to go after them. He had to either help them find their way to the Tinkerer or, if they didn't, make sure they didn't try to return to the school. If they tried…

They had been a disruption that James didn't want to be repeated. They had damaged his reputation. He was sure the others still looked upon him in the same way – as their fearless, invincible leader – but *he* didn't think that anymore. James needed to prove to himself that he was still the man trapped in the boy's body that he'd always been. He was their figurehead and he had to stand the pedestal up once more after it had been knocked form beneath him. It was only in his own eyes, but that was enough.

He didn't believe in himself anymore. He needed his confidence back. Staying here wasn't going to achieve that.

Eva opened her mouth to speak, but closed it again. She didn't have an answer for that. James had told her that he was going to find the girl and her group. He hadn't said why, apart from saying he wanted to make sure they were following the witch's orders. Eva didn't care if they were. Let Tamara take out her ire on them if they disobeyed her. But the fact they might return was something she definitely didn't want. Who knew what they might bring back with them? They could be being chased. The werewolf might be loose. The girl might weave her spell on James more than she had before. Eva had enough of a problem with Brie trying to get into James' affections. Her brother didn't need the distraction of either.

"OK," she said finally. "Go. Stop them or help them or whatever you want to do. Just come back."

"I will," James said smiling.

He turned and walked away, leaving his sister standing with her arms outstretched for the embrace that never happened. She dropped her arms down and sighed. He was walking with a stride that reminded her of why everyone looked up to her brother. He was strong. He was capable. He had his lapses, as recent events had shown, but he was still their leader.

Before all of this had happened, she would have loved for him to walk away. Eva, herself, could lead. She knew what was best for their group as much as her brother did, but he had the job by virtue of age. Being his second in command was a position she accepted but that she despised. She wanted to swap places with him. She wanted to show them all just what she could accomplish.

But that was then. Now, she just wanted her brother.

"Where's he gone?"

Eva turned.

"Hello Brie."

"Whatever. Where's James going?"

"He's on a mission," said Eva.

"A mission to where? To do what?"

"None of your business." Eva turned her back to the other girl. She didn't want her to see the tear creeping into the corner of her eye. "Just leave me alone."

"Don't tell me what to do!"

Eva heard the feet on the hard wooden floor and ducked before Brie could jump on her. She twisted and brought her foot up, connecting hard enough with the other's ribs to crack three. Brie fell against the wall, slumping to the ground. She glared at Eva, panting.

"I'll tell you anything I like," snarled Eva. "And if I tell you it's none of your business," she paused to grab the other girl's throat, "then that's what it is."

Eva stood and turned. She left the room by the same doorway her brother had, but went down into the cellars instead of out through the exit. She was smiling. The very brief fight with Brie had lifted her spirits enough to put her sorrow at James' leaving to one side for a while.

In the classroom up above, Brie held her chest. She was wheezing and wincing with every breath. She stared at the doorway and fury was a writhing serpent across her features. It twisted them into a sneer that showed very well what thoughts whirled through her mind. Her fist clenched and unclenched by her side.

She'd find out for herself what James was doing. She'd make sure he saw how much he needed her.

Then, for the last time, she would deal with Eva.

49

Sometimes, you want to hide from the world. Sometimes, it's much more than merely wanting. It can be a need. It can be a compulsion. Sometimes the world is descending upon you like a tsunami, waiting to wash you away with its angry power, and you have to take refuge for fear of drowning.

When you do, however, the world can seek you out and interrupt your sanctuary. It can tear at the shield you place before you. It can creep into your hiding place and sneak up on you. Then, when you are complacent and settled in your solitude, it can leap out to surprise you before dragging you back into its fold.

Of course, it doesn't take the form of the world. Though you might feel the interruption is planet-sized, such a thing would clearly be impossible. It can be a word in the silence. A light in the darkness.

A voice to break your reverie.

"Julian?"

Julian didn't move. He opened his closed eyes, but remained still. He looked at the dead man, hoping the voice was either his imagination or the ghost of the corpse. A spirit would have been welcome. A haunting preferable to the alternative.

He did not want Dorothy to be there. Nor did he want the man that had been with them. He ran for good reason though, when he fled, it was more instinct than intent. The hunger that overwhelmed him had spurred him on to escape the situation and hide. If either of them found him, he could not be sure of his reaction.

He knew what he'd felt. What he'd wanted. His stomach growled at the thought. He shut his eyes again and wished. If wishes were fishes, his would be wriggling through his fingers and swimming off into the depths of the ocean.

It didn't matter what he wanted. Life was like that. It had its own agenda and its own idiosyncratic departures from that agenda. Life cared little for wishes or desires. Life and the world were cousins who took great pleasure in riding roughshod over those who wished or desired.

"Julian!"

He sighed. Part of him longed to be still under the influence of the Terror. Though he had existed among shadows, Dorothy had been his light. She had been a beacon for him to follow. His sickening urges aside, he'd been driven by need rather than thought or hope. These things were dangerous. He was a boy, that was all. He wasn't a soldier. He wasn't strong. Or brave. He was afraid.

"Dorothy," he answered quietly.

His voice was clear. The syllables were distinctive, forming the word as if caressing each letter. He had stepped from the darkness and his friend's name had been there to welcome him. He held the feeling of it tightly, repeating it over and over in his mind to savour the sensation.

Dorothy.

He would feed on that. On the fact that he could think of her name properly. Completely. He wished she would go. She'd sense his distress and leave before he attacked her and made sure she couldn't. Concentrate on her name, he told himself. Forget about the Terrors' influence, and what remained of it, bubbling away deep inside of him. Just her name. It was a rock that he could lash on to with the entrails of his despair.

"Are you OK?" she asked.

Her voice wavered, as if it was a fragile jewel that might break if mishandled. Her worry tugged at him like a small child, urging him to turn around. He held his place. He couldn't turn around. What if his resolve broke? What if he turned her into... into *him*?

He nodded. He wasn't, of course. He was back, mostly at least, but he wasn't even close to being alright. He was mentally urging her to leave. He was shouting in his head, but she couldn't hear him. He couldn't say it out loud, in case she actually did it. Julian was torn. He needed Dorothy there with him to save him from slipping back into the darkness, but he was afraid her presence might push him deeper under. A nod was the only physical response he could trust himself to make.

"Julian," she said. "Turn around."

He almost did. He was so close to doing as she wished and facing her. He'd taken the deep, steadying breath. He'd clenched his fists against the potential internal battle he might have to fight. His head even started to move.

Then, for a wild second, her scream froze him in place.

The growl that chased the scream around the room yanked him around with an invisible force. He knew the sound. He knew its origin.

Dorothy was cowering down, hunched into a terrified ball. Above her, snarling with its mouth dripping with salival anticipation, was the werewolf.

Julian didn't have time to think. He didn't have time to suppress the instinct that spurred his actions. He also didn't have time to save his friend as another figure lunged into the fray, ramming into the werewolf and knocking it to the ground.

The creature twisted on impact, throwing its attacker off. Julian ran to Dorothy and pulled her away towards the wall. She was trembling, feeling so close to death, she was sure she'd felt the Reaper's breath on her neck. The intruder pushed himself to his feet and swung a huge axe up into the air, advancing on the werewolf. He looked odd, as if the parts of his body didn't quite fit together properly. Some of those parts glinted as if they were covered by a metallic shielding.

The werewolf crouched, ready to pounce. Its growl was low. Deep. A warning to the axe bearer.

Edward was unconcerned. He had found the trail of the boy easily, storming through the forest. Edward had followed him. He'd seen the transformation. He had wished such a change could occur for him, magically morphing his metal components into flesh and blood limbs and organs. He didn't mind the killings and dismemberment. He enjoyed them. He was making the world a better place, something his father would never have believed of his son. Something that would have given his father more of a reason to hate his son.

The beast's teeth were sharp and long and plentiful. Its talons were equally so. Edward needed only one tooth and it was much larger than anything the animal could hope to have. One swing was all it would need. His hands gripped the shaft of the axe. He kept the smile on the inside. The beast was a man, he knew. Perhaps beneath the fur and ferocity, the two being worn as a disguise to hide the dark heart of the person beneath the coverings. Perhaps in the pulsing blood that coursed through its veins that could be seen filling the red rimmed, bulging eyes.

But that man was still a monster. Even without the metamorphosis. Melody, the innocent girl in the decimated village was dead. Who knew who else had lost their lives at his hand? Or claw? Who knew what might happen in the future?

Edward saw the muscles in the legs of the werewolf tense. The fur bristled. The breathing slowed. It was preparing. The man who wasn't a man was ready for the leap from the man who, also, was no longer a man.

In other circumstances, a sense of kinship might have brought them together. They were not who they were meant to be. But no. Not this time.

There was only one outcome. Except, there wasn't.

Adam was a monster, but he was also part of their group. Or team. Or gang. Whatever it was called, the witch had entrusted each of them to the other. Dorothy, regardless of where the *thing* with the axe had come from and the current form of Adam, had to do something. She pushed Julian away and jumped forward, grabbing hold of the weapon. The werewolf took its chance and leapt, uncaring which victim would be first.

"No!"

Julian pushed himself from the wall. Dorothy's sudden absence from his side and appearance in the midst of the battle caused his control to crumble. Julian, in that instant, disappeared and the Terror resurfaced. It lunged, slamming into the werewolf in mid-air, throwing them both across the room. Edward roared in anger. He pulled back on his axe and Dorothy's grip was broken. He grabbed her hair and swung her around, letting go to send her crashing and screaming into the bones of the dead man.

Julian tried to stand and get to his friend but the werewolf jumped up, landing squarely on him and pinning him to the floor.

Edward strode across to the girl, his face contorted with the fury he was going to vent through his blade's edge into her skull. He was raising the axe as he moved to the point where it was above his head and ready to hit home. He would only give those that deserved it the kiss of his blade, but how *dare* she interrupt him?

It whistled as its sharp edge cut the air. When it was inches from Dorothy's upturned face, another growl filled the room and a massive white creature materialised in a swirl of ethereal smoke. Its open mouth bit down on the handle of the axe, wrenching it from Edward's hands. Frank's body connected with the tin man's and the pair became a cacophonous jumble of limbs that hit the ground, sending the shattered bones of the dean man in all directions.

The werewolf raised a claw and slashed at Julian, barely missing him. It was the boy's turn to scream, not in pain but in rage. Julian was gone. Only the Terror remained. He leaned forward and bit down, hard, on the beast's chest. It howled and opened its mouth wide enough to rip the boy's head from his shoulders.

Then the shaking began. The werewolf started to foam from its mouth. A violent trembling shook its entire body and its eyes whitened into sickly, blank orbs. Julian pushed it off and climbed on top of the creature. The convulsions almost dislodged him but he held on and went to bite again. The werewolf's forearm, thick with muscle and unnatural strength, swung out, more from the tremors than from purpose. It connected with Julian's head and sent him sprawling to the floor. He lay still, eyes closed and breathing shallow, looking nothing more than just a boy.

The werewolf's spasms slowed to mild twitches and then stopped completely. The teeth shortened. The fur receded. The talons shrank. The whole body seemed to deflate. After a moment, next to the unconscious Julian, laid Adam.

Frank was snarling at Edward, the dog's immense bulk dwarfing the mechanical man. Edward saw his axe nearby but knew he wasn't fast enough to reach it before the dog attacked. He'd seen the fight between the boy, clearly possessed by something of his father's creation, and the murdering werewolf.

Dorothy saw that the man who had been about to kill her was kept at bay by Frank. Wonderful, bizarre, terrifying and adorable Frank. She saw, also, that Adam was back to being himself. More importantly, Julian was injured. Maybe even...?

She scrambled over, ignoring Adam and taking her friend in her arms. The wounds to his neck had healed, as had the ones on his chest. But there was more blood, now, from the side of his head. The skin was split, a section of it hanging. Blood filled the laceration and oozed out, but that wasn't what concerned Dorothy. In the cut, she could see something white sticking up through the broken flesh.

Bone fragments.

50

In certain circumstances, someone can be a nuisance. They can be so full of themselves that their egos threaten to spill out, washing over you in a flood of obnoxious arrogance.

But, circumstances change. Sometimes dramatically. Sometimes, the very person who you'd like to swat away like a troublesome fly is the one person you hope to never lose.

Dorothy held onto her friend. He was no longer the boy with the cheeky smile who would rather crack a joke than smile and be nice. Now, it was only his head that was cracked and, rather than laugh, Dorothy fought back tears.

She stroked his cheek, not knowing what else to do. She wondered if she should pull the broken pieces of skull out in case they were at risk of piercing his brain. Or should she move them back into place like a bloodied jigsaw? Or should she leave then and watch him die?

"I don't know what to do!" she cried, knowing there was nobody to answer her.

"He's possessed," said Edward. "It is best to let him go."

"Who the hell are you? Where did you come from? Why were you trying to kill Adam?"

"Edward. I'm Edward. I come from the blackened heart of a father who cast me out. And this Adam is a monster in so many ways. I'd only kill him because he deserved it."

Dorothy shook her head. She'd had enough of this messed up world. She either wanted to wake up or, if this madness was real, be taken by either the Terrors or Adam's other form.

"What does any of that even mean? Blackened heart? A monster? Don't you think I can see that? But he doesn't know!"

"Blame and knowledge are not mutually exclusive. A wasp's sting is instinctive, but you would still squash it."

"Who *are* you?"

"I told you. I'm Edward."

"Shut up!"

Edward closed his mouth. There was something strange about this girl, but he couldn't quite decide what. She had an odd smell clinging to her. Her clothes didn't fit any fashion or material manufacture that he, in his admittedly short existence, had come across. Her voice had an odd lilt that he was unable to place among the various dialects of Oz. And, why would she want to defend a monster? Either the boy or the man, both of whom would take her life without a thought.

He wondered if he would be able to defeat the animal that held him firm in his place. It looked to be some form of dog, but not a breed he was familiar with. It was too large. Too white. Too... ethereal. And it had appeared mid-air. Perhaps, he thought, it had come in through the broken down doorway, but he would have seen it. His senses were too finely tuned not to.

Being built rather than born, he was unsure if he had a soul. It was a difficult concept to grasp, but there were a great many people who did believe such a thing existed. He surmised that a ghost might be the memory of a soul. Not the soul itself, which would, according to beliefs, move onto to an afterlife he would forever be deprived of. No, more of a recollection of it. Kept 'alive' by the remembrances of those who knew the person or animal.

So, this beast would be the memory or a beloved dog.

Would he ever roam the world in such a form? He thought not. He also thought he was happier that way.

"I don't understand who you are, but *what* are you?" Dorothy asked, holding Julian tightly as if to protect him from this stranger. "Are you one of these aberrations created by this Tinkerer person?"

Edward stared at her. How did she know of his father? He would never call himself an 'aberration', but was she right? His father had made him and then cast him aside. Was he as the girl described? Was he something to be abhorred? He paused before answering.

"The Tinkerer created me, yes. But I would not consider myself one of your aberrations. I lead a life fulfilling destiny's need and my own desire."

Dorothy frowned. Nothing the man was saying made sense., but she felt the need to talk to avoid thinking about Julian's death. She wasn't ready to mourn.

"Can you please stop talking in riddles?"

Edward looked to the floor, searching the dust and rubble for answers to his own questions.

"He made me. I am remaking myself and, in the process, removing those who do wrong. And, when I do, I'll unmake him."

Dorothy shuddered at the intense, dark promise that dripped from his words. Edward looked up, his mood suddenly lightening.

"Perhaps I could have your friend's spine? Perhaps his windpipe? At least then he can live on in me?"

"What?" Dorothy gasped, horrified.

"Oh," said Edward, misreading her reaction. "I know he hasn't hurt you, but he had the intention of doing so. And, if things had been different, he would have. Besides, he's dead already. He won't miss them. It's for a good cause."

"Don't you *dare* touch him," Dorothy snarled. He's *not* dead!"

Edward nodded in agreement.

"Not yet, perhaps, but it's close enough to not really matter. A few moments of pain filled unconsciousness before he dies will not change anything."

Dorothy pulled Julian closer still. She moved her hand to his face, stroking him tenderly.

"I won't let him have you," she whispered.

She rested her hand against his cheek, hoping to feel some warmth but finding none. The witch's ring, which Dorothy had forgotten she was still wearing, touched him. A flash of heat seemed to spin around her finger and into Julian's face. The veins in the ring, previously faded to nothing, became a vivid crimson colour, spreading out across Julian's cheek like roots under the skin. The ring began to glow with a faint blue light that enveloped her hand and then moved on to wrap Julian in a blanket of luminescence. Dorothy tried to pull her hand away, but it felt as if the flesh of her palm and fingers had melded with her friend's.

She tried to scream, but her throat wouldn't respond, instead allowing only a dry rasping to be heard.

Edward looked on in amazement. He had yet to witness real magic and was intrigued by its purpose and origin.

Dorothy had only recently come to terms with the very existence of magic and didn't know how to respond other than to try and fight it. She pulled but her hand was stuck fast, to the point that she felt that her fingertips were being ripped off. She gave in, finally, and that seemed to be what the magic wanted.

The glow became brighter. Whiter. Sharper, somehow, as if their eyes were being super focussed on the phenomenon. It had fully enclosed Julian and his body was no longer visible.

Dorothy felt the hold on her hand release. She yanked it back and, with the break in contact, the light disappeared.

Julian looked up at her. He smiled.

"Kiss me, ya filthy animal," he said.

Then his eyes closed and he started to gently snore.

51

A person can have more than one version of themselves occupying their body or mind. Without stepping into the murky waters of multiple personalities, the toss of a coin can spin an attitude or flip a smile into a frown. No one is always the person they appear to be at any single moment. In the main, this is limited to moods. Happiness. Sadness. Anger. During a day, or even just a few moments, each of these can be exhibited in a chaotic whirlwind.

Sometimes, a person can, literally be more than one version of themselves. And those versions can exist in complete ignorance of each other. In such a case, are the actions of one the blame of the other? Should one be held accountable for anything the other might do?

Dorothy smiled. Edward frowned. Frank growled.

Adam groaned.

Dorothy flinched and pulled away, bending over Julian as if her arms would serve to protect him from the claws of a ferocious beast. She relaxed slightly when she realised he was just a man now. A man who would sooner hide behind her than step out into the fray. His claws were gone. His teeth were retracted. He was just Adam.

She sighed, not knowing how to feel about him. She hadn't warmed to the man, and it had nothing to do with the creature he could become. She just could not feel a connection to him. He was dumped upon her by the witch, supposedly for protection but she felt him to be a burden. Could she blame the man for the beast's attack? She thought Adam was weak. Pathetic, almost. Was he more so because he didn't know what was going on?

Pathetic or not, the werewolf would have killed them. She had to be wary of the man, whether he was aware or not.

"Let me kill him," said Edward.

"What? What is it with you? Why do you keep wanting to kill someone? I should have Frank kill *you!*"

"Your dog is a ghost," sneered Edward. "I doubt he can do much damage to me."

Frank snarled in response, baring his teeth, as long as Dorothy's arm.

"You don't know him. You don't know any of us."

"I know him," Edward said, nodding towards Adam. "He is a killer. He has to die."

"I don't understand. You're a killer too. So why do you get to live? Who are you to choose?"

"I only kill those who deserve it. He killed his…"

"I know what he did."

"So, you must understand."

"No, I don't. Well..." she shook her head.

It wasn't so black and white. The whole of Oz was a grey area filled with contradictions like a piñata waiting to be smashed to pieces. The only consistent thing about the country was its inconsistencies.

"He's just a man. He doesn't know what he is or what he's done. He can't be held to blame. Like Julian."

"Your friend?"

Dorothy nodded.

"So you believe, if they don't know what they've done, they're not to blame?"

"Not always, of course."

"It either is or it isn't. They are or they're not."

"It's not that simple!"

"It is."

"What the hell are you? Some sort of robot?"

"If you mean am I mechanical," Edward said, "then that's exactly what I am."

Dorothy wasn't expecting that answer. After all the strange creatures, dragged from the annals of Hollywood, fiction and folklore, she didn't know if she could handle another addition to the list. But, it didn't matter. It couldn't. If one of the X-Files Greys was to materialise between them, beamed down by Scotty, she would no longer be surprised.

"It doesn't change anything. Julian was bitten by a Terror. It changed him. It wasn't his fault. It couldn't be. He didn't know what he was doing. As much as I don't like Adam, it's the same. It's not their fault."

Edward was silent. He was unsure what to think. He, to a certain extent, didn't know what to *feel.* Though feelings were beyond him, inside, something akin to sensitivity was swirling. Was it the effect of the body parts he had transplanted? Was there some lingering spirit of the lives he had taken that he had... soaked up? He could actually understand what the girl was saying. But it didn't make sense. It couldn't! They deserved to die. They *deserved* it.

Even if they hadn't known what they'd done, that changed nothing. Guilt was defined by act, not knowledge.

Wasn't it?

Adam groaned again and lifted his head, propping himself up onto his elbows.

"What happened? Where am I?"

"You're alive," said Edward, his tone flat.

"What? Why? Who are you?" He looked around when Edward didn't answer immediately and saw Dorothy. "What's happened? What's wrong with your friend?"

Dorothy could have said that he'd been attacked. She could have said that a werewolf had tried to kill them all and it was only Julian's intervention that prevented it. She could have said that Adam, himself, was that werewolf and it wasn't the first time they had almost lost their lives from its attack.

Instead, she didn't. As Edward was about to tell him exactly what had happened and what he was, she said: Edward was about to tell him exactly what had happened and he was, Dorothy spoke.

"We were attacked." She looked down at Julian. "But we're ok now."

"Attacked? By what?"

Adam looked around frantically, too fast for his still-groggy head. He gulped, holding back the suddenly rising vomit. Was the attacker still there? Worse, was he injured? He felt his body and his head, checking for injury.

"Don't worry, you're OK," said Dorothy. "We all are, thanks for asking."

"Good, yes, good," stammered Adam, his face flushing.

He wasn't usually such a self-centred man. He was caring, someone who would often put the needs of another above his own. Had his ordeals had a bigger effect on him than he'd realised? He wasn't strong, he knew, but he also wasn't this selfish coward he saw when he looked at himself.

Or was he? Was there someone else just below the surface, eating away at the decent person he had always striven to be? He closed his eyes, trying to picture himself from their point of view, as if he was standing beside the girl and looking down. He was ashamed of what he saw.

"Don't worry about it," said Dorothy. She didn't care if the man was bothered about them or only concerned with himself. Perhaps he would leave them now, particularly with talk of an attack. He was a coward and a monster in equal measure. They would be well rid.

Except, Tamara had sent them out together. Whatever her reasons for doing so, they were meant to be a team. Adam could tear that team apart or be its strength. Dorothy had a feeling it was the former, but she couldn't go against the witch. And magic was clearly real, she only had to look at the boy in her arms. The healed, sleeping boy.

Adam slumped back down, keeping his eyes closed. If he couldn't see them, perhaps they couldn't see the wretch he had become.

"Tell him the truth," said Edward. "Why protect him? Doing so doesn't protect you, it only leaves you in danger."

"No," Dorothy said sharply. "It won't do any good. It'll only confuse things."

"He should know. I would prefer him to be aware of why I have to kill him."

"I would prefer you didn't kill anyone!"

"He deserves to die. And I need his leg."

"Need his...?"

Dorothy looked at the strange man, feeling as if it was for the first time. He said he was a robot, but her experience of robots extended no further than a remote-controlled dog she'd had as a child and Will Smith movies. She would have said they weren't real, particularly not in such a way as to be almost human. But this was Oz. So much shouldn't be real. That wasn't all she saw. There was more to him. He wasn't all metal. Parts of him were clearly made of flesh and, she supposed, blood.

His leg. The robot needed Adam's leg.

Adam had managed to keep his vomit firmly in his gut. Dorothy didn't quite have that fortitude. She managed to turn her head enough to avoid splashing both herself and Julian.

"I sicken you?" Asked Edward, genuinely surprised at her reaction.

Dorothy nodded. What else could she do but find such a thing disgusting? He was clearly using the body parts of his victims! He was...

"Tell me what?" Adam asked, quietly.

He was sitting up, his head turning between the girl and the... not quite a man. He could smell the vomit that spread slowly as if the pool of bile and half-digested food was trying to be blood. He didn't need to look at it to know it was there. He'd heard her throw up. Heard the splatter. Looking at the other man, Adam could see what had made her empty her stomach onto the floor. Those words – needing his leg – made his strange appearance obvious. But why? Why would anyone want to kill Adam? He was nobody! Just a nice man who had yet to be given the chance to mourn his loss!

"Nothing," Dorothy told him. She had other things to think about. Other things to do. Priorities far above letting Adam learn any truths about himself.

"Tell him," Edward insisted.

"*No!*" Dorothy retorted. "It's not important!"

"Who are you to...?"

"*JUST TELL ME!*"

He was on his feet. His fists were clenched. A vein pulsed angrily in his neck, as if warning that non-compliance with his demand might bring dire consequences. Dorothy and Edward stared first at him then at each other. Finally, Dorothy shrugged.

Fine, she thought. *He would find out in the end. If he discovered that he was a werewolf, he may know how to control it.*

"You killed Melody," said Edward.

Silence is sometimes nothing more than a lack of noise. It can be a hush fallen like light snow on a room, carpeting everything with a layer of quiet that no-one wants to tread on to break the virginal covering. Silence can be calming. Soothing. Restful.

Silence, sometimes, can be none of these things. It can be a noiseless pounding against, not your ears, but your emotions. It can be an overwhelming onslaught of nothing that, by its very presence, can reduce a person to tears.

The absence of sound. It can also be the shocked response to a stunning revelation, where noise is as afraid to be heard as the air is to be inhaled or a breath released.

Edward looked at Adam. His expression was one of disdain and a smug appreciation of his words' effect. Dorothy stared at the mechanical man. She had expected some modicum of subtlety in the announcement. She also expected it to be told differently.

If she had been telling Adam who he was and what had happened, she would have led with the fact of him being a werewolf. As bizarre as even speaking about such a thing might be, the unnatural was natural here. She could have spoken to him about his failed attacks on them and how he wasn't in control. How it was all the Tinkerer's doing. She would have played it down. Eased the guilt he would be feeling. Defended what was, in many ways, the indefensible.

Yes, Dorothy could feed him to the metaphorical wolves, though in Oz, she wasn't entirely sure they were a metaphor and she wasn't entirely sure what form they took, ignoring the man in front of her. She owed him nothing, really. When it came down to it, however, he was still part of her group. Still 'one of the gang'. She had dealt with death with her parents. She knew the heartache that would come when he found out Melody was dead, so the fact that he was responsible only compounded it. She would tread carefully and lead him slowly into the dark cavern where the truth was hiding.

She would not, as Edward had done, drop the bombshell and watch as it exploded across his face in horror.

Silence filled the room to bursting, leaving little room for air. When the feeling of being crushed by the enormity of what had been said became too much, Adam spoke:

"I don't understand."

He didn't. Whoever the man was, what he was saying was absurd.

"I... I didn't."

"Yes," said Edward flatly. "You did."

He was watching Adam carefully. He wanted to see the reaction on the man's face. See how his body moved. He wanted the response to be that of a man fully aware of what he'd done and fully prepared to pay for it. He didn't want the indecision. He'd always had clarity.

Adam looked at Dorothy questioningly. She didn't know what to say. Should she tell him the truth? Should she hammer home the stake that Edward had planted in his chest? Or should she lie? Was it better to let him think some strange beast had taken Melody's life and he'd had no part in it? It wasn't entirely a lie, when put like that. Adam had not been himself. He'd had no control.

But Edward wouldn't allow her, she knew. He was unconcerned with feelings. Being a robot (and she couldn't believe, even on top of everything else, that she was even in the presence of a sentient machine), he wouldn't understand about sparing feelings.

She nodded.

"You did," she said quietly.

Adam's eyes grew wide and the vomit rose in his gut once more. He put his hand to his mouth, trying to keep it back and managed to swallow the bile back down, making his throat burn.

"*How?*" he cried. "How could I have? I'd know! I'd remember! It was a beast of some kind. The witch said so!"

"It was, indeed, a beast," said Edward. "You are that beast."

"What's he talking about? How can I be the thing that killed Melody? Tell me he's talking nonsense."

"I can't," said Dorothy. "He's not. I'd have told you differently. But it's the truth."

"HOW!" Adam pushed himself up, instantly regretting it, but standing anyway.

He wavered on legs as unsteady as his mental state. He turned between Edward and Dorothy, not knowing which one to address first to find out what was actually going on. He put his hands to either side of his head and squeezed, as if to stop the spinning of his thoughts. He failed and fell to his knees.

"So?" he asked.

He stared at the floor, not wanting to look at either of his accusers. He knew he hadn't killed the love of his life. They were mistaken. Even with their seeming conviction, they were wrong.

So, no matter his denial, why was there a sliver of him that wondered if it were true? Why wasn't he just telling them that they were crazy? Why wasn't he walking out and leaving them behind, determined to find the real killer for himself?

"You're..." began Edward, but Dorothy held up her hand. He was not normally one to be silenced, but the man puzzled him. Or, rather, made him question himself. He remained quiet.

"Something happened," Dorothy said.

She leaned forward, not letting go of Julian, and put her hand on his shoulder in a gesture of comfort. She felt him twitch as if he'd thought about pulling away but the need for the contact won over. Dorothy left her hand there for a moment, then returned it to Julian's chest. If Adam changed on hearing the news, she didn't want to be holding on to him.

"Something happened... to you. You changed."

Adam's head lifted slightly, but he didn't look at her. He just wanted to hear what had happened. What he really was. His posture was that of someone ready for the guillotine, but not realising there was no blade hanging above his head.

"You're..."

The words were, said out loud, laughable. She had fallen through the silver screen, like Alice through her looking glass, and was now in the made-up work of Hollywood. The problem was, the monsters were neither people in costumes or CGI effects. They were real. She knew this, but to say it was madness.

Then she must me mad.

"You're a werewolf."

Adam did look up then. His eyes bulged, his face reddened and his fists clenched.

"What?!"

"She said you are a werewolf," said Edward. His voice was an indifferent monotone that cried out his indifference to the man's plight.

"He heard me!" Dorothy snapped. She part wished Adam would transform and show the man just what being a werewolf meant to the victim. He would need no legs then.

"I..." Adam couldn't complete the sentence.

He could barely open his mouth fully to form any words. He looked at Dorothy beseechingly. She would, he hoped, tell him this was one big joke at his expense. A heartless, malicious joke, but a failed attempt at humour nonetheless. She wanted to look away but held his gaze. Her heart went out to him and she could feel it grabbing a hold of his sorrow and holding on.

"It's true, Adam. You're a werewolf and you killed Melody."

"How can I be? I'd remember something like that! I'd never hurt her! We were going to be married! We were going to have children and raise horses and... and..."

"I don't know the details. I just know... You attacked us."

Adam gasped. He was shaking his head. He knew he couldn't have murdered Melody, and now she was telling him that he'd tried to kill them too?

"No!"

Dorothy nodded.

"You did. Once at the school and then you chased us here. It was supposed to be just the full moon that could turn you but... something... I don't know. You changed again. If it wasn't for Julian, we'd be dead."

"Julian?"

"Yes. Tamara said it was something to do with us not being from here. You clawed Julian and it had some sort of effect on you. It turned you back."

"How can I be? I'm even afraid of spiders! How can I suddenly be a monster?"

"It's not your fault. None of it is. It's the Tinkerer. It's something he's done that's created the Terrors and you and even him!"

Dorothy indicated Edward but neither of them looked towards him.

"Who is Tamara?" Edward asked. "Is she your leader?"

Adam and Dorothy looked at each other. Both would protest that they had no leader, but they *were* following the instructions of the witch. She had put their little team together, so...

"Sort of," said Dorothy. "She gave us this quest. She's trying to stop what's happening. What your father has done."

"His father?" Adam asked, surprised. The man was clearly mechanical in some way, even though he looked as if he was a jigsaw put together by a confused child.

"My father, yes. He created me. He even, I suppose, created you."

"And that's who we're trying to stop," said Dorothy. "Tamara is the Tinkerer's sister. She's given us a cure and is hoping he can bring back her sister."

"Sister? What do you mean?"

"Tamara. She's a witch. One of three. And they're your father's sisters." She neglected to mention one was already dead. "Your aunts, in fact."

"My aunts?" Edward was incredulous.

He had, in his travels, heard of the three witches. He had yet to encounter them or to meet anyone who had. But he had other family? And this girl, the boy and the werewolf were travelling to find him? And *stop* him?

"We should work together," he said. "We both want the same thing. To end this and him."

"You want to kill him," said Dorothy. "We just want to stop him."

"Perhaps, to do one, you must do the other."

"Before we do either," Adam said, looking at Edward, "you have to do one thing first."

"What is that?"

"Kill me."

53

Intentions. Good or bad. Kind or cruel. They can lead a person to the light or drag them into darkness. Even the best can end up being a mire of catastrophe that swallows the spirit and spits out the bones into a neat, clean little pile that is as sparkling as the intention but as lifeless as the result.

The Tinkerer had intended to be a good person. In his mind, he had achieved that. His actions might show otherwise, but murder with a sprinkling of mayhem is sometimes necessary to enable a person to become the best that they can.

He had *intended* to cure everyone. It had gone awry. He miscalculated. He had a habit of doing so and, rather than learning from his mistakes, he only seemed to make bigger ones. It was a fact he was aware of, but something he ignored. Mistakes were the world's way of pointing you in the right direction if you had lost your way, so his were simply Fate's compass. He would get it right. He would do something so monumentally profound that all of Oz would know and revere his name.

So, the odd waver from his one true course was allowed. Expected and embraced, even.

He was leaning over his table. Strewn across it were small lengths of tubular metal, mixed in with tiny cogs and glass discs. The birthplace of his spiders. He felt as if he were a father and, in some small way, even a god. He was creating life were there was none. Of course, he had done so with Edward, but that was a mistake. No, a false start. A lesson. His spiders were different. They were more than automatons. They were more than remote controlled mechanical creatures. They were sentient, to a small degree.

He had learned from the building of his son - learning from the lesson – that too much knowledge is dangerous. As such, he ensured his spiders had none, not really. They knew and revered him, but that was all. Further than that, they followed his commands. They did his bidding. They, in their own way, communicated between themselves and some had... he could only call it evolved. Some had begun to live in communes, of sorts, in the large rooms he'd set aside for them to stay in when they weren't required. Rather than simply resting until called, powering down or switching off completely, they were communicating and socialising. Working together independent of his will, while still following it.

He kept track of it, of course. He found it intriguing. Edward had moved past the Tinkerer's original design and so had been cast aside. The spiders, his huge family, were remaining loyal to him but were also becoming *more*.

They were even, he discovered, repairing themselves. This was something he had not anticipated. He was their maker and their doctor and their father. But they, if any damage was caused, were fixing the broken parts.

He had yet to see if they were modifying his design. Improving it at all. That would have been unacceptable, but until then - if it happened – he would let them continue. In contrast to Edward's growth, the Tinkerer was proud of his spiders. He couldn't entirely understand why. Perhaps it was because they were no threat to him. He could control them. They didn't question either him or their existence.

Perhaps it was because, finally, he had created something that had not failed.

He picked up one of the partially made legs from the table and turned it in his hand. The light from a lamp glinted off it and reflected his own face. He smiled at himself and, for once, didn't find the expression unsettling.

One of his children climbed up onto the table and ran across to him. He held out his hand for it to mount and it ran up his arm to his shoulder, then continued around and up onto his face. It was eager. Excited. He smiled again as it spun around and mounted his eye socket, extending the thin tube into the Tinkerer's pupil until it locked in place.

The smile faded, suddenly.

He wasn't expecting this. No, not at all. His plan was to find his sisters. To entice them to his home so he could talk to them and, one way or another, get them to help him. What he saw was something that he would never have guessed, and his feelings about it were mixed.

Edward.

The view through the lens in the body of the spider was akin to looking at a fish through its bowl. There was a distortion that stretched the image and, if there was any fast movement, it could make the Tinkerer nauseous. Other than that, though, the picture was clear and, through a recent upgrade, there was also sound, though it was slightly muted and given a hollow tone.

He didn't know where his son was or why he looked odd. He didn't know who the strangely garbed girl and sleeping boy were. He'd not met the other man before.

He did, however, recognise the dog. He hated that dog. It had never liked him and had always growled whenever he and his sister were together. It didn't leave his sister's side either, so she must have been close. The dog was bigger, somehow, and it wasn't just the effect of the lens. There was something different about it. Something that blurred its form while leaving that of the others untouched.

But all that was secondary. What really mattered was the conversation they were having. Their intent. They were coming for him.

The Tinkerer dislodged the spider from his face and stood back from the table. He turned and moved to his throne, hoping the seat of power would steady the rage he could feel building within him. Anger was a waste of energy. It dissipated too quickly and ineffectually. It clouded the mind and diluted the resolve. He could have none of that.

He sat up and held out his hand. The spider that had been attached to his face and was now sitting, waiting on the table, skittered down onto the floor, across and up onto his hand. It sat there waiting. He stared at it for longer than he would have liked. He was a man of action, not one of indecision. Not one of compassion. Such things had been exorcised from him by the ridicule he had faced when younger. He was a solid block of resolve that his forthcoming, and entirely necessary, actions would not chip away at.

Gently, he put the spider back onto the floor. It ran off to the open window and sat looking out. To a witness, other than its creator, it would have, possibly, have been contemplating which corner of the frame in which to start building its web.

It wasn't.

The rundown building, in the mind of the man who had constructed it, should have been a castle. Maybe, purely because of the now decayed man's intentions, it actually was. Maybe the grand designs instilled a reality of the heart that the eye just didn't perceive. Whether this was the case or not, outside it's barely standing walls there was a rustling in the undergrowth. Slight. Little more than the whispering of the wind.

But, actually, so much more.

The spiders swarmed. Thousands of them, in mere minutes, amassed in an area only a short distance away from one of the only still fully standing walls. They ran silently, the only sign of their movement the nervous twitching of leaves.

The arachnid automatons separated into three groups, with groups becoming piles as they climbed up atop each other. There were quiet clicks as legs locked into bodies. Hushed whirring sounds as components realigned.

When they had finished, the spiders paused, waiting for the signal. The single spider sitting in the throne room of its father didn't need to turn around to know his command. As soon as he had made the decision, the thought was transmitted.

The quiet whispering of leaves became the loud cracking of branches and the crashing of broken brick walls as three colossal metal beasts, spiders formed of spiders, descended on the group.

The command had come and the Tinkerer's creations – all except one – acted upon it.

Kill.

54

Edward had pondered on Adam's request. He didn't answer or act immediately, which was unlike him. He would normally know what he wanted or needed to do and simply do it. He didn't like the indecision that seemed to be hampering his thought processes. He felt as if the cogs and wheels and bands that made up his brain, until he found another suitable one, needed lubricating to stop them moving so sluggishly.

He knew it wasn't that. He wasn't used to dilemmas or contradictions or the greys that seemed to be seeping into the crevices between the black and white he was accustomed to.

He had meant to allow his axe blade to taste the innards of the other's skull. Cleave the brain then sever the leg. But... now... he wasn't so sure, and Edward had always been so *sure*. It was unsettling. Before he could make up his mind and wonder how he might get passed a dog that wasn't really there...

He felt it before he, with his mechanically enhanced ears, heard it. Vibrations through the floor he was sitting upon. Not from the rumbling of thunder like the recent flash storm that had shook the ground and felled trees. No, this was somehow sharper, as if someone with huge hands and long fingernails were tapping nervously against the stone. Or as if...

Dorothy's eyes were wide at Adam's suicidal request, but she looked around, momentarily forgetting his words. Both hers and Adam's eyes were on Edward, mistrustful of his movements. In that moment, they were the team the witch had hoped they'd become, however short-lived it might be. The robot was not moving, though. He, too, looked confused and concerned.

Frank suddenly spun to the side, his warning growl aimed not at Edward but at the wall. A wall that seemed to be trembling. Adam scrambled back. Edward, closest to the wall, shifted sideways. Something was on the other side. He could feel it. And, now, he could hear it.

Chittering. A high-pitched sound that scratched at the inside of his head.

Dorothy followed Adam's example and moved away, pulling the still sleeping Julian with her. She shook him to try wake him up, but he couldn't be roused. Adam reached over to help her, a move that brought a half smile in thanks.

The shaking of the wall abruptly stopped and there was a long pause in which everyone including, it seemed, Time, held their breaths. Then the tapping began. Suddenly and loudly, as if giant fingers, with nails in dire need of cutting – or, perhaps, claws – were tapping on the other side of the wall. After a few second, the wall started to shake again, more violently now and in time to the tapping. A brick shook loose and fell, hitting the ground where

Julian's head had been only seconds before. Through the hole the tip of a long, sharp leg emerged. It paused in its movement, as if sensing from the air if there was anything – or anyone – of interest to investigate, and then it dipped down and pulled.

There was a moment when it seemed that the wall would resist. It would be able to withstand the pressure on its surface that was trying to force it to cave in. But it was too old. Too tired. Too ready to follow the rest of its brethren and crumble, giving in to time, the elements and decay.

The wall fell away in a cacophony of dust, broken rubble and noise. The disparate group backed away, moving together for the first time, any thoughts of uneasiness with each other banished. Even Edward closed the distance and helped Dorothy pull Julian across to the other side of the room. Frank's head was low and his hackles up. He was snarling and had grown even larger than he had been previously.

Edward could feel something but, though his eyes were superior to any flesh and blood variants, he couldn't see through the thick cloud of dust. He would have to think through his dilemma over the werewolf another time. For now, priorities had suddenly changed.

Dorothy shook Julian again, her actions more frantic. He needed to wake up. She needed to be able to get him – all of them – out of there. Her sensible, decisive head had become firmly attached to her shoulders once more and she had to save them.

Including Edward.

Julian murmured softly and turned onto his side, as if the only thing missing for his complete comfort was a duvet.

"Julian!" She hissed, tapping his cheek.

The boy smiled in his sleep and continued to quietly snore.

"Let me," said Edward, reaching forward.

Dorothy nodded. She had no choice. She could mistrust him another time. Nothing had, as yet, come through the space where the wall had been, but she could make out large shapes and faintly glowing spots of red that reminded her of nothing other than eyes.

Edward extended his finger and blinked in a manner that implied intent rather than automated response. There was a low, barely audible buzzing, and the tip of his finger sparked reminding Dorothy of a disposable lighter that had fumes where the liquid had once been. He touched Julian's side and jabbed. There was a loud crackle of electricity and Edward's eyes brightened momentarily.

Julian jumped, his own eyes wide. He was clutching his side.

"What the *hell?*"

Dorothy grabbed him and he turned to her. He opened his mouth to speak, but stopped himself. He could see the look on her face. She turned towards the shaped in the dust. He followed her gaze.

The spiders were huge. Their bulk made them look as if they would be slow, cumbersome weights that would shamble rather than walk. Looks are the bedfellows of assumption. Both need to wake up and take a leaf out of reality's book. The spiders were not slow. They were not hindered by their size or mass. Even though they were constructed from thousands of tiny, individual versions of themselves, they moved as one. And they moved quickly.

Dorothy screamed. Julian gasped. Adam, sort of, whimpered. He realised that, perhaps, his request for death was premature. Edward didn't make a sound. He clenched his fists and gritted his teeth, steeling himself.

Frank's snarl became a bark that became a roar that no dog could ever have made. He lunged, leaping onto the back of the closest spider. It shook itself, rising up onto its rear legs sharply enough to dislodge the ghostly hound. There was a loud whirring sound and a shift in the surface of the metal arachnid as the slight gaps between its component parts closed. The others followed suit as they moved. Frank jumped again, but slid straight across the creature, unable to gain purchase.

The dog landed, perfectly, in front of Dorothy, Adam and Julian but facing the attackers. He was growling. Protecting.

Julian stared at Frank, desperately trying to figure out what was going on. Where they spiders? Was that a dog? Was it a ghost? Who was the man with them? Who... or what... was the other guy? He looked... weird! His thoughts spun faster than he could grasp at them to make any sort of sense. He felt supremely weary, as if he had overslept by weeks. The last thing he remembered was... being on the bus? It didn't matter. Things had clearly moved on from his ride into town. He took a deep breath and moved in front of Dorothy.

"What are you doing?" she shouted, pushing him out of the way. "Move!"

"I'm protecting you!"

Dorothy glared at him. *He* was protecting *her*? She bit her tongue, holding her retort back. She saw how quickly his return to normality had dragged her own opinion down with it. He didn't deserve that.

Besides, how could he protect her from them?

The spiders were advancing. They had moved into the room too fast for any of the group to properly react and then they had stopped in the centre, appraising the situation. Information was being fed directly back to the Tinkerer, who had reattached a smaller one back to his eye. He could see everything.

His command had not changed. Even as he saw the changes in his son, he remained resolute.

Kill.

The spiders moved slowly now. They had the advantage. There was no escape, and they were much faster than any of their prey. The Tinkerer smiled. Their manoeuvres were not under his control and he liked that. He could feel something that should not have been there. Anticipation. Excitement. His creations were enjoying their impending strike.

One of the spiders had turned to Edward. He stood his ground in front of it, preferring to size up the enemy, as was his custom, rather than jumping in as the canine had done. He had moved to the side, drawing the attacker away from the others. He could see his axe a short distance away and was making his way closer.

A second was closing in on Dorothy, Julian and Adam. Their backs were against a wall and they had nowhere to go. And they knew it.

The third spider didn't move. It seemed to be watching the others and letting them take the lead. Back in his throne room, its creator knew exactly why it was stationary. It could see that the others had things under control. It would wait to see if any of them tried to run.

Then it would stop them.

55

Frank leapt again, hurling himself at the lead spider. It ducked its head down and pushed its body hard forward, slammed into the animal. The dog's yelp was one of surprise rather than pain as it was thrown back towards the group. They ducked, shielding themselves from his impact, but it didn't come. They opened their collectively closed eyes and, at first, couldn't see anything except a milky white haze. The mist, like a thick fog, shifted to the side and they saw that, rather than hit them with his massive bulk, Frank had made himself insubstantial again. Dorothy shuddered and Adam swallowed back his vomit. They'd been inside a ghost!

The spider stopped in front of them. Dorothy couldn't tell if it was waiting for them to react or to see which one of them to pick off first. If Frank couldn't fight it, they certainly had no hope. She looked at Edward who was still now on his back with one of the spiders over him. It had one its legs pressed against his chest and was pushing against his metal plating. Julian was griping her hand tightly and she held his with equal force. Adam had squeezed in against her the other side, taking solace from the contact. Dorothy stared back at the unmoving arachnid and shook her head.

This was it.

Frank moved, standing between the creature and its intended victims. Even if he couldn't gain purchase on its body, he would do what he could to protect them. His form shimmered and solidified and he growled a warning. The spider stared back. Dorothy wondered if it was smiling.

"The dog," whispered Julian.

"What about him?" Asked Dorothy quietly. Neither wanted their voices to prompt the spider into action. They were not at an impasse, rather choices at a buffet.

"He's not always a ghost!"

"Of course he is!"

"No, I meant, he changes, doesn't he?" Julian shrugged, struggling for the words to explain what he was seeing at a time when his mental state was in danger of spinning away from him.

"Yes! So?" Dorothy couldn't see his point.

Then she could. She had a sudden urge to do what she had been so dead set against doing on the journey that had resulted in them being in this situation. But a kiss would have to wait.

"Frank!" she hissed. "Jump *through* it!"

Frank didn't move for a second, then Dorothy saw his tail wag ever so slightly, showing he understood. The spider, sensing something was about to change, lifted one of its forelegs, but wasn't fast enough. The dog pounced, his body fading, allowing him to pass through the metal shell before becoming solid again. The huge beast's momentum dragged the spider backwards, crashing into the one behind it. Just before contact, Frank blurred again, his front end entering the second creature, then coalesced. He was entirely inside the two spiders. There was a crunching sound, as if mechanisms were struggling to keep moving and were breaking apart, then a high-pitched squeal. Frank jumped backwards, coursing through the now rippling metal like a fish from a river.

The behemoths shook violently, then exploded. Tiny legs, carapaces and cogs were thrown in all directions, with most of the smaller, component spiders in pieces. Those that survived the explosion were stunned and motionless.

Edward's chest was in danger of being punctured. He didn't have the strength to push his attacker back off him and was struggling to keep a hold of the leg threatening to impale him. And the *noise!* It was as if he could hear thousands of minute creatures inside of his skull. It was making him lose focus. Lose the concentration he prided himself on.

He heard, rather than saw, the blast from where the others had been cornered, but he couldn't move his head to see if they were injured, or worse. The spider atop him ceased its thrusting and lifted its head, turning to see for itself.

He took his chance and hammered his arm sideways into the leg that pinned him, knocking it away. He twisted and, reaching, managed to grab a hold of his axe. The spider spun back, lifting its leg to return it to his chest, but Edward brought his legs up. For a fraction of a second, he wished he'd had time to relieve the werewolf of his, but had no time to dwell on his regret. He planted his feet on the underside of the monstrous creation and pushed.

Again, he had a second to regret. This time he rued the changes he had made to himself. If he had still been, wholly, his father's son, he would have the strength to propel it off him. Legs of flesh and blood and bone did not have that capability.

He was about to bring his axe up and smash it into the spider's massive skull when, suddenly, there was a roar and his foe was no longer on top of him.

He turned to look, expecting to see Frank on top of the metal monster.

He didn't. What he saw left him dumbfounded.

Adam.

Or rather...

The werewolf.

Adam, for even a werewolf needs a name, was on top of the spider, his jaws locked on one of the legs, trying to wrench it free. His claws were raking at the armoured surface, barely marking it.

Edward turned to Dorothy and Julian, both of whom were regarding the spectacle is if they, too, couldn't believe what they were seeing. Then the ground started to move. Or rather the small spiders that littered it did. Having recovered from the explosion that broke them apart, they were joined together once more.

Edward gripped his axe and used its shaft to push himself up. He held it high and glared at the pair.

"Run!" he yelled.

Dorothy didn't need to be told twice. She scrambled to her feet, dragging her friend up with her. Not letting his hand go, she scanned the room for an exit. There was one obvious choice. There had once been a wall but now there was, hopefully, safety.

Dorothy and Julian, with the ghost of a witch's dog following, ran. As they escaped, she risked a fleeting glance back. There was no sign of Adam, but she could see Edward.

He was vanishing under a writhing pile of crawling metal creatures. She couldn't tell, above the clicking of their fangs, if the sound he was making was a cry of battle, or one of agony.

Then, the forest swallowed the scene and the sound as they left their comrades behind, along with, what could only be, a piece of themselves.

56

When horrors abound and can come from any direction, particularly behind you, do you remain where you are? Do you hunker down and hide, camouflaging yourself to prevent detection? Would there be any point when Terrors and any manner of other abomination could hunt you, or even just stumble across your location and devour you where you cower?

These thoughts and a million more ripped through Dorothy's mind faster than she fled. She could be running towards a monster. She could be running to her death, but staying and taking shelter could be just as dangerous. So she ran, dragging Julian along with her.

Julian, for his part, was following his friend blindly. She clearly knew much more of their situation than he did. Where were they? What were those things? Who were those people, if one of them could even be called a *person*? He felt as if he'd been asleep. No, not asleep. Not in a daze either. Just... out of himself.

He remembered the bus. The conversation. The storm. Then there was a gap. But it wasn't empty. It was filled with sadness and pain. A struggle. A *battle*, in fact. But he couldn't recall with what. Or with whom. What he did know, was that the only thing he had to lead him out of his darkness was her. The girl he quite liked and enjoyed throwing jibes at that were much cheekier fun than harmful insult. The girl who he had often casually thought about asking out but had never followed though. The girl he had liked more than he'd admit. She- her voice and name and warmth – were there with him.

So, if she ran, so did he.

He had no comprehension of the monsters that dwelt in Oz. He had no knowledge, even, of Oz itself. The scene he had just witnessed notwithstanding. He had yet to process that. It would wait, or he would be able to ignore it completely.

Although that wasn't likely.

"I need..."

He couldn't catch his breath. He was fit! He wasn't a fan of sports, but it didn't mean he wasn't able to run that 100 metres and beat most of his fellow students. So why was he struggling so much now? Why was he trailing Dorothy who, as far as he knew, preferred exercise books to actual exercise. When did she become so...

Dorothy stopped suddenly. Julian didn't. He crashed into her, sending them both sprawling. They rolled together, their arms intertwining. When they came to a stop, Julian was on top of Dorothy, their faces almost touching.

They stared at each other, neither speaking, shocked. Usually, Julian would have made a quip or a comment that, though good natured, was lined with barbs. He couldn't think of one.

"You stopped," he whispered.

"You wanted me to," she answered.

"I..." He faltered. He never faltered. "Thanks," he said. "I was struggling to keep up."

"You've been through a lot," Dorothy said. "I'm not surprised."

Julian took a breath, paused and pushed himself up. He was beginning to feel decidedly uncomfortable atop the girl who suddenly seemed to be such a large part of his life. He needed to know why.

"What do you mean?" he asked. "What have I been through? Where are we? What the hell were those things?"

"You're not going to believe this," she said, staring intently at her hands as if she could read the words she needed in the curves of her palm.

"Try me."

"Well..."

Dorothy looked off to the side, avoiding his gaze. Julian waited for her to continue, but she didn't.

"So...?"

She didn't answer. She had heard something. It had sparked in her a need.

Running water. They were back to the river. Follow the river, Tamara had said. They all lead to the Emerald City. To the Tinkerer. She needed to find him. She needed to make him pay for the death of his sister. For the deaths of Adam and Edward. For everything he had done to Julian.

She needed to end this.

"Dorothy?"

She stood, still not looking at him. Even though he was healed, he was still a victim. Still, in his ignorance, a casualty of a war neither of them had volunteered for. She knew she was just a girl. One who avoided fights and mourned parents she had to fight to remember.

Well, that was a fight she won. Perhaps this would be too.

She started walking, so used to Julian following her, it no longer occurred to her that he might not. He did. She seemed to know where she was going. He had no choice.

When they arrived at the river, Dorothy paused, looking each way. The waters were fast moving and appeared treacherous. She was always the sort of person to walk tooclose to buildings rather than skirt the kerb. It was something her friends would tease her about, as if she was afraid that she might be sucked into the path of oncoming traffic by the slipstream of a vehicle. She *was*. She'd smile and take the jokes, but she still let them walk between her and the road.

Looking at the Aren Rush's current, she could imagine that one false step, too close to the edge, would have her slipping from the bank and being dragged under. She moved away. Wanting to avoid any awkward but necessary questions from Julian, she tried not to look at him, but couldn't help herself.

She'd become so used to the devastating injuries to his throat and one-word vocabulary, she needed to make sure he was still *him*. She needed to see his neck. Hear him speak. Watch him walk. So she looked at him.

"This way," she said.

"Where are we going?" Julian asked, though the question didn't stop him remaining by her side.

"We need to... to right a wrong."

"What does that mean?"

"I really don't know," Dorothy said, shaking her head.

She didn't know. She had a destination. A task. But, how she was going to carry it out once she was there, she had no idea.

"Can I ask a question?" Julian said quietly.

This was it, she thought. This was where it started. This was where she had to explain the unexplainable.

"Of course," she said.

"Can you see the dog?"

57

Frank took that moment to run between the two friends. He had returned to normal size and was, once again, just a dog. A dead, ghostly one, but a dog nonetheless. He scampered around them and then pelted forwards, passing through the trunk of a tree and emerging out the other side.

Dorothy couldn't help but smile.

"Dog?"

"There," said Julian, pointing. "Tell me you see that!"

Dorothy shook her head, trying to hide her smirk. It was cruel, she knew, but in a friendly way. They needed a smile. They needed Frank's energy and his enthusiastic bounding. It was infectious, and not in a Terror's way.

Julian stared at her and then back at Frank. He frowned.

"I'm joking!" Dorothy said, laughing. "Of course I see him!"

"But... he's..." Julian couldn't bring himself to say the actual words. He left the sentence heavy with inference.

"A ghost?"

Julian nodded. He was glad Dorothy had been the one to say it. It didn't sound strange coming from her. Well, it did, but not as weird as if he'd said it himself.

"Is he?"

Dorothy's smile faded for a moment. Yes, Frank was a ghost. She'd forgotten what that actually meant. Her mind returned to the bus and the crushed bodies of the dog and his mistress. She felt the weight of their death on her own shoulders. The bus was the one they'd arrived in. It was from their world. So what if they were only passengers and had no control over what happened? It was still, at least partially, their fault, wasn't it? If they hadn't been their way to the mall, would the storm have snatched the bus up and tossed it down atop the witch and her pet?

No, of course it wasn't their fault. Of course, the storm would have occurred anyway. The witch and Frank would still have been dead and Julian would have almost been and Dorothy would have barely escaped

She knew this… but…

"Yes, he's a ghost," she told him. Her sadness and guilt filtered into the mood of her answer, but Frank circled around them and dispersed the shadows before they could take a strong enough hold on her. "He's one of us."

"One of who? What do you mean? None of this makes sense!"

"I know," Dorothy answered. She didn't know where to start or even if she should tell him everything. "What do you remember?"

"I remember being on the bus. We were going to the mall. You were ignoring me as usual."

"Are you surprised?"

"Yes! I'm always nice to you, yet you do everything you can to ignore me!"

"Yes. That's right. It's me."

"Are you implying it's me?" Julian seemed genuinely shocked.

"What do remember?" asked Dorothy again, diverting the conversation. She didn't want to get into the story of how his cocky attitude both put her off and attracted her. And it didn't matter here. She needed to get back on track.

"Good diversion," he said, smirking. Was Dorothy pleased, or would she miss the semi-Julian she had grown so fond of? "I remember the bus ride. A storm. Us trying to escape because some animals or something were attacking. Then… Just being sooo hungry but you were there like… a light? Like a torch? Something I had to follow. Somewhere I had to go."

"Close enough. Except for a few points."

"Go on?"

"Well, you've just missed one or two things," began Dorothy." There's the fact that you've been a kind of zombie." She held up her hand at her friend's forthcoming protestation and carried on, speaking over and effectively silencing him. "We were almost fed to other zombies, or Terrors, by some schoolkids. A witch gave us a task to do, along with a werewolf and we were attacked by a robot that had human body parts before it decided to save us from those mechanical spiders. I think that's it."

Julian had no idea which piece of information to grab on to, but he felt he need to reach for one of them, or he'd be swept away by the current of chaos that was descending upon him.

"I was a zombie?"

"Well, sort of," Dorothy said, nodding. "I don't really know. You saved me when we were escaping the attack on the bus. Those things bit you. They..." *ripped out your throat…* "I mean you were sort of like a zombie from a movie. Docile. Hungry. But you seemed to somehow recognise me and wouldn't leave my side. You protected us so many times."

They talked, or, at least, Dorothy did, until dusk fell like a dusting of darkness wishing it was glitter. She told him almost everything then, when dusk turned to night and the glitter to a veil of black, the pair and their dog took shelter against the trunk of a massive tree. Strangely, Dorothy didn't feel afraid. She knew they might be attacked by wandering Terrors or other beasts – now there were huge spiders to contend with – but she felt prepared, in a 'bring it on' sort of way. If they came, they came. She and Julian would prevail or they'd not. Julian had already proved that any scratch of his skin (though Dorothy hoped that didn't come) was an anathema to anything that prowled in this world. Frank would do his best to protect them too. Julian put his arm around her shoulders and, rather than push him away, she welcomed the embrace.

When morning came, they woke unhurt and, it seemed, unapproached. Many of Julian's questions had been answered, though that posed even more questions, each more fantastical than the last. He didn't want to dwell on the madness. He had agreed, at some point, to help Dorothy in her task for the witch – after more than a few protestations. He needed to get his head around that, daunting though it was. They set off once again on their journey along the bank of the river. Its flow appeared subdued, perhaps in reverence or anticipation of their forthcoming ordeal.

"Do you know how far we have to go?" Julian asked.

Dorothy didn't answer. It took a moment for Julian to realise she'd stopped walking and was staring. He followed her gaze and saw what had grabbed her attention.

Looming large and imposing, but possibly beautiful in other circumstances, was the Emerald City. That it was their destination was undeniable. Tall, grandiose spires reached for the morning sun, embracing it in a dazzle of reflection and sparkle, with everything having a distinctive green tinge. A single tower stretched higher than the rest, and this was coloured deeper green than the rest of the city. It reminded Dorothy of her mother's eyes. Their colour had been the most vibrant shade of jade she had ever seen, then or since. And this tower looked as if it and they had been carved from the same precious gem.

"Is that where we need to go?" asked Julian. His voice wavered slightly, but Dorothy ignored the obvious fear.

"I don't think so," she said. "Tamara said nothing about grandeur. I got the impression her brother wanted to be normal while wanting to be special."

"That doesn't make sense."

"It kind of does. In my head at least. He wasn't a witch, but he wanted some of that power, but he was also pleased that he was 'one of the people.'

"OK…"

"So I think we need to go there."

She pointed.

On a hill, somewhat separate from the surrounding buildings was a sombre building. The rest of the city kept a respectful, or perhaps fearful, distance from the structure and even the emerald shine that embraced everywhere else was notable absent.

Julian nodded, giving Dorothy pause as she glanced at his neck, expecting its – and his - completeness to be some sort of illusion. Sinews and spine could reappear at any moment, and her friend's vocabulary could suddenly drop to a single word. But it didn't.

He grinned the smile that seemed to have been his pass through most of his life.

"Let's go then," he said.

"Wait a minute," Dorothy said, putting her hand on his chest.

Julian looked at her, the shock on his face growing as she stepped towards him, leaned up slightly, and kissed him briefly, but firmly, on the lips.

"I guess we're off to see the Tinkerer."
Frank barked, Julian stared and Dorothy set off towards…

58

Emily paced her cell, mentally pushing away the walls she felt were closing in. She was suffocating in the room and, though not normally claustrophobic, was beginning to feel the pressure of being trapped.

The room wasn't small. It was, almost, comfortable, even. Her brother had ensured she had everything she needed. Everything except freedom.

What was he up to? Why was she being kept there and why wouldn't he even speak to her?

She knew he had visited her cell on multiple occasions. Even though he tried to soften his footsteps, she could feel his presence. She sensed his heartbeat. She tasted his breath, though he was on the other side of the closed and locked door.

He sent his pet spiders in to spy on her. They tried to move discreetly so she wouldn't notice, but failed. After all, real, living ones crawled around the room, spinning their webs, keeping her company. His metal creations couldn't compete, as talented as their builder was, with the arachnids they mimicked. At first, she allowed them their mission. When she grew angry, she would smash them, either with a fist, a heel or a spell. It depended on her mood. Then, she ignored their tiny tinny tapping as they scurried into the corners and up to higher points so they could get a better view.

She spoke to them, on occasion. Sometimes to them specifically, as if they were friends who listened to her rants and kept their opinions to themselves. Sometimes, knowing her brother could see her through them, she spoke to him directly. Arguing. Beseeching. Warning. Nothing worked. Nothing changed. She remained his captive.

When he visited, hiding beyond the thick wood of the door, she would stand close to it. She'd hold her breath. Walk barefoot. Wait for any sound to signify his presence. Or she'd throw herself at its unyielding surface, as if hitting it would transfer through to impact on him. He was adept at remaining silent, but he was her brother. She knew he was there. She felt it. It was part of being one of The Three.

Though there were really *four*, even if one of them had lost his way.

But they could always tell where each other was. It made playing Hide and Seek as children a waste of time apart from an excuse to run around and climb trees or hide in thick undergrowth. They just *knew*. Her brother had no magic of his own he did have that. Perhaps he was fully aware and was taunting her. Perhaps it was always a game. She would know he was there and he would get a bitter thrill from teasing her. Or he would tempt her to use her powers to see if she could escape.

She wouldn't. She couldn't. The Tinkerer was well adept at creating locks that his sisters couldn't figure out. The intricate tunnels of barrels interwoven with each other crossed like the synapses of his ever working mind, disconnecting and reconnecting in endless random sequences that only he, with his key, could open. And, because he was their brother, they couldn't hurt him either.

As children, they'd tried. Children can be like that. Siblings can be especially cruel to each other. So it was with these four. Magic and mechanics would often come to war when they were growing up. They would never intentionally do each other any real damage – they did love each other – but the sisters found that their magic wouldn't harm their brother. It was as if their hearts held sway over their intentions and the ribbons of incantations could never fully bind him.

Science, however, had no such limitations. It had no heart, unless it was the artificially created one that beat in the chest of a son. Hence Clara had the tip of the little finger on her right hand missing, Tamara a scar on her abdomen that would never fully heal. Emily had a bald patch at the centre back of her head where the hair would never grow again. It was covered by the rest of her long locks and mostly forgotten, but it served as an occasional reminder that, though the Tinkerer was their brother, he was not confined by their limitations.

Not that Emily actually wanted to hurt her brother. She wanted to help him. To find out why he was doing the things he did. Besides, her magic might not work, but a swift kick to his...

Emily held her hand over the lock on the door. Her eyes were closed and her breath was coming in short gasps. The palm of her hand itched and the wood of the door surrounding the lock was smouldering. Thin wisps of smoke curled out around her fingers as if holding them to aid her task.

It didn't work. The heat she was generating didn't seem to affect the metal of the lock or the wood of the door. She moved her hand away and the tendrils reluctantly released their touch. She slumped down to the floor, finally defeated. If only he'd speak to her. If only he would tell her why he held her captive! They had been close, particularly when they were young. They'd almost been each other's favourite sibling. There seemed to be no reason for his actions.

Emily tried to feel where her sisters were. She reached out with her hands, as if doing so extended her power. It didn't, of course, and her sisters would poke fun at the gesture, but it did give her focus. Her eyes closed. Her breathing calmed. Slowed. She listened to, and felt, her heartbeat, the slow breaths through her nose like soothing strokes down the back of an upset child. Easy, it said. Slowly, it said.

Her heart stilled, its beat dropping to a light pulsation every few seconds. Though Tamara and Chloe would make jokes about her methods, they were envious of her ability. Emily, once in this state, was able to find anyone or anything, wherever they were in Oz. It had even worked, once, when Tamara had found herself lost in somewhere called Kansas.

The air became like the surface of the Aren Rush. It was a moving, flowing plane of sensation. Every person, animal and thing in the land was a ripple on that surface, as if they were a stone skimmed across the waters. Though the flow was rapid and fluctuated wildly in places, the ripples barely moved. Emily knew them all, purely by the way the air moved about them. It gave a distinctive signature. A taste mixed with a smell that neither mouth nor nostrils could fully grasp.

She took her time, running her mental fingers over each of the ripples to find her sisters. In actual fact, her mind was flying across Oz at a speed no bird could ever hope to match, but inside of her head, she was simply grazing the surface with her fingertips.

There!

Tamara!

Emily's heart fluttered briefly, almost causing her to lose concentration, but she managed to compose herself. She was in silent awe of her older sister. Though, in the main, their powers were equal, each had their own strengths. Clara could, with the merest smile, calm the most savage beast or the frightened baby or the angry husband. The upturned corners of her mouth seemed to prick the bubble of tension surrounding a person, letting the emotions free, while the smile was transferred from witch to woeful.

Tamara was different entirely. She was commanding. She, though sweet and caring, had an aura of conviction and determination that was in contrast to her usually soft-spoken persona. People listened to her. They couldn't help themselves They were drawn to her and would do as she wished. If that included leaping off a cliff through a ring of flames, they would be falling afire while telling her they'd really rather not. Over time, Tamara gained the reputation of being someone in charge.

Emily lingered for a moment on the other witch, reluctant to let her go, but she needed to find the third of the Three.

Clara.

She left Tamara and let her mind wander. She had long since learned that a methodical approach was far less successful than a random, meandering route. The former took time to carry out while the latter was based more on heart than hunt. She wasn't forced on a path, but there was a sense of a current that would carry her to where she needed to be.

Before long, she could feel its gentle pull. She let herself float along, going where she needed to. The current slowed and started to move in a circular motion, something Emily hadn't experienced before. She knew the area where her magic had taken her. It was a forest that had a *huge* clearing filled with poppies. The vast blanket of red stretched so far that it seemed to bend to the curve of the world. It was always quiet there, as if it held a position of reverence, with both animals and people holding the same deference to its field of flowers. Emily, when she had the chance to be in its vicinity, would lose herself in its midst. Not physically, but mentally and emotionally to the point where she could easily drift off to sleep.

The circular motion of her senses increased, picking up speed. Back in the room her brother had incarcerated her in, Emily's body swayed in a similar way to that of her mind. She was being pulled in by a tornado of nothing that was centred in a smaller clearing close to the poppy field.

Abruptly, the sensation stopped.

Emily felt dizzy, but was pleased to have found...

Clara?

Her power had never been wrong. It had never failed her. Not once. But now...

Where was her sister?

59

A city can be a bustling metropolis. It can a hive of people shaped bees that are desperate to make just that little bit more honey. They buzz. They whizz. They rarely sleep with their too focussed lives, concentrating on the flower in front of them rather than the whole poppy field.

Oz's capital city should have been a better version of this. It had, for so long, worn its emerald mantle with pride. It was a glowing crown on a glorious country. The precious gem had sat in the centre of each home's door as a symbol of the richness of life. A vivid green was inlaid into the stones that made the roads, given the naturally yellow bricks a colour that seemed to shift as you walked past or across it. It should have teemed with activity. Smiles. Laughter. Endeavours that were made for the greater good of the community rather than the individual.

It once was exactly that.

Now, the streets were deserted. The laughter subdued. The smiles, frowns. The emerald shine had faded, to be replaced by a melancholy hue that seemed to sap one's spirit. The residents preferred to remain indoors when they could and walked with stoops and hooded faces when they couldn't.

They had a new Prime Minister too, something that was usually a cause for celebration. This one, however, had come to power through supposedly unorthodox means. Ones that included science rather than magic. But, he was proclaimed a wizard and he had cast a spell over the city, and beyond, that was like a slowly tightening noose about its neck. Whether or not that was his intention – rumours were that he had actually wanted to do something wondrous – it was his result.

The people of the Emerald City, and Oz as a whole, had always been the sort to love all living things. Birds. Insects. Animals. Whether it walked, flew or crawled on more legs than were right on such a small body, they were treated with care. They would carefully remove crawling critters, for example, and safely deposit them outside. Now, the spiders were different. They were metal and they moved with a suspicious intent. They moved too fast to be caught and, when one could be surprised and crushed, it was found to be made from the tiniest cogs. The smallest levers. For something so small, they held a menace that dwarfed even the tales of the Terrors that filtered into the insulated minds of the citizenry. Guards posted on the outer perimeter were there to stop such monsters from ever getting near the city walls, and they succeeded.

"Quick!" cried Dorothy, dragging Julian alongside her. "Help us!"

The guard that had been patrolling raised his rifle, aiming it expertly between the pair as they burst forth from the treeline, ready to flip it either side if one or the other made a sudden, threatening move.

"HELP!" Dorothy shouted. "*It's after us!*"

There was the roar of a viscous beast from within the forest and the guard swung his weapon in the direction of the sound, his face suddenly drained of colour. He had yet to face a Terror, though others in his squad had already had the pleasure. That was why he was alone. There just weren't enough soldiers anymore! Even the proposed conscription the new Prime Minister was suggesting wouldn't, in his opinion, improve the situation. You couldn't force people to fight against a monster when you risked becoming one yourself.

"Get behind me!" he yelled at the boy and girl. When they faltered, he shouted sharply: "*NOW!*"

Dorothy and Julian wasted no further time and did as the guard ordered. He crouched down and started to move slowly towards the trees, approaching the sounds of branches crunching beneath a great weight and a loud growling.

He didn't see Dorothy stand and pull out the large rock. He didn't see her walk to him or raise her hand or have the chance to feel it connect with the back of his head, though that particular pleasure would be waiting for him when he awoke. He simply groaned and slumped.

"Come on boy!" Dorothy called.

Frank bounded from the dark recesses of the forest, a rapidly shrinking blur of white.

"Good boy," she said to him as he leapt up into her arms. "Great touch with the growls and stuff."

Frank wagged his tail and, when she put him back down, sat happily wagging his tail.

Julian stared at his friend. She'd changed, he thought. She was so much harder now. He didn't know whether to be pleased or afraid. He looked at the dog, a creature that surely couldn't exist and must surely be a figment of their imagination. A ghost that could change size. Alter its appearance. Become solid and... *ghostly* in an instant. Was he still asleep? A coma, perhaps? Was he...?

"Let's go," Dorothy said cheerily to Julian.

She tossed the rock into the shadow of the trees and set off for the city walls. He followed, again, but with neither the energy nor enthusiasm of Frank.

The walls that surrounded the Emerald City were tall and grand. They'd been designed, not to keep anyone in or out, but to give the city a pedestal on which to stand in the minds of the populace. They were inlaid with thin tubes of constantly flowing water that had long, iridescent jade fish swimming through them. It gave the effect, particularly at dusk when the angle of the sun was just right, of green blood. The lifeblood of not just a city, but of the whole country. People would look at those walls and feel energised as if they could feel the pulse within themselves, whether it was an illusion or not.

Well, once upon a time, they would. Now, in a time of Terrors and terror, pride and hope were being bled from the land as if from an open vein.

Dorothy and Julian watched the fish for a moment, transfixed by their bright undulations.

"When we get home," Dorothy said quietly, "my counsellor will have a field day with all this!"

"You have a counsellor?"

"Yeah, grief counselling over my parents and stuff." Her shoulders slumped at the thought of her dead parents. "It's OK. It kind of helps."

"I'm sorry to hear that," said Julian. He put his arm around her shoulders and pulled her close. It was automatic and it was needed on both sides.

Dorothy shook her head, but didn't move away.

"Don't worry," she said, her voice almost a whisper. "Dead is dead. Say it enough times and it loses its meaning. That's what Dr. Connors says."

"Connors?"

"My therapist. Counsellor. Psychiatrist. Whatever you want to call it. The guy who's meant to help me lead a normal, well-adjusted life."

"Ah." Julian didn't know what to say. He wasn't expecting this doorway to open into her fears. He tightened his grip on her slightly. It was all he could do.

"Normal is overrated," he said, forcing a smile and hoping it would transfer into his tone.

Dorothy laughed. It was almost genuine. She shook her head again, dispersing the cloud that had somehow descended upon them. *Sensible head back on*, she told herself. *Such is life.*

"He tells me that he sees something special in me," she said, lifting herself back up straight. "Let's find out if he's right!" She looked at Julian. "Ready?"

Julian nodded and dropped his arm reluctantly. He was pleased the fighter had returned to her. He needed her strength to help him get through everything they were facing. He knew she needed the strength too. It didn't quite mask the grief she clearly couldn't shake off, but it pushed it off into the shadows for a while.

"He's right," he said.

Not far from the pair was a massive doorway. They crept towards it. A large handle hung in the centre with a chrome ball attached. It was obviously wanting to be lifted and hammered against the door. It was an invitation and one they were happy to accept.

Dorothy pulled the handle up and brought it back down hard against the wood. Expecting a loud bang, they were surprised when the impact made no sound at all. They looked at each other, confused and Julian took a turn.

Again, the slamming of metal against wood made no sound. He went to take hold of it again when, suddenly, the door opened wide. A guard stood in the opening, a long staff with a dangerous looking blade attached to the end pointing at them.

"Who're you?" he snarled. His face was tight, as if all the features were tensing together.

"Please," begged Dorothy grabbing hold of Julian for feigned support. "Let us in! We were being chased by a Terror!"

The guard looked past them, his anger changing to not very well contained fright.

"Where is it?"

"We don't know. There was another guard out there. He went to find it. Maybe he killed it?"

The guard looked at them, fear and duty dancing a waltz through him. He should go and investigate. He should bring the pair in and give them sanctuary. He should turn and run and let them do as they wished. But maybe shut the door first to stop the monster getting in.

He chose duty. He chose the friendship and camaraderie of his relationship with the guard outside.

"Come in," he said. He kept his blade up, but it no longer pointed at the friends. "Shut the door behind me."

He ran through the entrance, choosing speed to outrun his indecision. Dorothy did as he'd asked and closed the door. It was large and heavy, but slid easily on well-oiled hinges. There was a soft click as the locking mechanism ensured anything outside stayed there.

"What if he finds the other guard?" asked Julian.

"Then we'd best hurry," answered Dorothy calmly.

She was already on her way, moving close and low to the walls. Julian, of course, did the same. Frank fizzled into view and crept after them. Julian hadn't even noticed the dog had disappeared in the first place.

The Emerald City was quiet. It was a city in mourning. Not just the inhabitants, but the bricks and mortar too. And it was waiting.

60

Cities never sleep. They have a breathless pace that careens along with no direction or hope of stopping. When such a place *does* stop, it feels dead. A cemetery where the buildings are mausoleums dedicated to those that once lived and thrives and rushed. The people that venture out are ghosts of their past selves, lingering anon in the hope that life might once more be bequeathed to them and they can rise again.

Dorothy and Julian moved swiftly through the deserted streets, both feeling the ominous sense of desolation that dripped from every structure and ran through the streets like a river of sorrow. It hung heavy upon them, causing them to slump and drag their feet. They weren't sluggish but, rather, they were weighted. They couldn't stand up straight, feeling the need to be crouched as they ran. It didn't slow them, but it made the journey more of an effort than it perhaps would have done otherwise.

Frank had no such restraint. He was in his more usual insubstantial state and bounded through everything as if it wasn't really there when, in fact, it was the dog who wasn't...

Dorothy shook her head, stopping the thought before it could be fully realised, in case voicing the though even mentally might make it real.

Frank was real. Ghosts, clearly, were real too. Deal with it later. Or don't. She was sure Dr. Connors would find a home for her, complete with its own fashion line. One with jacket with straps and buckles up the back, if her mind melted in the heat of everything that had happened and still was.

But, sensible.

She did her best to absorb some of the dog's energy and used it to straighten up.

"Don't let it get you down," she whispered to Julian.

Her friend had kept close beside her, their hands occasionally brushing against each other as they swung. At first, she was unsure if it was deliberate but, as time went on, she had no doubt. She didn't pull away, however. Rather, she came to anticipate and hope for the 'accidents.'

"What?" he responded, looking confused.

"This," Dorothy gestured around them. There was nothing to see except emptiness and the sense of abandonment even though they were sure there were still people about.

Somewhere.

"What do you mean?"

"I don't know about you," Dorothy said, "but I feel like I'm wading through the Aren Rush!"

"The what?"

"The big river. It feels like we're swimming against a tide, even though there's nothing here."

"Maybe the city was built on the site of an old, dried up river, and it's come back to haunt us?"

"A ghost river?" Dorothy snorted, not in derision but in mirth.

Julian pointed at Frank and shrugged. Dorothy saw his point. Anything seemed to be possible. She grabbed his hand and pulled him close. Yes! Anything was possible. If nothing else, Oz had shown her that – though not always in a good way. But that didn't mean it couldn't be in a good way.

"Let's do this," she had intended to say, a defiant 'IN YOUR FACE' to the Tinkerer and anything he might throw at them.

Julian's lips on hers stopped the words in their tracks. They stopped any thoughts of anything for a moment. There was a brief thought of pushing him away and asking him who he thought he was to do such a thing, but that evaporated to be replaced by another.

He certainly wasn't a zombie anymore!

He broke the kiss, not her. Both of them were left breathless by the unexpected (on both parts) intimacy and Julian prepared to flinch at the oncoming slap. It didn't materialise and he smiled. Dorothy returned his smile.

"Let's do this," she said, her voice soft.

"Damn right," he answered, his croaky from a mixture of bravado and embarrassment

The kiss came out of nowhere. He hadn't thought about or planned it. She took his hand, he took her mouth. It felt as if it had been a single, fluid, movement from one to the other. Something natural in an unnatural world. It had the effect of pushing away the drag of the city as if they were kicking off a duvet on a too hot night.

Their hands remained held, fingers interlaced, as they set off again through the empty streets. Dorothy thought of the syringe Tamara had given her. Forget the Tinkerer for now. Apply the cure, then go to him. If they did it the other way around, they might never get the chance to fix his mistakes.

"We don't want to go there yet," she said, nodding towards their destination.

"Why not?" asked Julian, confused. They had a plan, of sorts. Why do anything to drag it out? Surely that put everything in even more jeopardy than it already was!

"We need to make a delivery."

"What?"

Dorothy had deliberately left out the details of the additional task Tamara had given them. She had tried not to think about it too much and concentrated on just getting to the city. Now it was an issue that needed to be resolved.

Quickly, she told Julian the rest of the story. He contained his anger well, he thought. He didn't release her hand and was sure he only squeezed it a little. From Dorothy's point of view, she disguised the expression of pain from the pressure quite well. He understood that she was sparing him from too much information too soon, but he was a 'big boy,' as his mother would often tell him when he did something she was proud of.

"Who's my big boy?" she'd cry, her pride threatening to burst forth and smother him in a shower of love.

Sometimes, he was jealous of Dorothy's lack of parents. She had her aunt and uncle but, though they loved her, there was always a sliver of separation between them. Julian's mother was sometimes overbearing. Most times, she was very vocal. When he was in trouble at school, she'd go wading in, oblivious to his protestations, and tear strips off his teachers. She would battle for her son's point of view, evenly if he was blatantly in the wrong, to the point where the staff questioned their own facts.

Julian hated that. Since his father had disappeared with the daylight when he was seven years old, as if the night swallowed him as he walked along the street, Julian's mother had acted as if she had two roles to fill, but with the energy of at least six.

She was too much. With school, at mealtimes, his clothes, his friends, his lack of a girlfriend. She had an opinion about everything and he just wanted to... drift. Let Life's current carry him on to wherever it might decide.

Dorothy, he thought, didn't have that problem. She had no parents. She had guardians who were purely keeping the seat warm until her future decided to become the present and take *her* on her own journey.

But still...

He wouldn't have complained if his mother took that moment to come bounding around the corner and insist on an audience with the Tinkerer. She would give him a piece of her mind, complete with a side dish of attitude and a seasoning of 'don't dare disagree.'

"Are you OK," asked Dorothy.

He'd been silent for some time and she was worried about where his thoughts were wandering. Would he change his mind about helping and leave her to do it all alone? Would he explode and vent his anger at her, only to storm off again, leaving her to succeed or, more likely, fail? Or would he huddle into a ball and retreat into himself, chased into the darkness by all her revelations?

Julian nodded. He took a breath and squeezed her hand. It was a gesture of affection rather than of anger.

"Do you know where we have to go?"

Dorothy thought that she did. She had an idea, but it seemed ridiculous. She had a syringe. It was obviously some sort of cure. Injecting the Tinkerer would do nothing. He'd created the problems – the monsters and the monstrous – but he, himself, wasn't afflicted. She needed something that would affect everyone.

"*All road and rivers lead to the Emerald City*," the witch had said.

Perhaps *that* was the answer. She was sure there was no piped, running water. She'd seen no evidence of such. Just occasional hand pumps to deliver water to the populace. That water must come from somewhere. The Aren Rush, she had no doubt, fed much of that supply. Dorothy had found Geography, at school, to be one of the more boring subjects and now wished she had taken more notice when the teacher had spoken about tributaries and ox-bow lakes and all that nonsense.

But...

How had the Tinkerer been able to infect so many people? The water! It was the only explanation. Well, next to the possibility that his spider army had spread across Oz and injected everyone... No. The more she thought about it, the more she knew she was right.

She pointed.

Ahead of them, in a small plaza surrounded by a low wall and once grand topiary bushes that barely resembled their original designs, was a fountain. A large ball covered in carvings of horses in a variety of different colours was a centrepiece surrounded by a series of smaller spheres. On these were etched other animals. Lions. Tigers. Something Dorothy couldn't identify that had a long striped tail and stood upright, it's snout extending out to a sharp point. From the top of each of these, water flowed. Or tried to. Intermittent spurts pulsed erratically, only to dribble down the surface of the globes.

"Oh my," whispered Dorothy to herself.

It would, once, have been a grand display, she was sure. A celebration of nature fed, she guessed, by the mighty Aren Rush. Disrepair had caused its pumped to start to fail and the once spectacular fountain was now little more than a of the Emerald City's, and Oz's, fall.

"There."

Julian looked at the fountain. It was unremarkable, though he could imagine that, once upon a time, it had been a dramatic display.

"There?"

The question was obvious. Why would the dilapidated remains of a fountain take precedence over their original destination?

"We need to get this into the water supply. Something is feeding that fountain, however badly. We do that, then we can..." Dorothy faltered. They could do what? "Come on!"

They ran towards the plaza, any stealth forgotten. They had made it this far without seeing anyone. If no one was there to stop them, why take care in their advance?

Once at the fountain, the pair circled it, trying to find an opening or sign of its inner workings. The carvings were intricate and, close up, in much finer detail than had appeared from a distance. The horses' tails and manes were shown with every strand of hair marked with meticulous care. The same was the case for the other animals. Each one looked to be almost lifelike in its composition.

Except one.

A horse in the middle front of the large globe stood out by the fact that it was not etched in the same detail as the others. It was little more than an outline, with only an eye and the inner parts of the ear shown. The rest was empty. It was, also, the only green animal in the entire display.

Dorothy and Julian put both hands on the horse and...

The spiders swarmed.

61

The Tinkerer was pacing.

He didn't like to pace, even though he did so more times than he realised. It was a waste of energy that could be better expended creating and, of course, tinkering. It wore shoe leather and carpet and it showed a level of agitation he didn't want to admit to.

Pacing was for those who didn't know the path they were meant to take. It was the foot's way of mirroring the mind's indecision or confusion.

Of all his experiments, the Tinkerer's mechanical creations were the only ones that hadn't let him down. His 'cure' had turned the people of Oz into monsters. He was ignoring the automaton that he had cast out. That part of his life was locked away in a dark room at the very back of his mind, where old memories and darker thoughts wandered the halls, trying to find their way out. His spiders, however, and the spyglass and Sidney's hand and more – they were innovations of exquisite achievement.

Why couldn't everything be filled with spindles and cogs and springs? Then, if anything went wrong, his screwdriver would be the wand to bring forth the magic he had within him.

The girl's groans stopped his striding. He was relieved but resentful at the same time. On the one hand, his pacing had ceased. His mind could focus and his energy could be expended in much better ways. On the other hand, however, this girl had been the one to stop him. Just who did she think she was? How dare she try and...

She groaned again, her head moving slowly from side to side as if she were looking around even though she wore a blindfold. The Tinkerer knew she couldn't see. Neither of his captives could. The blindfold was made from the same material he'd crafted for his bedroom to keep the early morning sun out. He hated being woken up by anything other than his own body. *He* knew when it was time to wake up. He didn't need any bright lights or warmth to do the job for him.

The Tinkerer stood in front of her, examining her closely. He stood silently, but wasn't particularly hiding his presence. He ignored the boy. The boy, as he had seen, was a follower. This girl was a leader. It was she with whom he needed to speak.

His spiders had given him much. He knew her name. Both their names. He knew she was from somewhere far from Oz. He knew that there was something about the boy that helped him withstand the effect of the Terrors' bites. That could be useful.

She would tell him more. He had ways to make sure that happened.

"I know you're awake."

"Who are you?"

Dorothy's tone was one of confidence. She was surprised with just how fearless she felt. Perhaps it was because of everything they had gone through. It had changed her. Made her stronger. Resilient. Perhaps, though, it was stupidity. She knew full well who this man was. How could it be anyone else?

"You don't know who I am?"

Dorothy shook her head. Let him offer her information. She would lure him in and then wait for a chance before fulfilling her task.

"You're not from around here, are you?"

Dorothy wasn't expecting that. She wasn't prepared for such a direct question and wasn't sure how to respond. Her body had reacted for her, though, with a gasp that confirmed his inquiry. She could have denied it, of course, but if he was asking, he already knew. She didn't know to what lengths he would go to extract the truth but she didn't want to find out.

"I didn't think so," he said.

Dorothy could hear the smile in his voice and wanted to punch it off his smug face. Far too recently, she would never have thought about using violence. Things had changed. She would do what was required and worry about worrying about it later. But first she had to release herself from her bindings. In the meantime, she'd tell him nothing.

Ask whatever you want, she thought. *You'll find nothing out until it suits me.*

"Where are you from, Dorothy?"

"Syracuse."

That surprised her. Not only did he know her name, she'd answered him without the slightest pause or resistance. Beneath her blindfold, she squeezed her eyes tightly, as if to rid herself of her stupidity.

"I've not heard of that. It's not in Oz. Is it in Ix? Or Ev? Merryland, perhaps?"

"No," said Dorothy. She tried to grit her teeth but they refused to stay clenched. She tried to hold her breath, but her lungs insisted on sucking the air in and pumping it back out. She was beginning to feel sleepy and part of her hoped that just telling him would make him leave her alone. "It's in America. New York."

"New York? What happened to Old York?"

"I… I don't know. I think it's in England or something."

"England?" The Tinkerer resumed his pacing. He'd stopped when, thanks to the injection he'd given her – a mixture of sycamore sap, crushed poppies and the venom he'd given his spiders, lest they needed it, the girl had told him her home.

"I don't know geography very well, and I've never been to England. The closest I've been to a holiday is a trip to Niagara Falls."

"All these names are very fanciful, but I don't recall any of them, and my spiders have been far beyond the Deadly Desert."

"I don't know," said Dorothy, though she was fighting an intense internal battle to not say anything. "I was on a bus. Going shopping. There was a storm and we ended up here."

"A storm?" The pacing stopped suddenly. "It brought you here?"

Dorothy's head nodded and she conceded that she had no choice but to allow it.

"Interesting." He stroked his chin thoughtfully. "I was just playing with the weather. I thought it hadn't worked. I didn't know it could bring things – and people – from far away. How many of them are you?"

"Just us," Dorothy said, tears welling at the thought. "The rest were eaten."

"Eaten?"

"Yes," she shouted, finally managing a moment of self control. "By *your* monsters!"

The Tinkerer stopped in front of her and raised his hand. The temptation to slap her was difficult to ignore but, with an effort, he let the arm drop to his side. Time enough for that. The monsters, the Terrors and other creatures, were an unfortunate by product of his cure. It hadn't worked, but at least it had given him valuable information to try and perfect the serum. The fact that the storm he had caused had created some sort of method of travel to far off places was a significant step towards his plans. He'd avoided spending too much time on the idea before now as there were too many obstacles in his way. A desert that caused anyone who touched it to turn instantly to sand for one. If he could perfect the tornado powered transportation method, he could test his experiments anywhere and, in the end, give the entire world the benefit of his inventions.

"So everyone else died?" He wanted no other lose ends to deal with. These two children were more than enough of a hassle to contend with.

"Yes, even the witch and her dog."

"The… the witch…?"

A hollow seemed to suddenly open up in the Tinkerer's heart. It threatened to consume him and he gulped the sensation back down. It must be *another* witch. Magic was prevalent in Oz. Witches and wizards wandered freely.

"Yes. Clara. She's one of your sisters. Our bus fell on her. It killed her and her little dog too."

His hand was up and in mid swing before he knew it and he pulled back, barely missing the girl's face.

"My sister?" his voice wavered. His eyes pricked. Clara was dead? He'd killed her? He would go to many lengths to exact his plans, but not Clara! She was his *Poppet!* He was her *Coggles!* The dog, he felt sorry for, but the beast was always growling at him so he wouldn't let himself be too upset. But, *Clara*!

"The bus crushed her."

Dorothy couldn't help but tell him, bluntly, the truth, but she could take pleasure in how he felt. She wasn't a vindictive person, but far too many had died because of this man. It served him right.

"Tamara told me to give you this."

She held up her hand with the ring on the finger before she could stop herself. She couldn't let him take it, but she couldn't control herself!

"The ring!"

"Yes," said Dorothy, her futile attempts to refrain from speaking making her head hurt.

"Give it to me," the Tinkerer commanded.

It wasn't a request. He was ordering her and Dorothy couldn't refuse. She held out her hand and the Tinkerer pulled his sister's ring from the girl's finger. He held it in his hand and the circle glowed faintly when it came in contact with his skin. *It still worked!*

"Was she still wearing this when she died?"

"Yes. Tamara told me to remove it and bring it to you. When I took it off her, she vanished. So did her dog."

The Tinkerer turned away. While the tears still welled in his eyes, he was smiling. There was hope. He had Clara's ring. He could get Emily's. That might give him the power he needed and, if not, he was sure Tamara wouldn't be far behind. She could never resist sticking her nose into things that didn't concern her. Maybe he should give her a nudge, though?

He lifted his hand, the intention not to slap the girl but to do much worse.

"I no longer need you," he said quietly, as if even the words were an afterthought and his mind was already on other things.

He was about to snap his fingers, an unnecessary gesture but one that gave him the feeling that he really was the ruler of the country and not just one that had seized control.

"NOOOOO!"

The Tinkerer spun as Julian leapt, his bindings dropping from his wrists as he pulled his blindfold from his head.

The Tinkerer smiled.

SNAP!

62

Julian screamed as the mechanical spider dropped from the ceiling onto the back of his neck and jabbed deep into the flesh, cutting between the vertebrae.

The boy dropped instantly, a shudder wracking his body before he went rigid. His eyes were open wide, but blank. A dead stare.

"Julian!" Dorothy cried.

The effect of the serum had weakened to the point that she could move under her own volition and she jumped forward to cradle her friend.

Her *boy*friend.

"Julian!" She glared at the Tinkerer and pushed herself back up. "I'll kill you!"

"No," said the Tinkerer calmly, his fingers clicking sharply. "You won't."

A second spider dropped.

This time there was no incision. No drop to the floor and certainly no blank, lifeless stare. The Tinkerer gasped, looking up at where the spider hung, frozen in mid air. Dorothy stepped back, tripping over Julian's body, falling to the ground. She moved forward and pulled him close. His figure was rigid with his skin beginning to harden beneath her touch.

"No more!" Emily bellowed from the doorway.

"You!" yelled the Tinkerer.

He ran towards her, flicking his wrist to cause a long, pointed metal shaft to spring from his sleeve. A larger version of the spiders' sting. She remained impassive and unmoving as he closed in, the weapon held high.

"Me," she whispered, bringing her hands together.

The Tinkerer was thrown back, slamming into the far wall. He tried to move, but seemed to be held fast. Emily, advancing, had her arm up, her finger pointing, the tip glowing faintly.

"You build your locks to keep me in," she growled, her voice furious, "but you didn't make your spider sentry magic proof."

As she walked purposefully towards him, she reached up and pulled the spider from the air. She held its extended sting out and, as she reached her brother, brought it down against his neck.

"I should kill you," she hissed.

"Do it!" cried Dorothy, sobbing over the boy she could so easily have loved.

"Do it!" the Tinkerer agreed. "*Do it!* Stop all this madness! Stop everything going so terribly wrong! Stop *me*!"

He began to sob too. He pushed his neck up, trying to impale himself on the tip of the spider's sting. Just a scratch would work. His creations didn't need to actually jab into the flash. They barely needed to break the skin for the poison to be effective. They seemed to enjoy it. The knowledge of that and everything else that had happened seemed to be revealed to him as if a curtain had been pulled back. He created monsters. He had become one himself.

Emily tried to push. She tried to force the spider's weapon – *his* weapon – into her brother's neck, but she couldn't do it. Whatever he was, whatever he'd done, he was *still* her brother!

"I can't!" she said, her voice cracking. "I'm not a murderer."

"Allow me."

"Edward!" yelled Dorothy, relief filling to the point it spilled out amid her tears. "You're alive!"

The mechanical man stood beside Emily, and had his axe held above his father's head. He wouldn't need to use any force. Gravity would do just a clean job as he might.

"I am," he said simply.

"How? We saw you get killed!"

"I am my father's creation," Edward said. "Just as the spiders are. We are cut from the same cloth and I am more a tailor than my father."

He pulled at the tattered clothes that hung to his form and they dropped to the floor. Everyone stared at his body. Dorothy could see the human body parts that had been affixed to his torso were gone. In their place were hundreds of spiders, quivering in place as if remaining there was either an effort for them or something of immense excitement.

"Who…?" Emily stuttered. She didn't know what to say in response to this strange metal creation.

"Edward. I'm Edward. As this man is my father, I assume you are my aunt. It's a pleasure to meet you. Perhaps we can become more acquainted after I do what I came here to do."

"Your father?"

"Father? Would you like to say anything?"

The Tinkerer shook his head. Shame prevented any response. *Father?* He had often thought of the mechanical man of something akin to a son, but he had no idea that the feeling was reciprocated. And he'd given himself a *name?*

"That's fine," said Edward. "He made me. He cast me out. I tried to rebuild myself in his image before coming here to kill him."

"Rebuild yourself?" It was the Tinkerer. The words were croaked, but clear.

"Yes, but people who are deserving of death that fit my dimensions are less numerous than you might think."

"You mean…?"

Edward didn't answer. He gripped the shaft of his axe with both hands and brought it down. In the same second, the Tinkerer grabbed Emily's hand and brought the ring he held up, slamming it into hers. There was a piercing whistle for a fraction of a second and then a blast that threw everyone back. Smoke filled the room. No, not smoke… steam! Steam filled the room, hot and humid. Cloying in their throats. Something in it making their eyes sting slightly.

There was a whir as fans in the ceiling sucked the mist from the room, then silence.

Emily smacked into the wall next to the door she had entered the room by. She pushed herself up slowly, looking around. Edward had been thrown into the air and crashed down against the floor, his bulk causing the tiles to shatter. As he stood, shards were sticking out from his back.

"Leave or I'll kill her."

The Tinkerer pressed his knife to Dorothy's throat in warning. She was laid against him with his arm tight around her chest. Her face was a mask of fearful imploring.

"Don't do it," Emily said, her hand out towards her brother.

"Put your hand down!" he yelled. "Don't even think to use your magic on me!"

"Alright!" she agreed, her hand dropping instantly. "Just let her go!"

Edward could see his axe across the room, but knew he didn't need it. He had been built from his father's hands. It was only fitting that the father should die by the hands of his son.

"Stay back, *Edward!* I'll slit her throat!" Eyeing the mass of spiders that clung together to make his son's leg, he sneered. "Away!"

The spiders, however much Edward commanded them, where still the creation of the father and, in the end, they would answer to him. They broke their hold on each other and on Edward's body. The leg they formed dissolved, as did the arms. There was a rattle from inside him and more spiders crawled from the openings the lack of limbs had made. Edward fell, a faint mewling sound coming from his mouth. He was crying.

"We're not going anywhere, brother," said Emily. She stepped forward, ignoring the collapsed automaton. If she could get close enough, she might be able to use her power on his and stop him. "Just let her go!"

"Do not tell me what to do! You've been trying to do that my entire life! I've had *enough!*"

He pulled the knife away slightly to make the promised cut.

"Don't!"

A new voice.

"I wondered when you would show up."

"You don't need to do this!" Tamara said, standing beside Emily. She still glowed slightly from the magic that materialised her there. "It's over."

"It's not over. It will never be over!"

"It is," insisted the witch. "Dorothy stopped it! It can all end!"

"What?!" Dorothy and the Tinkerer exclaimed simultaneously.

"Before your spiders captured her and…" Tamara glanced at Julian, fighting back her emotions. The boy didn't deserve that. "Before they were caught, Dorothy dropped a cure I created from your potion into the waters that run from the Emerald City! The cure is already taking effect! You can start again!"

No! How dare they interfere! How dare they mess with his plans!

"No!" He pulled his hand away, spinning the knife. Slitting her throat wasn't enough. He needed to feel the blade entering her throat and stopping her life as a lack of magic stopped his.

"Here!"

Tamara stepped slowly forward. She held out her hand. In her palm was her ring.

"Take it," she said.

The Tinkerer stared, mistrust clear on his face.

"Let her go and I'll give you my ring. Then you'll have all three."

The Tinkerer thought for a moment. He knew his sister. She didn't lie. She couldn't. Slowly, he lowered the knife. When Tamara was close enough, he dropped the weapon and grabbed her ring, pushing Dorothy away. Tamara, turn, grabbed the girl and pulled her to a safe distance.

The Tinkerer's face was fierce with triumph and he opened his mouth. He didn't get the chance to speak. A great white beast appeared next to him as if the air was coalescing. Frank raised his paw and slammed it into the man's chest. There was a crunch of breaking bones and the barest grunt from the witch's brother.

It was Tamara's turn to shout:

"No!"

It was too late. Frank was unrepentant. He pulled his paw from the crushed chest, shrinking down to his normal size. He paused to lick himself clean of blood then he ran to Dorothy's side.

63

The witches ran to their brother's side, Tamara releasing her hold on Dorothy. They fell to their knees beside him, both sobbing uncontrollably. Dorothy watched them, thinking that, surely, she should feel sorrow or remorse. She didn't. She wasn't, either, pleased or even thankful. She felt as dead as her Julian.

Emily touched her sister's shoulder and held out her hand. In the palm were the rings. Tamara took hers and slipped it onto her finger, with Emily doing the same. Tamara knew what Emily intended and nodded.

It wasn't meant to be this way. The rings were supposed to be brought to the Tinkerer for *Clara!*

Clara wasn't here, though. Their brother was. They would never choose one over the other, but without him there would never be a chance for her.

The witches laid their hands next to each other on his broken chest. They closed their eyes and began to chant softly.

"D… Don't!" Edward panted, unable to do anything other than look on helplessly. He was ignored.

Dorothy had returned to Julian'. She could only hold him and watch the proceedings.

As the witches chanted, they moved their free hands over their brother's body. On their fingers, the veins in the rings throbbed in time with their words. Green rivulets of colour seeped out and spread across the Tinkerer, wrapping him in a web of magic. It tightened to the point where it seemed as if it must slice into his skin then...

The chanting stopped.

The glow faded.

The silence stretched out like a blanket of sorrow.

And…

The Tinkerer opened his eyes and sat up. He stretched, yawned and looked around.

"What time is it?" he asked.

"Time to get up," said Tamara, her smile sad but evident.

"Have I been asleep?"

"No, but you have had a bad dream."

"A *bad dream?*" Dorothy screeched, her voice reaching a pitch and ferocity she never thought possible. "How can you call *this* a..."

Tamara's finger pointed at the girl silenced her. Dorothy's mouth was still moving but no sound was coming out. The witches helped their brother to his feet and hugged him close.

"We've missed you," Emily said quietly.

"Have I been somewhere?"

"Yes, you have. But you're back now."

The Tinkerer looked at Dorothy, Julian and Edward and his eyes filled with tears.

"I did this, didn't I?"

"Yes," Tamara nodded. "And there's no fixing it, not even for you."

"But I can fix anything!"

"No," Emily said sadly. "You can't."

The Tinkerer looked at Edward again and his hand went to his mouth.

"My son!"

He ran over to the remains of the man he had created and ran his fingers over the gaping holes where limbs had been. Fragments of skin still clung to the shell of Edward's torso and the faint whirring of gears and cogs and belts from within could just be heard.

"Father?"

The Tinkerer stood and turned his back, his hands squeezing his head as if he were trying to remember something of who he was.

"Father!"

Edward's cry was that of a son needing his father rather than a discarded offspring bent on murder. Something had changed. The balance had shifted.

The Tinkerer held out his arms, closed his eyes and tentatively snapped his fingers. Nothing happened. With more determination, he snapped his fingers again. The tapping of hundreds of tiny metal feet forewarned of the spider army that swarmed into the room. Dorothy screamed silently, reminiscent of Frank's original inability to make a sound. The witches drew together, hands raised in readiness for the impending attack.

Instead, the spider scurried to Edward, burying him under a sea of rippling metal.

As quickly as they'd appeared, the spiders left the room, or most of them did. Everyone looked towards Edward as he pushed himself up to standing. His arms and legs were no longer absent. The spiders had repaired him. They hadn't joined together to become the limbs themselves, they'd offered pieces of their carapaces and their legs.

He looked down on himself and smiled.

"Thank you," he said.

Dorothy turned away in disgust as the Tinkerer turned and looked at Edward. For a moment, his face was impassive, as if he didn't know quite what to think or feel and was waiting for the decision to be made. Then, he turned, reached out and embraced his estranged son. Edward's arms hung by his side at first, but slowly, he returned the embrace.

Tamara and Emily held hands as they watched their brother and their... their *nephew* reunite. They couldn't forget what either had done, but, in being brought back from the dead, the Tinkerer seemed to have left the darkness that was in him behind.

Being brought back from the dead!

"Can you help us bring Clara back?" Emily asked cautiously.

It had been the combined magic of their rings that had resurrected their brother, but the rings would be spent now. He had built them but they only had one use. They were nothing but circles of useless metal.

The Tinkerer stepped away from his son and looked at them sadly. He shook his head.

"I'm sorry," he said, "but you've used your rings. I told you that you had only one chance with them. I'm grateful you chose me, particularly after everything, but there's nothing I can do."

"Please, there must be!" Tamara said. She was holding back her emotions. It was something she was used to doing. She was the more restrained of the three, but this was enough to break that resolve.

"I'm sorry. There's..."

He stopped. He looked from his sisters to his son. *Could* there be?

He walked to his desk and pulled the curtain that obscured part of it away. Behind was a sheet covering a long object. The Tinkerer rested his hand on the material and turned to the others.

"Edward - I like that name – you were not always... you." He took his son's hand. "I'd built your body, and it could walk and had a simple level of dexterity, but that was all. Something was missing."

He released Edward's hand and started pacing. Dorothy, though she couldn't bring herself to let go of Julian, watched him.

"There was an accident. Nothing to do with me, before you ask. A man died. A good man. A father and a Samaritan. It was a swift death and I wondered if his spirit would linger, not having time for the journey to... wherever to be prepared. I'd already made your rings. I told you they would help you if ever you were seriously hurt, or worse. I had my own. I used it. I took the dead man's spirit."

He stopped his pacing and stopped talking. He didn't seem able to say what happened next. Edward prompted him. To the mechanical man, feelings were a sensation he was unused to. His anger at his father, then his relief and, even, love, were alien sensations that he was still becoming accustomed to. He had an inkling as to what his father was going to say.

"Who am I?" he asked.

"You're Edward," said the Tinkerer. "You're my son."

"Who was I?"

"A good man. And that's all I'm prepared to say. The transfer into your body seemed to wipe your identity but gave you the *life* it needed."

"He was a *real person*?" asked Emily, visibly shocked.

The Tinkerer nodded.

"What's under there?" Tamara pointed though they all believed they already knew.

The Tinkerer pulled away the sheet to reveal a gleaming steel figure. It seemed to shine even in the subdued light of the room.

"It's female?"

"It seemed natural, when making two, to do so."

"You're not suggesting we put Clara into there?" Emily cried. "There's no way we're going to let you do that. No way." She shook her head vehemently and buried her face in her sister's chest.

"She was my sister too," said the Tinkerer. "Do you think I wish this? I don't. She won't know who she is. She will recall nothing. But she'll be *here!*"

"I agree with Emily," Tamara said. "We can't do this. It's not right."

"Then we should say goodbye to our sister for good."

There was a pause, then Edward spoke.

"We need to do this. *You* need to. *I* need you to! I'll not be alone, the only one of my kind. I won't feel the need to be something else and to go to such excessive lengths to get there. Clara, your *sister*, won't know us, but you would still have her. She would be *here!*"

The witches looked at each other wordlessly. They didn't need to speak. There was only one answer. They both knew it.

Together, they nodded.

The Tinkerer held out his hand and Emily gave him Clara's ring. He smiled, though the smile was sad. He was bringing back their sister, but she wouldn't be Clara. She'd be whomever circumstance made her, just as Edward's situations made him the person he was – and the Tinkerer couldn't think of him as anything other than a person, just as he would think of the returned Clara.

He placed the ring on the prone metal figure, resting it in a slight indentation that would be missed unless you knew it was there. There was a soft click as things they couldn't see snecked together. He began to twist it this way and that, as if he was trying to crack the combination of a safe. In a way he was. He was bringing the afterlife to life. He was breaking the seal on the spirit world. He was releasing Clara's spirit, which was held in the veined ring, into the metallic woman he had created.

He stopped and stood back. Nothing happened at first and Tamara would have spoken if he hadn't shaken his head without looking to stop her.

There was a low rumble through the floor seemingly from somewhere far beneath them, then the figure's eyelids fluttered.

Then opened.

Then closed again.

"Give her a little time," the Tinkerer said, struggling to hide his excitement.

Emily was going to speak, but was pushed aside suddenly.

Dorothy!

The girl was yelling, close enough for the witch to feel her breath and the odd splatter of spit, but still under the spell of silence. Tamara stepped in between them and, rather than pushing Dorothy away or reprimanding her, she pulled her close. Dorothy was shocked enough to stop her silent shouting. She tensed, but something in the way the eldest of the Three held her was immensely soothing. Within seconds, her shoulders had dropped and along with it, her anger. The tears began to flow and Tamara let her cry. She stood holding the girl and stroking her hair.

Finally, Dorothy stood back. She pointed to her face and Tamara waved her hand. Dorothy opened her mouth, unsure if saying anything would actually work. It did.

"What about Julian," she asked.

Tamara and Emily looked at their brother expectantly but saw the look on his face. It was a look they knew themselves.

"I can't," the Tinkerer said. "It wouldn't work. I have my own ring, but you and your friend are different, as was proven by his reaction to the bite of a Terror and the wound of a werewolf."

"But Clara's ring healed him!"

"Healing and resurrection are very different things, I'm afraid."

"Adam! Where's Adam?"

She turned to Edward, who shook his head. The meaning was clear. She thought, briefly, that perhaps it was better for the man. He couldn't control the beast within him and had killed the woman he loved. The fact that he had died fighting for his friends was a form of redemption. Wasn't it?

"Julian," she said, not really wanting to but needing to forget about the man who, at any moment could have killed her but who ended up saving her. "You *must* be able to help him!"

I really can't! I wish I could."

"Build another of those robot things! Put Julian inside it!

"It won't work! You're *different!*"

Dorothy turned to her friend's body. She could feel her sensible head returning.

"I want to go home."

"That, I can do," the Tinkerer said. "It's not precise and I can't promise to send you back where you started, but I can recreate the storm and send you home."

"OK," said Dorothy. "Do it."

"It's not exact," warned the Tinkerer. "It's not like riding a rainbow or something, where there's a defined termination."

"I don't care. Just do it." She walked back over to Julian, sat next to him and pulled his body to her. Frank lay in the crook of her leg.

"It may take a little time, Dorothy."

"I can wait," she said. "And call me *Dorthy*."

The End

About the Author

Shaun Allan is a bestselling, award winning author who writes multiple genres, including psychological horror, introspective and emotive poetry, young adult and children's. He has appeared on Sky TV to debate publishing, is a Wattpad Creator and Adim Founding Creator, and been commissioned to write companion stories for such movies as The Purge: Anarchy, Sinister II, The Boy, A Quiet Place, IT and Amazon Prime's Panic series. He also holds regular writing workshops at local schools. Many of his personal experiences are woven into the points of view and senses of humour of his characters, along with the places in and around his home town. His novel Sin has been adapted into a Chapters mobile game titled Straitjacket Lover and was optioned for television.

Shaun lives with his manic dog, Ripley (believe it or not). He works full time and, though his life feels as hyper as his dog, it probably isn't.

www.shaunallan.co.uk

Instagram/TikTok/Threads/Facebook: @singularityspoint

X: @singularityspnt

More books by the author

Sin
MirrorMirror
Hollow
Cell
A Child Called Wendy
Pieces of Me
And the Meek Shall Walk
Puddlebrain
Dark Places
Darker Places

Printed in Great Britain
by Amazon

48283710R00138